CLIVE THOMAS

· BY THE BOOK ·

WILLOW BOOKS
Collins
8 Grafton Street, London
1984

TO BERYL, for letting it be so,
and CARYN and ALLYSON for gracefully
accepting it

Willow Books
William Collins Sons & Co Ltd
London . Glasgow . Sydney
Auckland . Toronto . Johannesburg

First published in Great Britain 1984

**British Library Cataloguing in Publication
Data**

Thomas, Clive
    Thomas – the book.
    1. Thomas, Clive   2. Soccer – Great Britain –
    Biography
    I. title
    796.334′3′0924   GV942.7.T/

ISBN 0 00 218083 9

Typeset by Butler and Tanner Ltd, Frome and London

Printed in Great Britain by William Collins Sons & Co Ltd, Glasgow

CONTENTS

ACKNOWLEDGEMENTS

My thanks go first to all those friends in the Rhondda Valley and in football around the world for their help and their encouragement ... to Derek Goodliffe and David Cracknell, of the OCS Group of companies, for actively favouring the combination of refereeing and business life ... to Len and Geoffrey Carroll, for the use of their villa deep in the south of Spain where flesh was first placed on the skeleton of this book ... for the gentlemen of the press and television, to whose columns and programmes I may have occasionally added spice but who have unfailingly treated me with fair-minded accuracy and whose editors have allowed me to quote from various headlines and articles ... and to Lynne Pitman for her cheerful speed behind the typewriter.

But chiefly, perhaps, my thanks are due to my collaborator, Duncan Gardiner, to whom I never had to show the red card whether on location in Puerto Banus or Blaencwm or while he condensed half a million words into what you are about to read.

·1·
WHY DID IT ALL HAPPEN TO ME?

Zico, arguably one of the finest footballers in the world, was in mid-air. Brazil and Sweden were sharing two goals in the Argentinian seaside city of Mar del Plata. A corner-kick had been taken. And Olive Thomas, for so I was described on an official World Cup list of referees for 1978, turned to point to the centre of the field and blew the whistle for full-time. Behind my back – I saw later on television – Zico met the ball accurately with his head, leaving the Swedish goalkeeper with no chance of a save. Zico was too late. Possibly only four-tenths of a second too late, but too late nevertheless. I had blown for the end of the game, the goal did not stand, and the name of Clive Thomas became known around the world.

I didn't do it deliberately, of course I didn't. I was not to know that Brazil would 'score' when that corner-kick was taken. My watch told me that time was completed. To have blown before the corner was taken would have been dishonest: to have waited until the ball went dead would have been dishonest.

That is not a word, I believe quite genuinely, which would be used to describe me, even by those who have opposed me in more than twenty years of top-class football refereeing in more than thirty countries. I have always done it my way, yes, which is why perhaps I sing that Frank Sinatra favourite in my dressing-room before a game, but I have also always done things which I believe to be correct.

Certainly, I did not make that decision in Argentina, nor indeed did I make any of the countless decisions that were to bring me notoriety, in order to court publicity. Why would anyone quite deliberately jeopardise his chances of refereeing in the final of the World Cup? I did not set out with the intention of being accused in Portugal of being bribed to rig a match, nor to lead both teams in a Manchester City-Manchester United league game off the field when two players refused to be dismissed, nor to allow contentious goals at Wembley, nor to send off some of the best-known players in the world. Neither did I make a conscious effort to wage war on soccer administrators across the globe, whether by resigning from the South Wales Amateur League or by telling the President of FIFA that I felt he was not capable of recognising the problems that existed in the game. No, I did not make any deliberate plans other than to become the best player and, when that so sadly went astray, the best referee in the game. I never aimed simply to be a headline-maker. Well, hardly ever.

Yet as I sit here now, with a kaleidoscope of colourful memories ever changing in my mind, I am aware that it may sometimes have appeared that way. Most of the memories are happy and may help others to progress in the game, but I hope also that much can be learnt from the disputes in which I became involved.

That is the prime purpose of this book. From the moment that the idea of telling my story first came into my mind, I decided that it would be totally honest – that is the way I try to live my life – but only if such honesty could be constructive for the future of the game I love. There can be no legitimate reason for destruction for destruction's sake, though there can be a commercial value. No, to me the only valid excuse for baring my soul and perhaps running the risk of being banished from the game is that a moral can be drawn from most of the incidents described, good, bad or indifferent. Some may take offence at the revelation of details of meetings held behind closed doors, but I have used these examples because I feel the subject matter to be of relevance to all referees and to football.

Although I think it is patently ludicrous that I have to retire from refereeing, not through lack of ability or fitness but merely because the birth certificate reveals I have reached the statutory age of forty-eight, I would like to contribute further to the game. Perhaps some of the ideas that follow will do so.

Names both known and unknown inevitably punctuate these pages. Every one of them has in some way contributed, wittingly or otherwise, to the growth of a career which has taken me to Cup finals and internationals, has seen me travel from Aberdeen to the Argentine, from Ireland to Iran, from Moscow to Munich. I thank them all (well, nearly all), just as I thank those anonymous millions on the terraces who have so often provided the stimulus and backdrop for my performances. And as the curtain begins to fall on the stage that has given me so much pleasure, it seems that I have travelled far. Ambitions have come and gone, fame if not fortune has flitted through, delight has followed despair. I hope, I believe indeed, that nothing of this has changed me and I am still the same Clive Thomas who is known by those to whom I return after nearly every match in order to relax among the real and permanent friends where it all began: the Rhondda Valley.

·2·
HOW GREEN WAS MY VALLEY?

For the stranger, looking in from the outside, the Rhondda Valley presents an imposing frame for the natural and industrial grandeur. And while Treorchy may not be the most romantic of places in the world, it is arguably the hub of the Rhondda with its broad High Street, the widest in the valley, and its character and characters. And it was here on 27 June, 1936, that I was born, not of particularly poor parents, as is often the case in stories of this kind, but not rich either. Dad was an insurance man, my uncle was in business as an estate agent, so we were a well-known family in the valley. Discipline ruled in the house as a priority, with chapel morning, afternoon and evening on Sundays.

The war, of course, interrupted the normal routine. One of my earliest memories, like so many of my generation, is of a bombing raid, and the need to leave the bedroom to hide in the kutch – the cupboard beneath the stairs – until the all-clear sounded. On the most dramatic of these occasions we had to evacuate the house because of an unexploded bomb on the mountainside up the road.

Dad, naturally, went to his unexceptional war, which led to one major domestic crisis in which Adolf Hitler had no part. Mother had accompanied father to Cardiff at the end of one leave and, while they were away, my older brother, Alan, and I walked up the mountain and past the Dare Colliery at Cwmparc. We saw a pit prop at the side of the road, and decided it would make excellent firewood. We had carried it for more than a mile down to Cwmparc Bridge when round the corner came PC Skym, who had watched our progress from across the valley. Well, the next hour or two were traumatic. We were treated like two criminals and, because we were Thomases, our case became an instant *cause célèbre*. Uncle Jack was called to bail us out, as it were, while other uncles and aunties gathered as the word spread. When mother returned, Uncle Jack relayed the dire news to her in the front room before, eventually, Alan and I were called in. Mother was crying. Fancy, to steal while Dad went back from leave ... shameful ... and though we could not fully understand the reason for the histrionics and emotional outburst we promised, naturally, never to do it again. I was eight and it was an early and indelible lesson, to think more than twice before offending the law in any way.

3

From the earliest age, I was never more happy than when I was kicking a ball. Perhaps it was because I had the one rubber ball among the eight boys in the street, or perhaps because I was so keen on the game, that by the age of about ten I was captain of the junior school team at the end of the road. This position included being manager, organiser and selector, which, at that level, also meant ensuring that one of the chosen boys had a proper football. In all honesty, he wasn't really good enough, but he had the ball. With the deep understanding that characterised the Rhondda, the rest of the squad appreciated fully the selectorial process and the diplomacy involved.

At eleven, I went on to Treorchy Secondary Modern School, a grave disappointment to my parents because they had wanted me to take the eleven-plus and go to the grammar school. But I had always maintained that I was going to be a professional footballer, regardless of my education, and I could not see that it was necessary for my parents to go to the expense of paying for me at Pentre Grammar School. At the secondary modern, known in the Rhondda as Treorchy Senior, I tried to continue my soccer only to come up against a brick wall – the PE teacher, Haydn Williams, who not only disliked the game, but who would not even allow a round ball in his school. The head, Percy Griffiths, was somewhat more sympathetic and, although he accepted that rugby should be the game on the curriculum as it was throughout the valleys, he did agree to allow two soccer matches each year against other schools. Invariably the team for the matches was selected by myself and a teacher, Evans Twin (he was the father of twins), and we never lost a match. But no one congratulated us: the applause was reserved for the rugby side.

Like everyone else, I had to play rugby. I was placed on the right wing, presumably on the basis that someone had to make up the numbers and I could not really upset anyone out there. But the moment of truth came in a match against Pentre Grammar at the Oval, Treorchy, when I was actually given a pass. I was on my own twenty-five-yard line, near touch, as I heard Haydn Williams shout 'Run!'. I looked up, saw the big, burly, eleven-year-old forwards from Pentre who disliked Treorchy boys anyhow, and ran. Straight across the pitch. My fellow three-quarters watched in amazement as I streaked in front of them and finally kicked. I had run fully forty yards: I gained two. The writing was on the wall. Thomas was never going to grace the Arms Park.

With only two soccer matches allowed each year, neither was Thomas ever going to grace Wembley. Fortunately, there were others who loved the game, and three nights a week or more we would play – down at the bottom of the rugby field, as we were not allowed ·on the sacred Cae Mawr turf. The patch of ground in the in-goal area of the rugby ground and beyond, however, had another major advantage: we could play on as darkness fell because we had light from the EMI factory just over the fence, where they worked a night shift. We did not play merely for ninety minutes, but continued almost until we dropped, with the teams gradually reducing in numbers as people drifted off home and the goalposts disappearing one by one as each player reclaimed his coat.

At least two of the nights we would play a team from Pentre Grammar and Porth County captained by Peter Jones. Such was the length of these matches, the scores inevitably seemed to be 22-21 or thereabouts. Quite probably I loathed Peter at the time but today he is a close friend, secretary of Tonyrefail FC and a great promoter of the game. Many of his team later played for the Boys' Clubs of Wales at both soccer and rugby; while Gwyn Evans, a big, strong centre-half, went on to join Crystal Palace before emigrating to Australia.

At about that time I joined Treorchy Boys' Club, and received a marvellous grounding in sport from Tommy Grant and Alby Nicholas, who were both leaders with respective teams at the club. But Alby was more. If anyone deserves an honour, it is Alby, eighty-one at the time of writing and still going to the club most nights. He was also a good Welsh League referee, and he took all our five-a-side football at the club. He always used to give the best player on the night threepence. From the club we would go up to a local cafe, Angela's, which is, alas, no more, and confide in Alby all our dreams and problems.

I tried to play for the under-fourteen team at the boys' club but I'm afraid class distinction played a part, in that secondary modern school-boys were clearly not welcome; those chosen for the side were invariably from the grammar schools. Because I knew of many other lads in similar circumstances, I called a meeting – with some confidence, too, as I knew that there were better players around than those in the club team. So we gathered, and founded Treorchy Athletic in the old washery at Abergorki Colliery, close to an ungrassed, flattened tip about thirty yards by fifty, between the old railway and the river – the only remaining level piece of ground in the area. We practised there in rain and storm though, in retrospect, the nights seemed longer and the weather less grim.

Alan Thomas – no relation – was appointed chairman at our first meeting. He was slightly older, at fifteen, and his uncle, Phil Haines, was an official of the Rhondda Football League, with a reputation of having once been the best penalty-taker in Wales. Alan, now head of security for Shell in London, was extremely competent, so with some confidence we agreed that we should enter the Upper Rhondda League and apply to the welfare committee for the use of either the Cae Mawr ground or the one at Ystradfechan. Our applications for the pitches were turned down.

Was this because most of the members of the Treorchy and Cwmparc Welfare Committee were from the boys' club? Did the boys' club really need two grounds? Or was it merely the first example of bureaucratic bumbledom that I was to fight throughout my career?

The refusal meant that every match would be an away game but we went ahead anyway; we also had to contribute threepence per person per week to buy equipment – we played in the West Ham colours – and a football. We had to pay our own travelling expenses, meeting each week outside the Midland Bank opposite the Stag Hotel in the High Street. We would board the public bus and assure the conductor that someone behind was paying. The chairman had to put up with a great deal.

Despite such problems, Treorchy Athletic immediately made the local headlines, winning all our early games. But the big match was to come: bigger even than Wembley. We were to play Treorchy Boys' Club at Ystradfechan. They, however, changed the venue to Cae Mawr, outside their own club premises, where they knew they would be guaranteed support – even from those members more interested in playing table tennis, but who could watch from the windows.

We played our hearts out, and beat the Invincibles, quite the proudest moment of my life at that stage. But at the end of the season the fact did not quite live up to the fiction – we finished as runners-up in the league, with Treorchy Boys' Club as the winners. Nevertheless, we had proved conclusively to the boys' club management that there were players outside the grammar school environment at least as good as those inside. As they were now prepared to include members of our team, I rejoined the boys' club and Treorchy Athletic was disbanded after one happy year.

After my first season with the club, I was excited to receive an invitation from Cardiff City under their manager, Cyril Spiers, but I could not accept their offer of trials on a Tuesday and Thursday night because of the difficulties of travel. Besides, I did not have much confidence in Cardiff City; it wasn't my team. I supported Norwich City, because Noel Kinsey, the Welsh international playing for Norwich, was from Treorchy. I kept all the cuttings about Norwich, every time they were mentioned.

Because I was still determined to become a professional, I was reluctant to enter into any formal kind of apprenticeship on leaving school. At fifteen I went to Polikoff's clothing factory as a presser and when, after only a couple of weeks, I was asked by the managing director whether I would consider going into apprenticeship as a tailor in their cutting-room, I declined with thanks – much to the annoyance of my parents who, for the very first time, decided that my dedication to soccer was too much and that I must have a profession or trade. I had not long been at Polikoff's when a scout came down from Norwich and invited me for a secret trial with others from the valleys. I must have impressed him because I was offered terms to join the ground staff at Carrow Road. So, just a few months after my fifteenth birthday, I left home, seen off by all my pals and with a blast of publicity from the local paper. One of the most memorable moments of my life was when I was met at Thorpe Station in Norfolk by Noel Kinsey and his wife with whom I stayed for a few weeks before settling in with friends from Ton Pentre.

During the time I was on the ground staff (which meant arriving at Carrow Road at 8.30, to prepare the training kit for the senior players who were due to arrive at 9), I trained, along with the two other youngsters in the same position, with the first and second teams. I must admit I was surprised at the dislike with which many of the seniors regarded training. I also used to laugh at some of the stories which appeared in the newspapers, because I made it my business to know what was really happening.

After a few games with the A team as an inside-forward, I moved up to the reserves, including playing in a match at Highbury against Arsenal when Brian Close, the Yorkshire cricketer, was with them. Everything seemed to be going according to the Thomas plan. But my career was to be short-lived. A nagging ankle injury led me to the local hospital where the medical staff warned that permanent damage would be caused if I continued to play. I was very nearly heartbroken. My parents said Come home, C.T., but I was determined to stay in Norwich, seeking alternative employment. My parents pleaded with me, though, and the folks with whom I was staying, whom I respected enormously, advised me to return to Wales – so I left East Anglia.

It so happened that Norwich City were playing at Somerton Park, Newport, that sad Saturday, and the manager, Norman Low, suggested that I should travel down to Wales with the team on the Friday. I continued my journey by train from Newport to Cardiff and by bus to Treorchy. Coincidentally, my mother picked up the same bus at Gelli, where she had been visiting relatives. 'Why did you get me home?' was my first question. In fairness, she was primarily concerned about me and my health, but she also felt that she could find a better trade for me than being a brickie in Norwich, which I had intended to become.

I went back to Newport on the Saturday to see my old colleagues play and, on the short journey between Cardiff and Newport, I got into conversation with a man who, by happy coincidence, turned out to be a linesman for the game – Jack Bailey, from Ynysmardy. Sympathising with my sickening problem, he suggested that I should consider becoming a referee.

After the match, the Norwich players had a whip-round for me and collected about six pounds. Then they shook hands and wished me the best of luck. I left Somerton Park desolate, with eyes downcast lest anyone should see the tears. At sixteen, life had come to an end.

·3·

DOMESTIC BLISS...

My dreams of Wembley, confided so frequently at Angela's Cafe to Alby Nicholas, had been shattered. I had to wake up to reality. True, I did play the odd game for the Boys' Club, but one day towards the end of the season a referee asked for someone to run the line. Possibly because I was the only person present with a handkerchief in his pocket, I accepted. The referee was Alby.

After the game, he suggested that I should take up refereeing seriously and, during the close season, I bought the referee's chart and made up my mind that it was the only avenue I could travel to reach the top of football. I had considered administration, but I scarcely had the academic qualifications and besides, although I had some experience of running a junior team, I felt I was far too young to contemplate a life behind an office desk. In the meantime, as my uncle, John Thomas, was an estate agent, I had joined a building company, Ray Rosser, as an apprentice carpenter with his son, William.

There was an immediate setback to my refereeing career. I applied to the South Wales Football Association for a referee's examination but the association's secretary, Tom Russell, turned me down on the basis that any potential recruit must have reached the age of eighteen. I was sixteen. However, because there was a shortage of referees throughout South Wales, he would accept me for the intervening two years on a probationary basis. At the first meeting of the Rhondda Referees Association which I attended, with other newcomers like Danny Moon and Bob Martin, the first referee I met was the man from the train, Jack Bailey. I had to have special permission even to attend those meetings, because they were held in the White Hart Hotel in Tonypandy and I was under age for licensed premises. Nevertheless, I was soon stirring things up because I knew the laws almost quite literally back to front, and soon the older members were seeking my opinion. I also received an enormous amount of help from them, though this was to be marred much later when jealousy seemed to become their top priority.

Then came the big moment. I was still only sixteen when I was appointed to referee my first big game. Big game? Well, Blaengwynfi Boys' Club versus Treherbert Boys' Club at Blaengwynfi: Saturday afternoon, kick-off 2.30.

Blaengwynfi is three stops up the line and through the tunnel from Treorchy. One of the other stopping points was Treherbert, and the train duly picked up the visiting team *en route*, my first experience of travelling with one of the teams. My kit was an old army tunic dyed black, and we had to walk from the changing-rooms in Blaengwynfi Boys' Club about threequarters of a mile down the street, across the road, and up the mountainside. As this was an under-sixteen match, the duration of the game was to be thirty minutes each way.

In fact, the match lasted for one hour and thirty-five minutes. It was clearly understood and accepted by both sides that I would have to stop the watch every time the ball went down the mountain, and that whoever kicked it had to fetch it. Even so, we played thirty-five minutes of added time, always with the knowledge that the last train back was at five-fifteen. I remember that journey back to Treorchy: the visitors showed their disapproval of some of my earlier decisions by refusing to talk to me. It was an early lesson, but from that moment on the general assessment was that I was too strict. From that moment, too, I certainly made up my mind that I was going to be the top referee.

I moved on to referee in the Upper Rhondda, Lower Rhondda and Pontypridd Leagues, where I first started to make the smaller headlines. I was the youngest unclassified referee not only in the Rhondda but throughout the country. As I had also been playing for Norwich, I was good newspaper material and, during the next few years, I was able to gain invaluable experience from two close friends among local news-papermen – Arthur Trembath, and the *Western Mail* staffman, Tony James, known as Ken, who lodged at my home for a few years and who is now head of public relations for Brooke-Bond Oxo.

At one match down at Cae Mawr, Porth, an old greyhound track, I arrived at the ground an hour before the game to find that every line was incorrectly measured. The penalty area was only sixteen yards deep, the penalty spot only ten yards from goal, and so on. No game, I said, unless the markings are altered. The home club secretary, Ray Hacker, said in no way was he going to change the marks: he had no sawdust left, anyhow. No markings, I repeated, no game. There was pandemonium. Within half an hour all the players from both teams were out on the park, re-marking the lines, after a local carpenter with sawdust to spare had been found. The name Thomas soon did the rounds; here was a man who would tolerate no nonsense.

At another match, in Ynysyngharad Park, Pontypridd, where branches of a tree outside the touchline overhung the pitch, a player had to climb the tree to retrieve the ball where it had stuck. He was just about to throw down the ball when his opponents claimed a hand ball. But where would they take the free kick? Up the tree? I could have given hand ball, I could have given a throw-in. Instead, I dropped the ball right under the branch. To my surprise the press took up this incident, and in the football pink edition of the *South Wales Echo* on the Saturday there was a picture of a player up the tree and me below. What pleased me most was the fact that the top referee in Wales at the time, B. M. Griffiths, stated in the paper that Thomas had made the right decision, that he had used the unwritten eighteenth law of common sense and that, if this young referee continues like this, he too could become Wales's top referee.

At the age of eighteen I was accepted as a Class C referee (certificate approved), the youngest ever in Wales and the first to have a certificate without passing examinations. Indeed, between you and me, I have never been tested officially. I was, then, accepted as a Welsh League linesman.

On my very first appointment, down at Ton Pentre against Llanelli, the referee was schoolmaster Gerard Lewis from Port Talbot. Ton lost and, as we walked from the pitch to the little stand, the secretary and chairman were waiting. 'What a load of rubbish we have here then', said the secretary to the chairman – a clear reference to Gerard Lewis. In the dressing-room, Gerard turned immediately to one of the linesmen and asked whether he had heard the comment. No, was the response. But I had heard it. 'That's what we want, a witness', said Gerard, and summoned in the two offenders. The dressing-room was so small that the five of us had to stand. Both the secretary, Tom Alf Davies, and the chairman, Ron Davies, apologised. They were later to help me greatly in my career.

But this was my first experience of football management, albeit semi-professional, seeing only its own team. That experience was invaluable in that I could perhaps understand, if not condone, the reasons and I was pleased to discover also that, once a game was over and people had settled down a little, they were able to review incidents rather more accurately. From then on, Ton Pentre, renowned as one of the top semi-professional Welsh League clubs, allowed me to train with them twice a week. The team were somewhat surprised to find that an up-and-coming referee was one of the dirtiest of players in their practice sessions.

I continued to be the youngest referee in the Welsh League, received quick promotion to Class B at only eighteen and a half and, although refereeing, playing basketball, table tennis and attending night school as a carpenter to pass my City and Guilds, I still found time to include some of the other pleasing things of life in my timetable. At the Treorchy Boys' Club Christmas dance in 1954 I met a very attractive girl called Beryl Mars who, by chance, lived next door to the referee Danny Moon. I will never forget – or perhaps I am not allowed to forget – that at the end of the dance, while the rest of the boys were walking their girlfriends back home, I said goodbye to Beryl on the spot, after arranging to meet her the following night. The reason for the brusque departure was that I had to go to Angela's with one or two of the others to meet Alby and to tell him our escapades of the night. Alby's view was that no good would come of it, and he gave me his one word of advice to those who have started courting: stop.

It was one of the rare occasions on which I have overruled Alby Nicholas, and yet his watchfulness lives on in the most pleasant of ways. Although his name may now disappear from the trials and triumphs, the disasters and the delights of this book, he has since our marriage come to our home every Christmas night.

Because of my apprenticeship, the army was prevented from enjoying my talents for a couple of years for National Service, with the result that by the age of twenty I was promoted to the Welsh League referees' list. My first league match was Tynte v Abercynon one Tuesday night, and it led to my first serious brush with officialdom. On the previous Saturday I had sent off some players in an Upper Rhondda League match and posted the customary report to the secretary, T.E. Russell, only to receive it back from him on the Tuesday on the grounds that it had not been compiled correctly.

Furious, I telephoned Mr Russell and told him I thought it was very wrong to disturb me when I was about to referee the most important game of my career and that, if this was his attitude to referees, then I no longer wished to be involved. He told me politely in the way that only T.E. can tell people, 'Look, you as a referee interpret the laws of the game. You expect players to accept your decisions. You now have to accept my rules. If you don't, get off the phone and the list.' He was right, of course he was. But I do believe he might have used a bit of diplomacy – perhaps the administrator's equivalent of rule eighteen.

I was nevertheless accepted as the top referee in the Rhondda and was sent one day to take a match which was crucial to the Rhondda League between Blaenrhondda and Ystrad Athletic. It was played at Blaencwm, on a sparsely-grassed and flattened tip by the side of a railway line, under the shadow of a mountain. An old library acted as the changing rooms. Today, only the mountain exists at Blaencwm apart from the one shop, the one pub, the one post office and the road that leads to nowhere. As I stand now on the bleak, still level pitch that is no more, I look up at the steep mountainside with its Forestry Commission walks and wonder whether it also remembers that day, one of the most worrying that I have ever experienced.

Ten minutes from time, something happened that no referee had previously considered, let alone attempted. I sent off a Blaenrhondda player at Blaencwm. His name was John Jones, he was also the local boxer – and couldn't they fight at Blaenrhondda! In my opinion he hacked down an Ystrad player, and certainly could not remain on the tip, er, sorry, field.

I stopped the game and showed him the way to the early book in the library. John Jones looked genuinely astonished. 'You can't send me off', he remonstrated, and then shouted for assistance to the secretary of Blaenrhondda FC, Fudgie Lewis, who came on to the field looking for all the world like a representative of the Football Association. 'Don't be so bloody silly', Fudgie said to me. 'Get on with the game.'

In the meantime the rest of the players sat around waiting for the restart, almost certainly expecting that Jones would continue. Even the Ystrad team were not prepared to assist me at that point: they too had to go home, and the bus stop was some distance from the library/changing rooms ... Yet Fudgie must have seen the light, for he escorted his wounded hero from the field with the remark, 'Come on John, let's get off. We can get him after the match.'

When the whistle went, with Blaenrhondda beaten, and the thirty-odd spectators with JJ and Fudgie among them had run to make a passage for players and officials to walk through, the Ystrad Athletic players must have felt sorry for me. They had a big number nine, who looked on the field to be about eight feet tall but who was in reality only about six foot three, and he said 'Come on, walk off with us.' I did, put up with all the comments, had a bath, dressed and was ready to go when Fudgie came to pay me the seven shillings and sixpence fee and one shilling expenses. 'Now that I've paid you, you're on your own', he warned me laconically. 'Whatever happens now has nothing to do with the club.' I recalled the long walk down the library path, under a dark and sinister railway bridge, to the bus stop. 'If anyone lays a hand on me', I said, 'you'll never see another ball kicked in Blaenrhondda because I'll report you to the Football Association of Wales.' He must have been in charge not only of his team but also of their supporters, because no one touched me. And for many years since Fudge Lewis and John Jones have been among my greatest supporters.

National Service was now looming: my apprenticeship was complete, and I was a qualified carpenter. Because the army summoned me I was unable to take the referee's Class A certificate. But there was one vastly important piece of personal business to be completed and, on 18 May, 1957, I married Beryl Mars – my finest decision. By accepting that particular date, Beryl thus acknowledged from the start that the close season was the time for personal matters! We never discussed my refereeing career in fact. With her sister, Gaynor, Beryl had seen me officiate in only one important Rhondda League match. She said then that she would come to watch a game in the Welsh League, and so she did – a local derby on top of the mountain between Blaengwynfi and Caerau. That was the end of Beryl's visits to football until, I promised, I would take her to a Football League match when I was in the middle.

Because I am Welsh, and despite being one of the last unlucky few to be called upon by Her Majesty to do National Service, I went into the Welsh Regiment. There I found in my barrack-room the boxer, Dai Dower, who went on to become a world champion, and Gerry Hitchens, who was to become the longest-serving Briton in Italian football but who died so tragically young.

After only two days of failure to impress anyone in the Welsh Regiment, the medical officer recommended my transfer to the Royal Engineers as I was unable to wear army boots: I was duly transferred to Malvern. On arrival, I discovered that the secretary of the Welsh League, Selwyn Jenkins, had written to my commanding officer to request leave for me to referee an important match. Permission was granted and so, in my first week of National Service, I was sent home to referee.

As I was excused boots, I was automatically excused various duties and at the end of my six weeks' carpet-slipper square-bashing I was sent to the RE Postal Division as a pay orderly at Mill Hill in North London. Within a few hours of my arrival it was quite obvious why this was my particular posting: the chief clerk, Staff Sergeant Rouse, wished to become a football referee and, for six months, while I was refereeing Army League and London and District League matches, I duly coached Staff who later qualified.

I was also determined to gain promotion – not in the army necessarily, but to Class A level in refereeing. I applied to the South Wales FA but they decreed that the Army FA were now my governing body. I was assessed in an army match at Chelsea Barracks and I was really rather pleased with my performance. It was therefore with some considerable disappointment that I received two weeks later a letter from Sergeant E.A. Edgeley, Hon. Secretary Eastern Command FA Army Referees sub-committee, to say that my assessor, one Captain Allen, had turned down my application. He felt that I had not reached the required standard:

'Reference your application submitted on 21 April 1958.

I have to inform you that your application was considered by my Committee but it was not agreed that you are up to the standard required.

The following suggestions which should be helpful to you have been given by the assessors:

(a) Play the advantage rule more fully and use far less whistle.

(b) Make certain that your decisions are correct.
(c) Position yourself more intelligently.
    In view of the above would you please arrange to re-submit your application at the commencement of season 59/60. The Committee hopes that you will accept their decision in the spirit in which it is intended and that you will take the advice of the assessors.'

Ironically, and not instead, I was promoted fairly quickly by the army to Pay Corporal in the orderly room.
    Two games during my time in the army I will never forget. The first was a match between REME and the Medical Corps at Mill Hill when I was so disgusted with the attitude and behaviour of the REME team that I reported every member of the team, from private to officer, to the secretary of the London District, Sergeant Major Scurr. He had never known such a report, but I do not know, alas, what action was taken.
    The other match was when, as a linesman in the London District Cup semi-final at Aldershot, I was surprised to find photographers at the ground. I asked the referee, Captain Dennis, what the fuss was about, sir? He told me that he had just been named as FA Cup Final linesman and had that morning been promoted to Major Dennis. I honestly remember him saying, 'Corporal Thomas, you may be linesman at Wembley one day.' Little did I think that his words would not come true! In fact, I never did run the line at Wembley.
    National Service passed quickly and reasonably comfortably and, back home, I was immediately made up to Class A. I returned to my job as a carpenter with Ray Rosser and became involved in boys' club work on a part-time basis at Treorchy. I was later invited to become leader of the club, a tremendous offer as it was then renowned as the best in Wales, but instead I applied for the leadership at Treherbert, where there was going to be a vacancy, because I felt it was a greater challenge. The departing leader, a very fine rugby player called Emlyn Jenkins, was moving his job.
    I was accepted at Treherbert, where I stayed as club leader for five years during which I also continued my refereeing with the Welsh League. My name was firmly associated by both players and officials with the strict application of the laws and so it strikes me as slightly bizarre that my next row with officialdom came when I was invited to referee in the South Wales Amateur League, now called the South Wales Corinthian League.
    In my fourth game in this league, I was refereeing Maesteg Park against Fleur-de-Lys and, during the first half, the visitors were consistently straying offside. At half-time I went to their dressing-room to warn

them that if they continued to go offside in the second half I would caution the player and ultimately send him off. I had no further trouble in the second half.

I was, then, astounded to receive a telephone message on the Tuesday morning of the following week from the league secretary, A.J. Thomas, requesting that the next evening I attend a special management committee meeting at Cardiff YMCA, in view of the warning to the players of Fleur-de-Lys. At the meeting I was politely told by the chairman, Tom Rogers, that I had been requested to attend because of the strangeness of my decisions. As A.J. was an ex-referee, he was concerned that I must adhere to the laws of the game and that the committee, in its wisdom, was trying only to help me as they thought there was some potential in my performance. I appreciated their interest and told them they were absolutely right: I did have potential. But, I continued, you are also wrong, and, as from tonight, I am never going to referee in your league again unless you apologise for bringing me here this evening because, whatever respect you have for A.J. Thomas, he is obviously not aware of the laws of the game. I was quite justified in what I did at Maesteg Park. The chairman was sorry that I took that particular view.

The following day, I wrote to the secretary of the Football Association, Sir Stanley Rous, who at that time was certainly not aware of Clive Thomas. He confirmed in no uncertain manner that I had made a correct decision. I sent a copy of the letter to Alf Thomas, who in turn telephoned me to ask if I would forget the whole incident. I was quite prepared to do so if he would send me a letter of apology. He did not, so that was the shortest period in which I have refereed in any one league.

For the next few years, I continued to referee in the Welsh League, and changed jobs, first to become a carpenter with the NCB and later to become Sports Adviser to the Boys' Clubs of Wales in Cardiff. Shortly after this appointment, I received the most important letter of my life – from Alan Hardaker, secretary of the Football League. At twenty-seven, that made me one of the youngest men ever on the league list. I ran the line for a couple of seasons before the second best-ever letter arrived. I was now a Football League referee.

I was immediately advised by a top referee who had taken part in the 1966 World Cup finals, and who is still prominent as an adviser in the game today, don't referee in the Football League as you have refereed for years in Wales. They won't put up with it.

In February 1967, my first season, Beryl telephoned me at the office to say that a letter had arrived from Alan Hardaker but she was surprised it was addressed to me because it was so clearly intended for someone else. She then explained the contents of the letter which I have read at least once a year since to keep my two feet firmly on the ground:

'The Management Committee have been considering the averages of Match officials up to date, and they note that your average is below the accepted minimum of 2.5.

They appreciate that this is your first year on the List, and have asked me to draw your attention to the points which have drawn comment from the Clubs, which are as follows:

(1) Allowed far too much rough play;

(2) Hesitant and indecisive in control;

(3) Did not inspire confidence in his decisions.

In drawing your attention to these points, I may say that it is not unusual in the case of Officials who are new to The Football League List, but the Committee hope that now that the matter has been drawn to your attention, your record will improve in the knowledge that, so long as you control the players firmly and fairly, the Management Committee will give you their unqualified support.'

I asked Beryl why she thought the letter could not be meant for me. She was unaware that I had changed my style and could not believe I now refereed in the way outlined by Alan Hardaker, and which had clearly led to the unacceptably low marks given to me by club managers, under the assessment system in operation at the time.

I immediately changed back to my original style of refereeing strictly according to the laws of the game, and ensuring that the players adhered to those laws. But I was in an odd situation. Geoff Powell of Newport, the referee whose position I had taken, had been dismissed by the Football League and was now demoted to the Newport and District League. But he remained on the FIFA list by courtesy of the FAW – I would not be included until the next season.

Incidentally, I recall very little of my first league game – Swindon Town v Orient – other than that I was surprised at the amount of swearing done by the full-time professionals – but I do remember well my first First Division game, between Arsenal and Manchester City. There was a knock on my dressing-room door and a man came in to say that he always introduced himself to referees at Highbury. It was none other than Captain George Allen, the man who had deemed me to be below standard for refereeing in the army. I was delighted to say to him, and without the 'sir' this time, that I felt his original decision was unjust. But, you know, you can't win with officers. 'You have obviously taken heed of what I said', he commented, 'and that is why you are here today'.

Even Clive Thomas had no answer to that.

· 4 ·

...AND DOMESTIC WARFARE

Curious as it may seem to readers from outside Wales, I was taking part in international events some time before I was first appointed to the Football League referees' list. This is one of the undoubted advantages of being Welsh: the limited numbers and talent available in a rugby country mean that you can make rapid strides up the small ladder, even if the rungs are of suspect quality. This quick progress also gave me early and enormous experience of the pressures at international level, of some of the senior game's less savoury happenings, and of the strange attitude of the Football Association towards referees.

My first 'international' was to run the line at Aberdeen in February 1965, a game which gave me my first feelings of disquiet and even disgust at the antics of both players and managements at this level. The first half of the match, between Scottish and English Under-23 sides, was badly marred and scarred by fierce tackling and more than robust play by two particular players, one from each side. At the interval, the referee, Jack Lowrie from Neath, whom I rated as very competent indeed, asked me if, at the end of the match, and if these two players were near me, I would walk in between them to ensure there was no trouble. At the final whistle they were in the centre of the pitch, but, before I could reach them, they put their arms round each other and walked off together. Later Alf Ramsay, in charge of the England team, said at the banquet that there had been a few robust tackles, and probably one or two that should never have occurred. The players were Alan Ball and Billy Bremner.

Twelve months later, Ball helped England to win the World Cup, while Jack Lowrie had resigned within weeks of the match. The press had crucified him for not controlling the game, when he was trying to act as the establishment recommended by keeping players on the pitch. I vowed then that neither players, nor managers, nor establishment, would leave me in that position. The players would go first. I can still see now the dejection on the face of Jack Lowrie next morning as we sat in the plane at Aberdeen Airport with the snow falling. He was reading the newspaper reports, probably aware that his international career was at an end. 'Is it worth it?' he sighed.

The conclusion I reached was that you had to referee in a professional way, no matter what the match and no matter who the personalities.

There is no doubt in my mind, though I appreciated Jack Lowrie's problems fully, that both Ball and Bremner should have been sent off – I was later to deal with both of them that way. Under-23 internationals are important matches and young players should be taught at the start of their top-class careers that they cannot get away with footballing violence. I blame also the managers of such players for allowing them to exhibit this lack of discipline.

It was in Scotland, too, that I learned further major lessons three years or so later. The match seemed innocuous enough: Hibernian v Leeds United in the old Inter-Cities Fairs Cup in January 1968. Innocuous? I suppose that nothing to do with Don Revie's Yorkshire team could be thus described.

Waverley Station, Edinburgh, was not the most welcoming of places on a damp, cold night but the waiting official of the Hibernian club was certainly hospitable enough. Indeed, the following morning he took the linesmen and me shopping. In one particular store, where I fancied a Scottish blanket as a present for my wife, he asked the shop assistant to pack three (one for each linesman also) and told her he would pick them up later. The club, he said, would be delighted to present them to us.

Before the kick-off, familiarising myself with the pitch, I met Don Revie and the Leeds players and Revie, professional as always, inquired from what part of Wales I came. Some of my best friends are from the Rhondda, he claimed when I told him, including one of the greatest footballers he had known in Roy Paul, with whom he played at Manchester City. Revie may have thought he was tuning into the same wavelength as Thomas: neither of us knew that we would be clashing heavily for the next ten or twelve years. As it happened, during the final minute of the game, a Bremner free kick floated over the Hibernian defence for Jackie Charlton to head the winner. The Scots were out of the competition.

In the guest room later, the charming young man who had ordered the blankets and who had looked after us for twenty-four hours or more now totally ignored me. His secretary, a nice lassie, assured us that he would overcome his disappointment. But back in the hotel for the reception he still steadfastly refused even to acknowledge me, with the result that I lost my temper and told him not to act like a little schoolboy. I was restrained by my two colleagues, Ray Davies from Swansea and Roy Parker from Wrexham, but, when we left the following morning, there was no sign of our blankets. (In fact, I lived without Scottish blankets for a further six years until Bill Theurer, a Treherbert milkman who was by a curious coincidence a Hibernian fan, was told of the story and returned from holiday in his native country with a blanket for me, so as not to let down the club's reputation! Which all goes to prove something or other:

even if it is only that some milkmen are more sporting than some club officials.)

However, that match had more far-reaching consequences. During the game, I had to caution big Jack Charlton and, for the first time in the history of association football, a player appealed against his caution. Dennis Follows, who was then secretary of the FA, wrote to me on 22 January and enclosed an extract from a letter he had received from Revie in which the Leeds manager stated:

'I personally felt that the referee was a little bit weak because only a minute before the booking of Charlton he booked one of the Hibernian players and the crowd were incensed at this, and it looked to me as though the next foul a Leeds player did, he was going to put it in his book.'

I took great exception to this implication and told the Football Association so in my letter of 24 January. To me this was an opportunity for the FA to back up referees and to put Revie in his place for using the words he did in criticising the referee.

At the FA's Lancaster Gate headquarters, the first of many appearances I was to make there, the massed support and professionalism of Leeds United and Jack Charlton won the case and the caution was struck off. I had learned a hard lesson: I was now not only a football referee but was required also to be a legal expert, acting as judge on the pitch as well as prosecutor, leading witness and, apparently, being in the dock as well. There was no doubt in my mind that the FA had let down all referees with this decision. The FA deserved from that time all they received at disciplinary hearings. They didn't even comment on Revie's remarks.

The battle between Thomas and establishment, Thomas and managers, Thomas and players – which I have never sought – had been joined. In the next few chapters, I'll be telling you about some of the matches that made the headlines in the league, at Wembley, in Europe and round the world, as well as taking you into the gloomy depths of football's famous institutions.

· 5 ·
FUN AND GAMES

Maine Road, Hillsborough, Villa Park, Wembley, Highbury, Home Park, Plainmoor . . . Plainmoor? Yes, that's the Torquay United ground. The point is that all these grounds and more come to mind when I try to recall the more controversial incidents of my career. Several games are more suitable for inclusion in other chapters to illustrate other points, and you may therefore have to seek elsewhere in the book for an explanation of your own particular memory of Clive Thomas.

But let us first head for Manchester and to Maine Road, whose club and stadium seem to crop up very frequently in my cuttings. I think first of a Wednesday evening in March 1974 – the thirteenth, for those who have superstitious inclinations, which I have not – when, as usual, the local derby between Manchester City and Manchester United was a tough one to referee. During the first twenty minutes, it was plain that tension was high with tempers to match and, very early on, I booked City's Mike Summerbee, a player of enormous talent but who needed to be shown that he would be controlled.

Then in the twenty-eighth minute Mike Doyle brought down Lou Macari, who reacted with his normal Scottish fervour. He picked up the ball and thrust it into Doyle's face; the latter retaliated with fists flying. I ran up to them, cooled them down, and sent them off. To my surprise, they both walked away as if nothing had happened. Perhaps they had misunderstood my Welsh accent, I thought. I called them back, told them they were off, and again they refused to go. Mike Summerbee came up to represent the two players in his usual diplomatic way but I was adamant. 'Come on, Clive', said Doyle. 'You're spoiling the game. Let's get on with it.' Lou said simply, 'Forty-five thousand have come to see this match.' Again they both walked away.

I picked up the ball, blew the whistle, and motioned to both teams to come off the field. I was not aware at that moment that this was the first time in history that a referee had taken both teams from the field in a Football League match because two players had refused to obey orders. Somewhat surprisingly, perhaps, both teams did come off. Less surprisingly, the secretary of Manchester City was waiting by the tunnel to find out what was going on. I told him to inform the crowd over the loudspeakers that we would be back on the field, all of us bar two, within five minutes.

I told the respective managers, Ron Saunders and Tommy Docherty, that I would speak with the teams in their dressing-rooms. I went first to United's where, with all the players seated, I pointed at Macari and said we were going back on without him. Not even the Doc said a word. I repeated the message in the City quarters, this time to Mike Doyle, and we finally resumed the game without further trouble.

The headlines next day were, I suppose, predictable: 'Off – the lot of you', 'A disgrace to the name of football', and 'In the cooler' were samples of the genre.

Curiously, the assessor – and by now a referee's assessor reported on every game – took the view that he could not comment on the dismissals because the matter was *sub judice*: my immediate reply to the Football League was that he had chickened out of a major decision. The assessor also felt that I should have shown more tolerance. All right, I was known as Clive the Book, but such comments were a load of nonsense. That game had needed total control with very little flexibility, which any competent assessor would have realised.

At the inevitable personal hearing, Lou Macari said I had ordered both teams to the dressing-rooms before he had time to go off, although he did admit that he was at fault: Doyle merely denied any offence. What did surprise me, though, was the massed band of witnesses they produced – the representative of the Professional Footballers' Association, Cliff Lloyd, both managers, and a substantial proportion of the City board in Messrs Swales, Alexander, Humphries and Niven. Needless to say, each gave an identical version of the incident despite sitting some seventy yards away in the grandstand.

During the evidence to Vernon Stokes, chairman of the FA, Dick Speake and Harold Smart, it was pointed out that a videotape of each match was made for the Manchester City club. Mentally, I rubbed my hands together at this chance to produce real evidence. Alas, when I asked the chairman for an adjournment while we all watched the tape, Mr Swales said that they had looked at it and, unfortunately, just before the incident they were changing the reels. I am not afraid to say that I laughed out loud in front of them all.

The result? Macari was found guilty of misconduct and fined seventy-five pounds while Doyle was fined fifty pounds for misconduct. But the committee decided that Doyle was not guilty of striking an opponent.

Maine Road again, this time on Saturday, 23 April, 1977, for probably one of the most crucial local derbies in the history of football – but not a Manchester team in sight. Everton were playing Liverpool in an FA Cup semi-final, a difficult match in prospect not only because of its importance but also because some of the players on the park that afternoon were likely to take matters into their own hands.

One entertainer on the field was Duncan McKenzie, a gifted ball-player and a fine distributor of the ball, who needed a little looking after because of some very hard tackling from Liverpool; it was he who unwittingly became the villain of the piece. The score was 2–2 with only a couple of minutes left when a cross from the right resulted in what Bryan Hamilton and at least 30,000 Everton supporters thought was the winner: beating Liverpool and reaching Wembley, a double triumph. I was satisfied, though, looking at Hamilton when the ball was passed to him, that he was offside. I blew accordingly but the Everton players had drowned Hamilton in their celebration and, even more unfortunately, linesman Colin Seel was on his way back to the halfway line, also satisfied with the goal.

Although McKenzie was the best footballer on the field, I had to blame him for his last touch of the ball on to Hamilton because, by then, Hamilton was indeed offside. I could not blame the linesman for not seeing this final touch, nor indeed the Everton players, nor Gordon Lee, the manager, who was raging on the touchline. I gave an immediate interview on radio and told listeners to watch the match on television to see whether I was right or not. The cameras did prove me correct and, as Colin Wood said in the *Daily Mail* on the Monday, 'Liverpool owe it to eagle-eyed referee.' Mind you, I am also convinced that Bryan Hamilton handled the ball too. The angle of the pass meant to me that there was only one way in which he could have 'scored', and that was with his arm. If I had not blown for the convenient offside, you Everton fans, I would still have disallowed the goal for hand ball.

Liverpool won the replay comfortably enough by 3–0 the following Wednesday evening, again at Maine Road, when there were two further decisions which upset Everton supporters. I gave a penalty against Mike Pejic when he pushed Liverpool's David Johnson but when he turned away in anger I am sure it was in disgust with himself rather than with the decision. Everton wanted a penalty when I gave an indirect free kick against Ray Clemence for his threatening foot-up challenge against Duncan McKenzie and, while I would have been delighted to have given the penalty, the laws are to blame for this one and not me. Indeed, how many referees would have given a free kick of any kind?

The football followers from that particular side of Stanley Park have never forgiven me for those decisions and Hamilton always brings up the issue when we meet. I remember later trying to find the Holiday Inn in Liverpool and asking a taxi driver the way. 'I know you', he said. 'You're asking for trouble coming here. I'd like to show you the longest way round. But because deep down I respect you, the quickest way is ...'

He may well have been at the match in 1980 when I had the two teams again in the fourth round of the cup. I was delightedly naturally because it suggested that the Football Association had confidence in me and had for once backed the decisions I had made in previous cup-ties. It was not the first time I had refereed Everton since 1977: I had for example had them against Villa in the third round in 1978. On that day, from a crowd of 44,338, 44,336 booed me on to the pitch. The other two were my guests. I decided to try to take the sting out of the situation, so, after walking about ten yards on to the field, I made as if to run off again to the tunnel. I made a few more friends.

But all that was forgotten as I headed once more for Liverpool. This time I took my wife and daughters with me, and it certainly made them aware of the demands of football in that part of the world. Radio Merseyside actually interviewed me in the pool of the Holiday Inn within half an hour of my arrival in Liverpool on the Friday evening, Granada Television wanted me live with former Liverpool and Everton stars and the papers were full of the game. It turned out to be the most difficult of the matches I have refereed between the two clubs. Before the kick-off I had warned the linesmen that there could be plenty of trouble. But I was also on the look-out for the Everton fans who gave me their usual boisterous welcome. I wanted to show them very early that I would stand no nonsense from their players.

The opportunity came quickly. With only twenty-five seconds gone, I gave a free kick, for a foul by Asa Hartford on the halfway line – one which I would normally have let pass without mention, but this time I spoke severely to Asa who replied like the true pro he is. 'OK, Clive, I understand', he said. The crowd were howling and, before Phil Thompson took the kick, I saw from the corner of my eye a figure jumping up from the Everton trainers' bench. I went straight over to Gordon Lee and asked who had leaped up. It was one of their injured players, Jim McDonagh the goalkeeper I think, and I told Gordon that any repetition would lead to someone going up the tunnel. Gordon knew what I was up to. 'Sorry, Clive, let's get on with the game', he said.

There was one unpleasant incident between Jimmy Case and the Everton goalkeeper, Martin Hodge, in which some half a dozen players became involved. I was acting like a boxing referee breaking up clinches, and I gave Case a public warning. Souness was a very lucky man not to be sent off for a stupid flare-up with Mick Lyons. I was surprised at Mick because I respected him as one of the coolest players in the game. Souness we all know: he is a hard man.

In the end Everton were worthy winners, 2-1, and although I had to book six players I was immensely satisfied with my performance. For once, so was everyone else.

Bob Paisley told the *Liverpool Echo*: 'The referee Clive Thomas did well and came out of the game with tremendous credit, because it was a situation which would easily have got out of hand with a lesser man in charge.' And Gordon Lee said: 'He was very sharp. It was a terribly hard game to control and it took a top man to handle it.' In *The People*, Norman Wynn stated that 'only the firm handling of referee Clive Thomas stopped the game from falling apart', while Peter Thomas wrote in the *Daily Express*: 'Mr Thomas was not only excellent and sharp. He gave one of the bravest performances seen on a football pitch and it must be remembered that he is hardly the favourite member of the Thomas clan at Goodison.'

I had agreed with Eddie Hemmings of Radio Merseyside to go on a live phone-in after the match. It went on for about an hour and was going so well that they asked if I would stay an extra thirty minutes. However I remembered Frankie Vaughan's advice, to quit while the audience wanted more. Besides, my family were waiting for me and I was hungry. I took them to a restaurant to have a quiet dinner. No chance. Halfway through the meal, some of the Everton players arrived with their wives and girlfriends. For once we were able to speak to each other and have a drink or two. They paid . . .

One final quickie from those Liverpool-Everton matches. Following the World Cup in Germany, I was proud of my German blue suit given to every referee. I arrived at Anfield to be greeted by my dear but late friend Bill Shankly.

'What's that you're wearing?' he asked.

'My World Cup suit', I replied.

'Pity about the colour', he said. 'I'm supposed to mark you out of ten for your performance today. You're already minus two.'

Liverpool were involved in another regrettable episode in my story. Some one hundred and seventeen minutes had passed almost uneventfully during the afternoon of 14 March, 1981, in the Football League Cup Final between Liverpool and West Ham United. As Donald Sanders wrote in *The Daily Telegraph*: 'One could not avoid the feeling that the £603,000 (the crowd) had spent could have supported rather better causes in the meaner streets of West Ham and Liverpool.' In short, it looked odds-on for a replay at Villa Park on, ironically, 1 April.

Then, with three minutes of extra time left, Sammy Lee and Billy Bonds went up for a cross, Lee was bowled over and, as the ball ran loose, Alan Kennedy drove his shot over the prostrate Lee's body and into the goal. I saw Lee lying on the ground in an apparently offside position and my linesman flagged, but I overruled him as I did not think a player lying on the ground was interfering with play.

The League had at the beginning of the season reminded referees that they had a duty to decide before ruling on offside whether a player 'is interfering with play or an opponent, or seeking to gain an advantage by being in that position'. Was Sammy Lee seeking to gain an advantage? No. My only fault was that I did not – and this is in retrospect – go to the linesman and say 'I'm satisfied it was a goal'. I saw him flagging but gestured to him, as per my pre-match instructions, to put down the flag. The West Ham players asked me to consult the linesman, Mike Jerney, but I went only halfway to him and again motioned for him to go back to the halfway line, which, as I say, is the normal procedure if a referee has seen the linesman flagging but is satisfied justice has been done. He did not move and so I had to follow up the protest.

With West Ham a goal down, ironically I had to award them a clear penalty when Terry McDermott turned Martin's header on to the bar with his hand. Stewart promptly thumped the ball wide of Clemence's left hand and honour was surely satisfied – or was it? No, the trouble then began. On the Wembley turf after the match, alas, John Lyall, the West Ham manager and as nice a man as you will meet, started to point and shout at me. I quote now from the evidence I sent to the Football Association, as I felt I had to book John and report him:

'When I stood before him, he (Lyall) stated: "You and him are cheats." (I assumed he meant my linesman.) I told him, "Do not speak to me like that."

'He replied, "You are a cheat." I then stated "You say that again and I will report you." He replied "You are a cheat." At that time Mr Bob Paisley, manager of Liverpool FC, put his arm round me and told me to take no notice. I told Mr Paisley, "Bob, no one ever speaks to me like that."'

John claimed in his submission that I approached him on the pitch and said, 'In my opinion the Liverpool player was not interfering with play.' He then said, he claims: 'I will give you our opinion. We felt cheated and if you watch it tomorrow. I think you will understand why.'

Clive Thomas then said, 'Say that again and I will report you.'

Lyall said 'We felt cheated.'

Clive Thomas then said 'Say that again and I will report you.'

Lyall again replied, 'We felt cheated.'

Bert Millichip, chairman of the FA Disciplinary Committee, headed the three-man commission which took the hearing, along with A.D. McMullen, chairman of the FA Referees' Committee, and Dick Wragg, chairman of the FA International Committee. Millichip said the commission had the benefit of television evidence, but there was nothing on film to help them with the charge. Referee Thomas, he said, was not on a charge, only Lyall – and there was no question that he used the word 'cheat'. The dispute was about how the word had been used. In the end, John Lyall was cleared by the Disciplinary Committee of a charge of 'insulting and improper behaviour'. After the hearing, we had lunch together. As I say, he's a nice guy.

If I ever dropped a real clanger, it was at Highbury two years later on 19 March, 1983. The game between Arsenal and Luton Town was a very drab affair, surprisingly in view of Luton's precarious position in the First Division at the time and despite their manager, David Pleat, for whom I have considerable respect. The afternoon was hot and the whole atmosphere soporific. Wales were playing rugby in Paris, the policeman by the tunnel keeping me in touch with the score. But none of this is an excuse for what happened.

At Highbury, the referee rings a bell linked to the dressing-rooms to summon the players on to the pitch. By the time you walk past the admin offices and down the steps to the tunnel, the players are on the field. And so after half-time it was an orderly scene, with Woodcock ready to restart the match. I looked at both linesmen, received the usual thumbs-up, and away we went. The ball was played up the touchline for an Arsenal attack when I heard an outburst of laughter. Anything to liven up a dull afternoon, I thought, but I could see nothing to warrant it. Wanting to share in the joke, I turned just in time to see Pat Jennings, the Arsenal goalkeeper, trotting out on to the field and down to his penalty area. I stopped play and went down to see him. I had to laugh.

'Pat, why did you have to do that to me?' I asked.

'Sorry, Clive, but I was talking to the boss in the tunnel and never thought you would start without me.'

Before restarting the match back in the middle, I apologised with head bowed to the crowd, and then counted each player, to huge applause.

What if Luton had scored in those seconds of play? I would have made the same decision and restarted the half all over again, but, during the next week, there was much discussion among referees' societies round Britain. Of ten referees and four assessors I spoke to, only one assessor thought my decision to kick off again was correct. Most of them said they would have dropped the ball where I stopped play. Some said they would have carried on and waited for the ball to go out of play before allowing Jennings to enter the field of play. All would have cautioned Pat for coming on without permission. The assessor described it as a 'slight lapse of concentration following the half-time break. However, you got out of it well and with good humour.'

I am sure that in some circles the knives were out for Clive Thomas in the hope that he had made the biggest mistake of his career. But Law 3 states: 'A match shall be played by two teams, consisting of not more than eleven players, one of whom shall be goalkeeper . . .'

Talking of goalkeepers, I hope that as a breed they will forgive me if I talk about another record-breaking game in which I took part – a Football League second round (second leg) cup-tie one Wednesday night in October 1981, when Stoke City were beaten 8–9 at their Victoria Ground by Manchester City. There is of course a catch to the record score: it was Britain's most dramatic shoot-out ending with Joe Corrigan's save from the twentieth penalty shot of the evening by Stoke City substitute Peter Griffiths at four minutes past ten. Big Joe said afterwards that he had asked referee Thomas what would happen if Griffiths were to score. I had told him that he was next as the other ten had all had their shots. 'I couldn't face that', said Joe, and saved the shot from the unfortunate Griffiths. I did actually break a law in that match. After the extra time, I allowed the players to go to the touchline to talk to their managers before having to return to the middle of the field to take their penalties.

Penalties? That reminds me, just as no doubt it will remind all those Tottenham Hotspur fans who were either at Hillsborough, Sheffield, on 11 April, 1981, or who saw the televised version later. I suppose that the subject has to be raised somewhere in the book. So here goes.

The story so far, as they say in the serials: fifteen seconds from time in an FA Cup semi-final between Tottenham Hotspur and Wolverhampton Wanderers, Spurs are leading 2–1. Kenny Hibbitt of Wolves, a tricky personality at the best of times, makes progress through the Tottenham penalty area. Glen Hoddle, of all people, comes across to tackle and the Wolves player goes down. Penalty. Carr equalises from the spot and chants of 'Cheat, cheat, cheat' sweep round Hillsborough . . .

John Sadler, supposedly a friend, writes in *The Sun*: 'A penalty? Glenn Hoddle's tackle on Kenny Hibbitt was far from that. Nay, dammit, that tackle was perfection. Hoddle knew it. Hibbitt knew it, and even admitted: "I had to go down – it was the last chance we would get." No one blames him for trying. But I blame Thomas for being conned.'

I disagree wholeheartedly with John Sadler when he says that no one blames Hibbitt for trying. It must be wrong for a responsible journalist to write like that, especially when he has been a proponent of discipline in the game. There were conflicting reports during that weekend as to whether Kenny had admitted to conning me. But then, later, he denied that he had deliberately taken a fall.

When I went into the dressing-room after the match, both linesmen agreed that it was a definite penalty and, therefore, if I had been in doubt at the time, they would have confirmed the decision. I have, of course, watched the incident on numerous occasions and I do question now not whether Hibbitt was brought down by Hoddle but whether I was in the perfect position to make that crucial decision. In all honesty, I have to say that, if I had the chance to relive those moments, I would not now give the penalty. This brings us back to the point that the referee has to be a hundred per cent certain – because a penalty to me is a goal and you have to be a hundred per cent certain in awarding goals as they are what decide a game. But for referees the game is also about angles, and I have to say that I was out here, only slightly perhaps, but enough to prevent me from being absolutely sure.

It is one of the few decisions that I wish I could make again. But from the countless thousands I have made in football, I must surely have been wrong at least once, for I couldn't be right all the time! Nevertheless, I still sleep peacefully at night because I think of the correct ones, and of how many mistakes footballers make in every match.

If that was a match for me to remember, Plainmoor, Torquay, comes to mind as the match that never was, yet still I ran into trouble. No matter what the advertisements say about the palm trees down there – oh, yes, I know they are there – 9 February, 1983, was not the balmiest of tropical evenings. Indeed, threequarters of an hour before Torquay's home match with Bristol City was due to kick-off at 7.30, I had to postpone the game as the pitch had frozen up. The respective managers, Bruce Rioch and Terry Cooper, had agreed at 5.35 that it was playable, but the conditions changed dramatically.

Many Bristol City supporters had travelled a fair distance to reach Torquay and the police thought that in view of the cancellation it might be unwise of me to leave the ground for an hour or more. I suggested that it might be better if I went out to speak to the supporters and they agreed. In *The Star* the following morning, under a headline 'Top ref Thomas saves a blow-up', the article stated that 'police last night praised Thomas for helping to quell a potentially explosive situation'. I was therefore a little upset to receive on St Valentine's Day, 14 February, a letter from Graham Kelly, Secretary of the Football League, in which he enclosed a copy of a letter from Mrs Marjorie Warren of Wick, Bristol, complaining about the lateness of my decision and that she would be pleased to receive my observations.

I don't know. Firstly, the Football League tell you not to become involved in speaking to anyone about your matches. Then, in the next breath as it were, they want you to correspond, even though the Football League had been kept fully informed by me at every stage since 3.45 on the day of the match. At 6.50 I had phoned Graham Kelly to tell him of the cancellation, and described what had happened. He had accepted my explanation.

The game was finally played on a Sunday afternoon, 20 March, the day after the Arsenal-Luton match I referred to earlier. The Football

League was concerned about my two appointments in two days but I was determined to show the Bristol supporters that I was not afraid to meet them again.

Another incident concerning Bristol City had occurred at Ashton Gate, in October, 1982, when York City were the visitors. The York manager, Denis Smith, an old friend and sparring partner, approached me before the game to seek help. Because of the financial position of the club, York wanted desperately to catch an early train home to save costs. I could not, of course, cut into the forty-five minutes each way. But I could have the minimum time for the interval. The result was that we marched from the field at half-time and literally had the chance to swill only a mouthful of tea around before I rang the bell to summon the players back on to the park. It was the quickest interval I have ever had. The York players, of course, were prepared for it, but I wasn't sure how Terry Cooper and his Bristol players would react.

I went to their dressing-room, told them the reason, and Cooper said he would oblige but warned, 'You know the rules, Clive.' We restarted in about three minutes while the spectators were still going for their break, let alone coming back. There is no doubt that neither a single director nor the referee's assessor saw the start of the second half. But York City caught their train.

Two further examples now of managers I would also help – because they help the game. First, Brian Clough – he really backed me up at a match between Nottingham Forest and Middlesbrough early in 1982. Cloughie had been on holiday and, in his absence, under Peter Taylor's management, Forest had lost a game or two. They were little better in this game – though that is not the point. At one stage, I gave a free kick against Viv Anderson. He regarded me with such arrogance, which I felt to be out of character, that I had a quiet word with him. He showed no remorse, putting on an air of what the army used to call 'dumb insolence', so I cautioned him. After the match Cloughie asked me why I had cautioned Anderson: for dissent by word of mouth, perhaps? I explained, and Brian said, 'Right, I will fine him as well.'

Strong backing also came from Aston Villa manager Tony Barton in October 1982 after a match between his side and Tottenham. Jimmy Rimmer, the Villa goalkeeper, watched a shot thunder past his post and, instead of retrieving the ball, marched towards me, shouting about a decision I had given earlier. I remained in the penalty area and gave him the opportunity to stop. He didn't. 'Are you shouting at me?' I asked. 'Yes', he yelled. I then walked up to him, said 'You must be crazy' and cautioned him. After the match, I told Rimmer he must be as thick as the goalpost to behave as he did because, quite apart from his goal-keeping abilities, he was a player who usually accepted decisions. Tony

Barton said Rimmer had only himself to blame, and that his reason for his behaviour, that he was furious at not being prepared for a Spurs free kick which had so nearly caught him unawares, was unacceptable.

In the same game, in an off-the-ball fracas between two very tough players, Paul Miller and Peter Withe, I allowed the advantage as Villa had possession before walking back to caution Miller, the instigator. 'Don't bother to caution him', said Withe, coming between us. 'Leave him to me because I'll get him.' I told Withe he must be a prize idiot to speak like that as he could be sent off for threatening behaviour. 'No, I know you would not send me off for that', replied Withe, 'because I can speak to you, not like the others'.

I am still trying to work out whether that was a compliment or not.

One occasion when I had no support from either management or officialdom was during a local derby between QPR and Orient in October 1980. Stan Bowles had by now joined Orient in his chequered career and he was besieged throughout the match by his former QPR colleagues. Finally he was brought down so harshly by the Rangers skipper, Glenn Roeder, that I had no option but to send Roeder off. Bowles had to leave the pitch for medical treatment and on his return asked me, 'What made him do that?'

You would think that Orient would thank me for protecting their player. But no. Manager Jimmy Bloomfield and chairman Brian Winston wasted no time in defending Roeder, a former Orient player, in the press. 'I know Glenn better than anyone here', said Winston. 'He would never intentionally hurt anyone. He is the quietest and gentlest person.' Brian, it is a shame that you didn't go down to your own dressing-room to see the marks on Stan's legs.

I telephoned Peter Barnes, the Orient secretary, to tell him how shocked I was by the comments of his manager and chairman as it was one of the worst fouls I had seen for some time. I added also that if the chairman and manager wished to take my further comments to the FA and the Football League, I would be delighted to repeat them as the two men were a disgrace to the game. Mr Winston is on the Football League Management Committee.

I had come under attack for a sending-off the previous month, in fact, when I dismissed Lawrie Sanchez, the Reading striker, for a tackle on John Uzzell during a match at Plymouth. As I went to restart the game, I saw Sanchez sitting in the dug-out, which is close to the pitch at Home Park. This incensed me – just as it does when I see a manager put an arm round a player when he is sent off. To me, it's on a par with an employer putting his arm round a worker when he has committed a dismissal offence. Be that as it may, I went to the dug-out and sent Sanchez to the dressing-rooms. Two days later, a headline in the *Daily Star* reported,

'Touchline ban ref faces rap'. An FA spokesman was quoted as saying, 'A sending-off from the field of play does not mean the player has to go to the dressing-room. He is entitled to sit on the bench and only if he makes a nuisance of himself is the referee allowed to order him to the dressing-room.'

Technically, I suppose he was right, but the attitude is typical of an organisation where few people have ever refereed a match themselves. Actually, the FA never communicated with me on the matter: but my view is still that the very presence of Sanchez constituted a nuisance.

There were nuisances, too, at the Hawthorns, West Bromwich, on 30 November 1983, during and after the blood-and-thunder fourth round Milk Cup tie between West Bromwich and Aston Villa. I had to caution seven players and send off Albion's Gary Owen – a gentle man on the pitch but who, on the night, had to go. I pulled a muscle in the second minute of the second half, but there was no way I was going to hand over to my senior linesman, John Grainger – and that is a reflection on the ferocious match, rather than on his ability. Tony Barton, manager of Villa, said later, 'It was a softening-up process for the whole of the first half'. Yet Ron Wylie, the West Bromwich Albion manager, told the press, 'There wasn't a vicious tackle in ninety minutes'.

What chance does the game have when managers like Wylie appear to condone what I believe is brutality on the pitch? Nor did the nuisances stop there. Back in the dressing-room after the game, the table was bare: not a cup of tea, a glass of milk or a sandwich was to be seen, even though they had been there at half-time. It is traditional that referees and linesmen receive at least a cup of tea after a match. I pointed this out to a West Bromwich official when he came to pay our expenses, telling him I would be reporting it to the Football League. Within a couple of minutes, chairman Sid Lucas and secretary Tony Rance came to convey their apologies. The teapot duly reappeared, along with sandwiches and a selection of miniatures. I applaud the chairman, too, for his action in following up the incident with a letter of apology. Well done, Sid.

Mind you, in reflecting on these incidents and on many, many others at just about every ground in England and Wales, it seems to me that I have often been the one who is regarded as the nuisance. Even at the showpiece of football, the FA Cup Final.

·6·
WEMBLEY GOOD AND BAD

If you are not careful, the Football Association can even manage to spoil the Cup Final for you. Don't get me wrong: it is a tremendous honour to referee at Wembley, there are memorable moments, and, as a Welshman, I was possibly even more fortunate than most referees to receive the appointment. But, one way and another, somebody, somewhere seems to do his best to try to spoil that magic weekend.

One Sunday morning in the spring of 1976 I received a telephone call from Reg Payne, the FA referees' secretary, in which he said very simply, 'Congratulations, you have been chosen as the Cup Final referee.' My immediate reaction was of delight because I knew the problems involved for a Welshman having such a match. The appointment is made by a committee where a number of council members have their say. Invariably, the honour goes round the different areas of the country and each representative plugs his own referee. But Wales, of course, is not represented – and, besides, Wales has its own Cup Final and no English referee has the chance to take that game (wrongly, in my view). Other Welshmen, Mervyn Griffiths and Leo Callaghan, had taken FA Cup Finals, yes, but even if there is another Clive Thomas, in my opinion he is unlikely for political reasons ever to do so.

Reg Payne told me to keep the news under wraps although he did agree, apparently reluctantly, to allow me to tell my wife. Within hours, though, I was inundated with telephone calls from just about every newspaper in Fleet Street and Cardiff, quite apart from television and radio. Between you, me and the proverbial gatepost, I had been so confident a couple of years previously that I would be chosen for a final that I had been interviewed for BBC Television in Wales and said how much I was looking forward to the final and so on. The tape was kept in cold storage because I wanted the producer, Dewi Griffiths of BBC Wales, to have the first interview. Dewi's a real pro and a real friend and I had confidence in him, just as I had in having the final one day.

The first telegram my wife received on the Monday morning was from Lawrie McMenemy, manager of then Second Division Southampton who were, of course, to appear in the final. No doubt the establishment would say that it was wrong for a club manager to become involved in this way with the referee, and, indeed, in the case of some managers I

33

would agree that it suggested collusion. But not in Lawrie's case: he's far too professional, and he comes from the north-east where they have a feeling for the game unsurpassed anywhere else in Britain.

The confirmation of the appointment from the Football Association began the disappointments. Only eight days before the match, they notified me that in addition to the twenty-five-pound fee I would receive two tickets free – not enough even for my wife and daughters – and that I could buy only an additional four. I immediately phoned Reg Payne, but he said it was nothing to do with him although I was to communicate with him about every other aspect of the match. How was I to gather enough tickets to supply to all those people who had helped me on the way up?

Unlike many referees, I had never taken a member of any FA committee by car to a match and I was therefore unable to lean on them. But I did make contact with several managers and club secretaries who willingly came to my aid when I told them of my allocation. I thank them again – just as I thank my daughters Allyson and Caryn for not insisting on going to Wembley. I couldn't even ensure that my wife was sitting with our great friends, Howard and Maisy Jones. In fact, Howard ultimately sat by himself. I wrote in vain also to Ted Croker, secretary of the FA.

Then came the official itinerary and another altercation. I was told by Reg Payne that I would be the guest of Manchester United at their banquet after the match, despite having been told the previous day that no banquets were being organised by the clubs. It seemed curious to me that an FA official should be so involved with one of the participating clubs, let alone under the instructions of the FA, and, anyhow, I wanted to go out that evening with the Joneses and my linesmen. But, said the FA, that is our decision, and you can expect a letter from Manchester United. This duly came from Les Olive, the very efficient and capable secretary at Old Trafford, who said the invitation was for referee, linesmen and wives. I explained the predicament over our friends and he replied, quite understandably, that accommodation was very limited. In that case, I said, I thank you for the invitation but I will have to decline it. But, said Les, this is an FA instruction. Would I therefore discuss it with the FA?

At Lancaster Gate, Reg Payne decided it was too big a decision for him and referred me to Croker. Croker was not pleased and told me, in effect, that in refereeing a Cup Final I also had to accept all the FA diktats. I told him that I would referee the game, yes, but no one was going to tell me what to do after the match. He said that one reason why I should do what I was told was so that the FA would know where to find me in case of controversy or any other points they may wish to discuss.

Fair enough, I said, you will probably be able to find me at the *Talk of the Town*. That's not possible, he said. Good grief, I thought, the FA control the *Talk of the Town* as well! Croker said they had tried to book tables for visitors from overseas but there were no vacancies, again despite a letter on 22 April which said arrangements had been made for referees and linesmen to go there: lounge suits, said the letter, were to be worn. I told him I would notify him in due course where they would be able to find me. One telephone call to my old friend Frankie Vaughan, and, within an hour, the booking for a table for four was confirmed.

Even the night before the match was fraught with foolishness. The linesmen and I were told by the FA that we had to attend the usual eve-of-final rally organised by the London Society of Association Referees, an occasion which I had never attended but which is supposed to be a stupendous night, when the trumpets are blown, the arc lights come on and, lo, into the spotlight marches the big match referee and his henchmen. Well, sitting next to Sir Stanley Rous and being entertained by a cabaret, I made inquiries at about 10 pm as to the duration of the performance. Sir Stanley said we had a long way to go yet. Going through my mind was the total lack of professionalism of referees: could you imagine the players of Manchester United and Southampton attending a major function the night before such an important match?

I told chaperone Reg Payne that we were leaving. You can't do that, he said, it would be discourteous and no referee leaves before the end. This one does, I said – and I was duly reported, as the first referee to walk out of a Cup Final rally. Many of my colleagues, I was to discover, sympathised, and even Ted Croker, in fairness, agreed when I took up the whole matter with him later.

On the morning of the match I discussed with the linesmen my instructions for the game and was truly astonished, as I came to an end, to hear Alf Grey, the reserve referee, ask the other linesman whether he could choose which team he would be lining for, as he wanted to become acclimatised. Here we were, just five hours or so before the kick-off, and I had an official who, because he was a Football League referee and therefore had had no experience of lining for a season or two, was admitting that he was not very confident. (The Football League, incidentally, for their cup finals have the reserve referee on the bench with two experienced linesmen running the line, a system which I suggested the FA should emulate though it fell on deaf ears.) I told Alf that if he did not feel he was competent, I'd have him taken off the game, at which point he quickly agreed that he would line to whichever side I told him.

We were picked up to be taken to Wembley at 11 am, with wives travelling in separate limousines, and even after a salad lunch there were still two and a half hours to go before the kick-off, a foolishly long time to leave people wandering about Wembley. I walked out on to the stadium turf at one stage for a stroll and was immediately asked by Dickie Davies whether I would be interviewed for ITV. Chaperone Payne said I had better have permission from Mr Croker but I thought it would be very rude to interrupt his lunch, and went ahead.

In the referees' dressing-room at Wembley, there is scarcely room for the four officials to change, especially when the ubiquitous Reg Payne is also there. So threequarters of an hour before the start, when Lawrie McMenemy and Tommy Docherty came in with their teamsheets, I almost had to ask the reserve linesman to leave or, alternatively, take the managers out into the corridor to make the few points I wished to mention. Half an hour to go and I take my honey with a cup of tea from the paper cups so generously provided and I start to sing, as always in the dressing-room, *Land of my Fathers*, any Welsh hymn I can remember, *My Way* ... And not a word of protest from the linesmen of the day, maybe because they did not wish to hurt me, for others have said quite categorically that as a singer I'm a first-class referee.

Time to take the field. For the first time in many years Dickie Bird, Ted Croker's assistant, was unable to lead the team on to the pitch because he was recovering from an operation, which saddened me because I have always felt that Dickie had some sympathy for referees and I certainly respected him. This time, it was his assistant, Eric Dinnie, who led us on and I think he was as nervous as anyone. I told him not to worry: he would be leaving when we reached the halfway line. I felt quite relaxed as we entered the arena like the gladiators of old: I had been reserve referee at the FL cup final a couple of months previously, I was due to come back again shortly to do the England–Northern Ireland International in a week or so. I began to think Wembley was like my home ground of Cae Mawr at Treorchy.

For all that, it was a moment of colossal satisfaction, the boy from Treorchy, known only for its male voice choir, at the centre of the most glamorous soccer spectacle in the world. A jumble of other thoughts in my mind: Beryl visiting me when I was in the Army at Mill Hill, our walk round Wembley Stadium and my promise that we would one day be back. And then, suddenly, the presentations. It was one of the rare occasions when Her Majesty the Queen and the Duke of Edinburgh were at the match. I felt like a toy soldier standing next to big Lawrie McM, the ex-guardsman, when I noticed the linesmen waving. I asked what they were doing and they told me they were waving to their wives. I thought this to be extremely unprofessional and told them so, although I should probably have understood their reason.

I was presented to the Duke, not for the first time in fact because he had previously attended functions for the Boys' Clubs. We exchanged a few words, he wished me luck, and suddenly, I was in charge.

I have been asked why, in the centre of the pitch that day as we prepared for the toss-up, a certain photographer wanted pictures only of the two linesmen. Simple: they were publicity pictures for the company providing the referees' kit, and I had refused the instructions from the FA to wear it.

Away we went then. I had been presented with a gold-plated whistle by the Rhondda Referees Society and had promised that I would start the game with it. The whistle has been blown only that once – I put it in my pocket after that initial blast, accompanied by the Thomas kick – with the result that the pea is in excellent shape.

The game, as far as I was concerned, went according to plan. The players were a credit to football, though Manchester United put up possibly the worst playing performance I have ever known from them when I have been in charge, while Southampton, with so much to play for, scored the only goal in the one moment during the match when I thought things might not be going right. When Stokes, the scorer of the goal, had the ball at his feet, he appeared to me possibly to be ȯffside. I looked quickly to my linesman, was very relieved to find that it was the more confident of the two, and the flag stayed down. Another split-second and I saw another Manchester United defender playing Stokes onside. Then the players were jumping for joy, the supporters were going berserk and Southampton had won.

It was a marvellous moment to receive the gold medal from the Queen, knowing that only eighty-odd people have received such a medal, and a photograph of the presentation remains in our lounge at home today, not because it was the Cup Final but because it is Her Majesty. The Duke of Edinburgh referred to a point he made to me earlier on the field but to this day I refuse to divulge what it was that he said.

Back in the dressing-room, I was asked by Peter Lorenzo on BBC radio what Clive Thomas now had to look forward to. I said, and meant, another Cup Final. The listeners that day would surely be baffled if they could have looked ahead and known that in 1983 I would not have been given a single FA cup-tie.

I relaxed, reflecting what a marvellous afternoon it had been. I was delighted also, as a Welshman, that among the spectators had been James Callaghan, the then Prime Minister who represented a Cardiff constituency, and that the man who actually received the trophy was Peter Rodrigues, the Southampton captain and Welsh international full-back.

After showering – one by one because there wasn't room for more than a single person – we all went upstairs to a reception room where I went straight to my wife. 'Why didn't you wave like the linesmen?' was Beryl's first question. 'You didn't honestly expect me to, did you?' I asked. 'No', she said.

Back to the limousines, and to the hotel where I left the linesmen and their wives to attend the losing team's banquet after arranging to meet them at a nightclub at 1 am. My party of four went off to the *Talk of the Town*.

In Leicester Square, to our bewilderment, there were mounted police on duty. 'What's going on?' asked Beryl. 'I don't know', I said, 'I didn't have all that bad a game.'

Certainly, we could think of no reason for their presence and we quickly forgot them as we were met by the manager of the *Talk of the Town*, taken swiftly to our excellent table and found there an ice-box with a bottle of champagne in it and a card saying, 'Sorry I couldn't be with you this afternoon. I am sure you had a fantastic match, Frank and Stella (Vaughan)'.

I scarcely had the time to raise my glass and to toast Beryl before a huge paw landed on my shoulder and nearly knocked me to the ground. I looked up into the face of Lawrie McMenemy, and immediately understood the police presence outside. He had taken over half the *Talk of the Town* for his 'family' as he called them, and, indeed, virtually the whole of Southampton Football Club were there, including the old gentleman who looked after the referee and linesmen at The Dell. From that moment, Lawrie and I have been close friends.

The night, of course, was a huge success. We were with the winners while the unfortunate linesmen, who said the Manchester United banquet might just as well have been held in a morgue, had to join the losers. *Match of the Day*, in fact, was presented from the *Talk of the Town* that evening and I could not help wondering what the FA Council members and Ted Croker thought if they saw me being interviewed with the Southampton team.

At 1 am, with the morning still young, we went off to join the linesmen and their wives at the *Astor*. I told them to forget their evening with the losers and enjoy themselves: and we did. At about 3.30, there was the boy from the Rhondda, a gold medal in his pocket, eating eggs and bacon in a plush London nightclub.

Strange day, I thought.

I mean, I never eat breakfast.

EUROPEAN WARS 1975-83

'*Dear Mr Thomas*,

FC Amsterdam v IFC Cologne to be played in Amsterdam, 19 March.

We would like to draw your attention to the fact that the first leg match between the two teams concerned was played at Cologne on 5 March, 1975, in a most tense atmosphere. According to the reports received from the referee and the delegate at the first match, a total number of four Dutch and one German player had to be cautioned, not to mention the one Dutch player ordered off the field by the referee.

According to the officials of the first match and press reports it must be feared that the "war" started in Cologne may continue on the occasion of the return match. For this reason we ask you to strictly enforce the Laws of the Game from the beginning and, provided necessary, to take immediate action.'

I was somewhat shocked to receive by special delivery from Hans Bangerter, secretary of UEFA, the above letter dated 12 March, not particularly because of the content but because the UEFA rule states quite categorically that any correspondence between the association and a referee must go through proper channels. In this case, it would be through the Football Association of Wales, whose secretary at that time, Trevor Morris, was unaware of the letter and who may be surprised to read it now.

I had intended to keep the contents of the letter away from the linesmen in case it put additional pressure on them. Unfortunately, I had to tell them an hour or so before the game when the official delegate to the match, Sir Harold Thompson, came somewhat nervously into the dressing-room to explain what sort of a match was anticipated. He said he would be prepared to help in any way possible and was going to inspect the ground and its facilities.

Two or three minutes later, the manager of Amsterdam came in to complain that the Cologne shorts were a similar colour to their own and he was protesting officially. It seemed that the war promised by Hans Bangerter was starting at psychological level. I asked him to bring in the manager of Cologne with the kits, sent for Sir Harold, explained the problem, and, much to my lack of surprise, he passed the buck straight back to me. 'Clive', he said, 'I'll leave it in your capable hands. You won't need me now, I'll see you after the game.'

I decided that no change was needed in the colours. The game kicked off with extreme tension. There was no doubt that the number of players cautioned in that first match was going to increase – and so it was, as I took the names of three players in the first quarter of an hour. Just a few seconds before the interval, I awarded to Cologne what Amsterdam regarded as a dubious goal and, as we walked off at half-time, their goalkeeper dashed up to me to remonstrate rather violently. I was showing him the yellow card as we walked down the tunnel, but because I was not sure he had understood I went to the Amsterdam dressing-room to point out clearly that he had been cautioned. I had no further trouble in that game; a smiling and grateful Sir Harold Thompson came in to congratulate us on our handling of it.

I start the chapter with this particular story not because it was my first game in Europe – I had been involved in European competitions since 1968 – but because it serves to illustrate that the average league match in Britain is of naught when compared with the difficulties of European matches at international level and the politics and finance involved. Clearly, because there is more at stake than in the average match at Aldershot (or, indeed, even at Aston Villa) on a wet February afternoon, tempers fray, tackles grow more cynical, the whole atmosphere is more dramatic.

It was on a wet day, but in June in Yugoslavia, that I next came up against the 'Europroblem'. Through the Football Association of Wales I had been delighted to receive the appointment to referee in the final phase of the Henri Delaunay Cup, otherwise known as the European Nations Cup, in Yugoslavia, from 16–20 June, 1976. One point about the Welsh representation surprised me: although UEFA quite rightly rule that one of the linesmen must be on the international referees' list on the grounds that he would have to take over if the referee were injured, the FAW chose Ken Dodd as senior linesman over Rhidian Harris, although neither of them was on the Football League referees' list. Ken – no relation to his namesake, incidentally, though he did keep us in jokes for those few days – was highly promising, but as yet untried.

Once installed at the Hotel Metropole in Belgrade, a meeting was called for 10 am on 15 June by the late Herr Friedrich Seipelt, whose name will appear with some frequency in the ensuing chapters as chairman of the UEFA referees' committee and member of FIFA. I would ask you, understanding reader, to treat him throughout as what in other circumstances would be referred to as a hostile witness.

Seipelt told us very little other than that I would be refereeing the first match the following night at Zagreb and that, because the first match was of paramount importance in respect of control, he was looking to me to set the standard for the tournament. All the members of the UEFA executive and referees' committee would be at the match. He also confirmed at that meeting that the referee for the final, with linesmen from the same country, would be a certain Signor Gonella, an appointment which may or may not have had something to do with the fact that the president of UEFA, Dr Artemio Franchi (who was to die so violently in a car crash near his beloved Sienna in the summer of 1983) was a fellow Italian. I do not like to speak ill of the dead but the late Dr Franchi, like the late Herr Seipelt, and indeed Signor Gonella, will be reappearing in further acts of the European and world dramas.

That meeting was also told that should the final end in a draw, the referee for the replay had not yet been chosen.

We flew up on the day of the match to Zagreb, where it was raining continuously. I assumed therefore that my first decision would concern the fitness of the pitch. I walked on to the field, umbrella held aloft, but the decision had been taken out of my hands: UEFA had decided that the game must go on whatever the conditions because of television commitments round the world. So my inspection was a formality but, in fairness, I should say that I would have started the game anyway. (Throughout my career I have only once started a game and not finished it – an England v Scotland Under-23 International at Newcastle when there was such a heavy snowfall that one of the linesmen, Gwyn Owen, was not even aware that I had abandoned the game and withdrawn to the dressing-rooms with the result that he finally appeared looking like some particularly unpleasant abominable snowman!)

From the start, the match between Holland and Czechoslovakia was going to be difficult to control but we nevertheless went in at half-time without a single caution having been necessary, though the final figure was to be five in the book and three off. I restarted the second half with the rain still coming down like the proverbial stair-rods. In those last forty-five minutes, I cautioned four and sent off two players, including some of the best-known names in European football. Both teams had forgotten the word discipline which left me with no option but to show them that I was prepared to take them all on.

Johan Cruyff was one of the worst-behaved players on the field that wet and stormy night. He commented regularly on my ability as play went on and, although he could fully understand my warnings, the confrontation had to cease with me showing him the yellow card. It clearly hurt his pride: thank goodness looks cannot kill because I would not otherwise be here to write this book. But Cruyff was not the only big-name offender. During that inconclusive second half, I took the names of the Czech, Pollak, in the fifty-first minute before sending him off seven minutes later, booked Willie Van der Kerkhof and Cruyff, and sent off Neeskens after seventy-six minutes. Dobias of Czechoslovakia found his name in my book in extra time. Then, in the closing and decisive stages of extra time, I angered the Dutch by awarding a goal to the Czechs.

Van Hanegem particularly showed his fury, and in return I showed him the yellow card inside his own penalty area. He continued his verbal abuse as we walked back to the halfway line. I told him that if he crossed that line and continued his dissent he would be off. He did: I showed him the card: and he refused to go. Cruyff in the meantime was raring to restart and I could, I suppose, have ignored my previous decision and carried on with the game. But I was determined that Van Hanegem had to go, while he was equally determined to stay. I was prepared to abandon the game but, to give him one last chance, I picked up the ball, walked to the touchline and pointed to the tunnel. After what seemed a short lifetime, Van Hanegem finally got the message and, with head bowed, stalked from the field. Because the game had been televised and because of the number and names of the players cautioned and sent off, I knew we were in for a controversial time. For Ken, Rhidian and myself it had been the hardest hour or so we had ever experienced.

Back in the dressing-room, still sodden and unstripped, we had an immediate visitor – the match delegate, Sir Harold Thompson, seeking the details of the players warned and dismissed, the nature of their offences and so on because he had to make a report for the UEFA committee to decide what action should be taken. I told him in no uncertain Welsh way that he might at least wait for us to shower, dry and change. No doubt he wished to go quickly to his UEFA buddies drinking in the lounge. Seipelt was next in and I told him politely – well, in the same words as I used to Sir Harold – that he must wait.

Seipelt accompanied us back to the hotel for a late dinner and, over the goulash, said the executive committee of UEFA had arranged a meeting for the following morning to discuss my handling of the game and whether disciplinary action should be taken. Not only that: he went on to criticise the way in which I demanded that players on the field should come to me when I issued the cautions. It was, he said, the job of the referee to go to the player, an edict which surprised me insofar as I am not prepared to run around the field to seek out a recalcitrant footballer. He accepted that I was a strict referee but that I had to adhere to UEFA's rules, and that might well be the outcome of the meeting next morning. I said I would be leaving on the first plane home if that was the decision as I wanted nothing to do with an authority that held such views. Indeed, the discussion grew so heated that Ken Dodd inter-vened very diplomatically to suggest that we left the outcome to the executive.

Back in Belgrade the next day, I was not asked to attend the meeting but, an hour or so before the match between Yugoslavia and West Germany on the following evening, Dr Franchi telephoned me to con-gratulate me on the handling of the previous game and also confirmed that the UEFA committee had backed me in every respect. The three players sent off could take no further part in the competition and both countries were severely reprimanded. Seipelt never spoke to me about these decisions.

There was a strong rumour on the day of the final that, if there were a draw, the Welsh officials would have the replay. Then, half an hour before the kick-off, everyone was astonished when UEFA announced out of the blue that there would be no replay and that, if necessary, the final would be decided by penalty kicks. Brian Moore was there to give the commentary for ITV but the BBC had the replay rights. John Motson and the Beeb crew were there for nothing.

Repercussions? Well, as I say, the influential Mr Seipelt was never a friend. But shortly after I returned home I received a letter from UEFA secretary Hans Bangerter, dated 24 June, which said in part:

'On behalf of the Organizing Committee and the Referees' Committee of UEFA ... our best thanks for your collaboration and to assure you that your performance on the occasion of the match CSSR v Netherlands was very much appreciated.'

A couple of years later, on the last day of October 1978, I was involved in another controversial match, this time in Germany. Borussia Mun-chengladbach were playing Benfica of Portugal in the second leg of a UEFA cup-tie which had bubbled over in the first leg in Lisbon and which is possibly why I was named. True to the Portuguese temperament, boots started to fly, and names started to appear in my book almost from the start. For once this surprised me, because the Benfica manager at the time was an old acquaintance, the former Chelsea player, John Morti-mer, and he would surely have told his team what kind of referee I was. But some players forget their warnings when they are on the park and so it happened here in Munchengladbach. Tension mounted as the game went into extra time before, finally, I had to send off one of the Benfica team. Even so, they struggled on with ten men until the final minute when a German player was brought down particularly savagely in the box and I awarded a penalty. The Benfica players were thunderstruck: a last-minute penalty in extra time and an exit from the UEFA cup? Not for them. Every Benfica player remained steadfastly in the penalty area. There was no way that they were going to move. I started to caution them one by one until John Mortimer came out on to the field to plead with his players to allow the kick to be taken. After some delay, and with Mortimer still standing by the goal trying to calm his team, the Germans scored from the spot.

I was walking back to the halfway line when the ball hit me with considerable force on the back of the head. I looked round but was unable to identify the culprit among the suddenly innocent faces. Then on the following Saturday on ITV Brian Moore confirmed that it was the goalkeeper who had kicked the ball. 'Lucky fellow', commented Brian. 'I'm sure if Clive Thomas had known, the goalkeeper would have had his marching orders.' I'm not so sure. Any man who can strike the ball so accurately from twenty-five yards or more that he can hit me on the head has a talent that deserves more than a red card. I'm not so sure either, in retrospect, that I thank John Mortimer for his intervention. I would have been prepared to send off the whole Benfica team and abandon the match.

Mind you, management does not always come to the rescue: on the contrary.

Sarajevo is an indelible name in the history books. It is a city of beauty in the heart of the Balkans, and it was here, on 28 June, 1914, that the revolver shots which killed Archduke Franz Ferdinand, the heir to the Austro-Hungarian throne, fired the excuse for World War I. But on a personal level Sarajevo showed me soccer management at its horrific worst. The date was 17 September, 1980, the venue was Hamburg, and the match was a UEFA cup first round game.

There was no hint of trouble before the match. Indeed, at the lunch-time reception the Yugoslav national coach, Milan Miljanic, whom I had met several times, said that Sarajevo were a good sporting side. 'You will have no problems from them', he predicted. Quite obviously, he could not have watched them. At the same table also, incidentally, was the manager of Hamburg, Gunter Netzer, who had a long chat with me about Kevin Keegan as he had just left Hamburg to return to Britain. I pointed out that Southampton had seen little of Kevin so far, unfortunately, because he had been injured. Netzer replied that Keegan's best years of football had been in the *Bundeslige*, that he had pulled off a fantastic coup in persuading Kevin to go to Germany, and that he had made an even better judgement in releasing him when he did. Keegan, he predicted, was finished.

Back to the story, though. I realised when I booked Radelyas, a Yugoslav, in the second minute, that Miljanic's view of Sarajevo was either biased or ignorant. The crudeness of their tackling, quite the worst I have seen in European football, suggested almost that they wanted to appear in my little black book. If so, they were not disappointed. There was no possibility that all eleven Sarajevo players were going to remain on the field and at half-time I warned the linesmen to keep their eyes peeled. So they did, and the names, most of them unspellable, let alone pronounceable, continued to flow into the book. Hamburg, in all fairness and possibly because they knew my background, accepted my decisions and scarcely retaliated to most of the brutal fouling. I then started to send off the Yugoslavs, who were greeted by their management with arms outstretched in sympathy as they left the field. In all, there were six cautions while three players were sent off.

Those on the trainer's bench had no respect for anyone. When they substituted players, they ignored all UEFA instructions to introduce the number board for those coming and going, creating total confusion as players came to and fro as if instructed by some traffic policeman.

Sarajevo lost the match 4-2 and, when I was walking off, four Yugo-slavs from the bench, Messrs Zebec, Rieger and Meyer along with Dr Matthies, showed in no uncertain manner what they thought of me, shouting and waving their arms wildly. I do not understand Serbian or Croatian or whatever they were speaking: but I had no need to under-stand. I promptly took out my book and made it clear I was going to report them too. The following morning the German press hailed me inevitably as Thomas the Book – but this time with approval.

In my report to UEFA I stated that the Yugoslav side were a disgrace to European football and the management were no better. UEFA apparently agreed to some extent: the three players I had sent off were suspended for two UEFA competition matches and the club was fined 25,000 Swiss Francs for the incorrect conduct of the team and the im-proper comportment of the officials on the bench. A further fine of 2,500SF was placed on the club for the throwing of a few bottles by their supporters. Predictably, they appealed, and I was duly summoned to Switzerland for the customary very expensive few minutes of questioning. In front of the Yugoslavian representatives, however, I did reiterate that they were a disgrace to European football and, if I had anything to do with it, they would never play in a European competition again. The chairman quickly interrupted but I think I had made my point to every member present.

An appeal, also predictably, followed problems at a match in March 1983 which on paper at least appeared to have few pitfalls. Paris St Germain had comfortably beaten Waterschei of Belgium 3-1 in the first leg of their cup-winners' cup match but there was still considerable anticipation in the Belgian town before the game because the club had never before reached such an advanced stage of a European competition.

Curiously, when I arrived at the stadium, I found of all people a group of Chelsea supporters. They had read that I was taking the game, had intended to watch a European cup game somewhere, and decided this was as good and as near as any. Needless to say, my six complimentary tickets found good homes. I invited them into the guest room where we had a long chat about games I had done at Stamford Bridge and various decisions I had made – but even the notorious Shed inhabitants would be unlikely to be involved in the sort of scenes we saw that evening.

Waterschei were quite obviously determined to erase the two-goal deficit, and they deserved to be on level terms by full-time. We went into extra time and, with only two minutes to go and the scores still level on aggregate, Waterschei scored. It was surely the winner; a place in the semi-final was booked. With just a minute to go, the ball ran innocently over the touchline for a throw-in. What happened next I hope never to see again in football. A spectator who was sitting on a bench about seven yards from the touchline threw the ball back to Jean-Claud Lemoult of PSG who was rushing to get the ball as time was running out. He missed the return pass, and in his temper continued forward and struck the spectator violently across the face. Police and security men went to the spectator's aid and I went to Lemoult and pointed to the tunnel. 'You'll never come back on to this pitch', I told him.

Now it was the turn of the Paris St Germain supporters. As their depleted team were sliding to defeat, they threw fireworks and tins on to the pitch but, if they thought I would abandon the game, they had another think coming. I explained in broken English to the protesting defenders of Waterschei that they should put up with the missiles for literally a minute and they were of course happy to accept this. But still it was not over. With only a second left, Sari Boubacar decided that he could kick a Waterschei player in the back. I couldn't prevent him but I could ensure it wouldn't happen again. And off he went. In the final three minutes, then, we had a winning goal, two players sent off and, quite literally, fireworks.

Finally, in this chapter on the European wars, a memory of a man who perhaps in retrospect I might not have ordered from the field. Munich was buzzing that April day in 1976 when Real Madrid were due to play Bayern in the second leg of the European Cup semi-final. The first game in Spain had been marred by crowd disturbances and the referee, the highly experienced Linemayr of Austria, had been struck by supporters. But I was all tuned up for the game as I had been reserve referee for the English League Cup final at Wembley a month before and was due a month later to referee the Cup Final itself.

Thirty minutes before the kick-off, I went into the dressing-rooms and through an interpreter explained how I was going to referee the game. My inspector that day was Hans Bangerter who must have heard about this because by the following season UEFA instructed referees not to address the two teams.

The game lived up to its pre-publicity and, perhaps, so did I. But there were no real problems, although Real, only an insubstantial shadow of the team who have entertained so hugely in the past, indulged in shirt-tugging and other off-the-ball infringements in their frustration as they headed for defeat. With time running out, I gave a free kick against their skipper, Amaro Amancio, who was in tears after the game. I still believe that it was in disgust and frustration at his team's performance that he belted the ball forty yards down the running track. As I had cautioned him earlier, he had to go. It was a stupid sending-off offence.

Speaking to Alan Hardaker some months later in England, he said that the expression on my face as I issued the marching orders was one which had to be seen to be believed. It looked, he said, as if I really did not want to do it. 'It's the first time I have seen you look like that', he said. 'You should appear that way more often.'

No, I didn't really want to send Amancio off. It was a stupid offence, and he paid dearly for his moment of frustration. He played neither for Spain nor Real Madrid again, a sad end to an illustrious career.

·8·
ALL THE WORLD'S
A STAGE...

... and one man in his time plays many parts. I do not know that I played all of Shakespeare's seven ages of man during my escapades in the World Cup, but many of the roles cast upon me were eminently suitable for comedy, tragedy or high drama. Yet there were moments when it looked as if I would not even have a walk-on part either in West Germany in 1974 or in Argentina in 1978. Quite obviously I do not regret the experiences. Equally obviously, they were not the most happy times of my football career – and I am not talking about minor incidents like blowing for full time when Senor Zico was in the act of scoring a winning goal for Brazil. No, I am referring to the jealousy and the rivalry, the politics and the puzzles, that spoil for the referee, at any rate, what should be the finest moment of his career. And yet I would not have missed taking part in the World Cup for anything.

Mind you, as I lay in my holiday bed at the Hotel Bristol in Newquay down in Cornwall in August 1973, I thought I was going to miss it. I sat up with a start when I read in my tabloid that the Football Association of Wales had recommended two referees for the World Cup series the following year – and neither of them was Clive Thomas.

I suppose in retrospect that I should not have been all that surprised. I knew after all that the two who had been nominated, John Gow and Iorrie Jones, had their support from council members and that they were not bad referees, though in my opinion unlikely to reach the very top. In short, you may be surprised to find that I lodged no complaint but decided simply that I would referee in the League as well as I could. Then, one day in January 1974, I was told after a match at West Ham that the referee supremo of FIFA, the Englishman Ken Aston, had been at the game. Did I still have a chance?

Lying in bed one Saturday shortly afterwards (no, I don't usually read the paper in bed: it was simply coincidence, and besides I didn't have a game that particular weekend) I found in the *Daily Express* that Welshman Clive Thomas had been booked for the World Cup along with Jack Taylor from England and Bob Davidson from Scotland. Beryl greeted the information with a typical show of emotion: how long will that be for? she asked.

Within minutes of reading the news, I received a call from Ken Aston in Switzerland to confirm and to congratulate me on the appointment. The very next call was from John Gow, also to congratulate me, absolutely characteristic of the man he is for he would probably also have admitted that I was the right choice and had received the appointment on the ground of ability. Iorrie Jones remained silent on that issue and has spoken to me on only a few occasions since.

Written confirmation followed fairly soon afterwards from FIFA, with the details, the rules and the regulations to which we must adhere. I was rather surprised to find that the thirty-four referees would be sleeping two to a room at the Esso Motor Hotel near Frankfurt but assumed that, as one of the youngest in the squad, I would be billeted with either Jack Taylor or Davidson, as it was their third and fourth World Cup respectively. FIFA also requested details of measurements for us to be kitted out with suits, shirts, underwear and everything else, supplied by various companies.

This interested me at the time. As I was very conscious that the referee's outfit had not altered for twenty to thirty years, I was in the process of designing a new kit for Bukta. Immediately I suggested to the company that they should move fast; I supplied them with the relevant names, and Norman Dally, Sales Director of Bukta, wrote to Dr Helmut Kaser, secretary of FIFA. His proposal was accepted and all the referees were given the option of wearing the new gear. Only two objected: Messrs Taylor and Davidson, who had always worn kit supplied by another company. It may have crossed your mind that Thomas made a killing out of this. In fact, I was not paid a penny: not one. Although I had my own sports shop in Treorchy at the time, I was not given any preferential treatment over any other retailer. I did not even get a consultancy fee. More: I was not paid expenses for travelling to Stockport to outline to the designers the type of kit I wanted.

In the meantime, apparently, the FAW had written to FIFA to ask why one of their nominees had not been selected and received the reply that nominations from football associations round the world were only guidelines and that the referees' committee made the appointments. It was actually Ken Aston who had put his head on the block by including me.

And it was Ken who took our first seminar when we arrived in June in Frankfurt. (There I found that my roommate was to be the Canadian referee Werner Winsemann, though some referees had preferential treatment with a room to themselves.) Ken outlined some of the major problems to us, including the necessity of wearing identity cards at all times. Security was particularly tight, with the hotel guarded by the military, in view of what had happened at the Munich Olympics. Ken also informed us that there would be a fitness and medical test, including an electrocardiogram, in four days time on 11 June. After being kitted out, we were taken by bus to a small ground some ten minutes from the hotel where the German coach, Herr Heddergott, took us through the schedule watched by members of the referees' committee. Well, he took the European referees through it: the South Americans trained on their own and would not take part in the much more intensive activities prescribed by Herr Heddergott. We protested, of course, but apparently there was nothing he could do about it.

Ken Aston, as acting chairman of the referees' committee, seemed to be doing all the work. The official chairman, one H. Riedel of the German Democratic Republic, never seemed to be around for the early morning seminars and in fact only shortly after the World Cup he was replaced. It was Ken, then, who tried so desperately hard to ensure uniformity of interpretation of the laws and he was a real credit to Britain. But the fitness test was a mockery: in no way were all the referees fit enough to officiate at a tournament of such importance. To this day I do not know how some of them were permitted to take control of matches when they had failed their test – though I was to witness the same thing four years later in Argentina. One can only assume that it was too late to send them home and to find replacements.

Then came the moment when we gathered in the hotel to hear of the appointments for the first round matches from Sir Stanley Rous who, it was rumoured, was shortly to be ousted from his position as president of FIFA by the ambitious Dr J. Havelange from Brazil, thus heralding the end of European control of world football.

You may remember that during the World Cup in England in 1966, Sir Alf Ramsay, the successful English team manager, had described the Argentinians as 'animals'. The eighth game to be announced by Sir Stanley was that of Poland v Argentina, at Stuttgart, on 15 June. And the referee? Clive Thomas.

There was a surprised silence, intensified further when the linesmen were announced as Bob Davidson and a German, Heinz Aldinger. The reserve linesman was to be the highly experienced Rudolph Scheurer, who was also to referee the opener between Brazil and Yugoslavia. But it was the general view that the crucial game of the round in terms of control and, therefore, the standards for the competition, was the one involving Argentina. It was just what I wanted, though I had never anticipated that I would have such a World Cup baptism in view of the fact that there were many referees more experienced than I. Throughout the flight to Stuttgart, I don't think Bob Davidson said more than a couple of words to me. I suppose he was jealous of my appointment and upset at not having a first-round tie to referee. With Jack Taylor taking the relatively easy Bulgaria-Uruguay match, I knew that a good game could help me towards my goal: a place in the final. My inspector for the game was the charming Koe Ewe Teik from Malaysia, one of the nicest men I have met in the World Cup series but unfortunately not strong enough to stand up to some of the harder and more determined football politicians.

My World Cup career did not start smoothly. I had arranged with the linesmen to inspect the studs on the players' boots in the tunnel five minutes before going on to the pitch for the anthems. Heinz Aldinger reported that the studs of the Argentinians looked rather lethal and so, two minutes before we were due on the field, I held my own inspection as my decision had to be the final one. I certainly could not accept the studs of two players: they were sticking out like three-inch nails.

An interpreter gave the ruling to the Argentinian manager, but he refused to accept it. With the German organiser trying to lead us out on to the pitch, there was deadlock. But, I said, this game is not going to start with players wearing those studs. The Argentinians finally realised I was determined and took their two players back to the dressing-room. I wonder how many people noticed that the Argentinians were two short as we stood for the national anthem out on the field?

When the erring two finally came out, they had indeed changed their studs and we got under way. At half-time Koe Ewe Teik came in to congratulate me on my first-half performance but, as always, I told him politely not to come in until threequarters of an hour after the match. The game went exactly as I had wished. It was a five-goal thriller producing some marvellous football, and I was hailed by the press the following day as one of the strictest – nay, *the* strictest – they had seen in the World Cup.

My next appointment was as reserve linesman in Berlin for Australia and Chile, which pleased me because the referee was an old friend, Jafar Namdar from Iran. His linesmen were Vital Loraux of Belgium and Arie van Gemert from Holland, which should have meant an easy passage because Loraux was in fact being mentioned as a possibility for the final. Namdar was very nervous on the flight from Frankfurt and Loraux and van Gemert cut themselves off from him completely, to such an extent that they would not even check the goalnets when we inspected the pitch two hours before the kick-off. Apparently they were above that sort of thing. They also appeared to ignore Namdar's instructions before the match and I told them, in front of Seipelt, the FIFA inspector, what I thought of them, although technically it was not my place to do so.

The situation did not improve. Namdar received little co-operation during a rough, tough first half, the rain teemed down and, at the interval, he even asked me whether he should abandon the match. Then in the second half Namdar cautioned an Australian while a Chilean was lying injured from a hard tackle about a yard from the touchline. Namdar wanted him removed, the Chileans wanted him to have treatment on the pitch. As reserve linesman, and to help Namdar, I busied myself organising the removal of the player on to a stretcher as the game continued. When I returned to the bench, I was told by my interpreter that an Australian player who had been shown the yellow card by Namdar in the first half had again been shown the yellow card for a further offence and should therefore have been sent off. What to do? Let it go? No, the rules state that no player can receive two yellow cards and so I walked to the touchline and beckoned Namdar to stop play. I explained, and he sent off the Australian, who quite naturally found it difficult to accept the decision but at least I could talk to him in English and he reluctantly left for the dressing-room.

The match was unsatisfactory in every way and, back in the dressing-room, I again told the two linesmen exactly what I thought of their lack of co-operation, and explained my views to Seipelt. He suggested to Namdar that he should make an official report. FIFA never made public their decision but Loraux and van Gemert had only one more match each during the competition. If I had had my way, both would have been sent straight home: they did not deserve to take any further part in the World Cup.

My next appointment was as linesman for the match between the Netherlands and Sweden, which pleased me again because my roommate, Werner Winsemann, was in the middle. But in the first twelve minutes of the match, he overruled me on two occasions with the result that I threw down my flag as we entered the dressing-room at half-time and asked: 'Do you want me or not?'

'Tonight', he said, 'you are the linesman, I am the referee and you will do exactly as you are told.' It hurt my pride, but I had to look up to him for being in control. It was a disgrace, in fact, that he was not chosen for any further matches because he was a very capable referee. Maybe Canada is not a sufficiently fashionable footballing country.

Before the second round appointments were announced, I spoke with a number of referees about the problems of inspectors coming into the dressing-room at half-time and straight after the game. They agreed that this was wrong and so, at the next appointments meeting under the chairmanship of Sir Stanley Rous in the hotel lounge, I stated that I thought the inspectors should remain outside for at least thirty minutes. But when Sir Stanley asked whether the other referees felt the same, there was silence. They had set me up: it was obvious that they would not risk jeopardising their appointments. Sir Stanley peered at me in his very diplomatic manner and said, 'I'm afraid, Thomas, that you have lost this one.'

When he announced the appointments for the second round, however, the first match named was Brazil v East Germany, referee Thomas. And the inspector, added Sir Stanley, will be Ken Aston, who will be in the dressing-room half an hour after the finish. I had won my point and, equally important, I had another plum match – incidentally proving that you do not always lose by speaking out.

It was a tough game, too, played at Hanover, and won by a truly brilliant Rivelino goal from a free kick. An interesting interlude on that trip was when we were taken to visit at his home Rudi Kreitlein, who at Wembley in 1966 had sent off the notorious Rattin, the Argentinian captain. One wall of Rudi's house was covered with photographs of his sendings-off – a sort of black hack museum.

I flew next, by helicopter this time, on a two-and-a-quarter-hour journey which I would rather not do again, to Gelsenk, to line for Jack Taylor the match between East Germany and Argentina. Jack had no reason to look forward to the game as both sides were by now out of the competition as they could no longer qualify, and he had no chance of showing his ability while both sides were merely going through the motions.

By the time we made the return journey all the results were in, and we knew that Germany were to play Holland in the final. Jack's experience of World Cups led him to believe that there would be a European referee and that there was every possibility he would be British. He had information, he said, that FIFA were suitably impressed with my handling of my two games, that I had the highest marks ever achieved by a World Cup referee, and that, if this had been my second World Cup, I might well have been chosen. On balance, he felt that Bob Davidson would have the game if all had gone well when he was linesman the previous evening in the Holland-Brazil game. I disagreed: I did not think they would overlook Jack Taylor.

Back in Frankfurt, the Esso Motor Hotel was a hive of activity. All our colleagues were packed and ready to leave for the special train that was to take us to Munich for the final. And what a lavish train it was, sheer luxury for the five-hour journey with the opportunity to eat and drink free in the restaurant at any time. But it was also a travelling gossip shop and, as we swung smoothly through the German countryside, I was very quickly made aware by German colleagues with whom I had become very friendly, that something *had* gone wrong in the match between Holland and Brazil. The Germans in my compartment made a scathing attack on Bob Davidson. During the match, they said, a player was alleged to have struck an opponent behind the back of referee Kurt Tschenscher of West Germany, an incident which should have been seen by linesman Davidson. He had not drawn it to the attention of the referee and from that moment the match became more difficult to control. The Germans believed that Davidson was determined to keep his nose clean and did not want to be involved in an incident.

The journey was taking on sinister overtones. No sooner had a rumour spread the length of the train that Bob Davidson had been appointed for the final – a decision which was due to be rubber-stamped at a meeting the following morning of the whole FIFA executive committee – than I was approached in the corridor by George Suppiah, the Singapore referee who had been the second linesman the previous evening. He told me that he had been asked to attend a specially-convened meeting on the train of the referees' committee to give his version of the events of the match and that Bob Davidson had already spoken to him about the incident concerned. Suppiah had, in fact, seen it but because he had been on the far side of the field he did not think it was right for him to draw it to the attention of the referee as the match was still going on. He thought Davidson must have seen it because it was closer to him and I advised him to tell the truth at the meeting. I then sought out Bob Davidson to tell him I thought he was wrong to have approached Suppiah.

Within a few minutes of booking into the Munich hotel, where Winsemann and I were again sharing a room, I had a telephone call from a television commentator to chat about the train journey because rumour was already rife. I told him I was not interested in discussing the journey but that a glass of champagne would be very welcome. Two bottles later, and with my firm rejection of a £1,000-bait to tell the story of the journey, he left. But all that night journalists were camped in the hotel trying to get the story. I had had enough. I went to Ken Aston's room, asked whether I could speak with him on a personal matter and told him I was so fed up with the politicking that, unless he personally objected, I would leave before the finals. He warned me that the official appointment would not be made until the following (Friday) morning and questioned the wisdom of leaving early. 'I just want to get out of this football madhouse', I said. He said he could not stop me and that he would try to put over my point to the authorities concerned. I immediately contacted Lufthansa and changed my tickets from the Monday to the Saturday morning.

Next morning, all the referees were due to go on a tour of Munich at midday and I was in Jack Taylor's room with Bob Davidson when his phone rang. Jack answered, looked considerably surprised, and hung up. He said he had been appointed the referee for the World Cup final.

I was so delighted that I threw my arms round him in congratulations. 'It is a tremendous honour for the Football League', I said. Davidson did not so much as shake Jack's hand. 'It's a mistake', he said. 'I've got it.'

The BBC rang to ask whether the British referees would be filmed in the hotel's grounds to show their pleasure in the appointment as Jack was not allowed to comment himself. Davidson declined, but I was happy to be involved before going off on the tourist trip which both Jack and Davidson missed. When we returned that evening, Jack was extremely disappointed with Davidson's attitude. There had been a colossal row and the Scotsman had accused the committee of changing its mind. Rumour had it that he had already made arrangements for his wife to fly out for the match: instead he had now left to fly home.

I think we can all imagine his disappointment well enough. But in appointing Jack, FIFA could not have made a better decision. As we all know he had a splendid and courageous final, including the award of two penalties – one to each side – in the first ten minutes.

It was not only the politicking and backbiting that disappointed me about that 1974 World Cup. On my return home, I sent a report to FIFA to complain about a number of issues concerning our stay in Germany. There was, for example, the ridiculously low subsistence allowance of 120 Deutschmarks per day (at that time only a few pounds), which meant that many referees were unable to eat properly as only breakfast was included in the payment by FIFA for hotel rooms. (I was fortunate: setting out one evening after a match in Frankfurt, I called in at a restaurant where I was recognised and met with open arms by the owner, Herr Helmut. He would be delighted to look after me, with my Canadian colleague Winsemann, whenever we wished. I remember Helmut's Hungarian goulash with some pleasure. He was also director of a nightclub, which we visited once or twice, and a close friend of a jeweller, Helen Sinn, who had her own shop and who advised us on presents for our wives.) We also had to wash our own clothes or pay for the laundry and there was the question of the shared rooms for some of us. We were, in short, second-class citizens. In the reply, FIFA said that referees were the only 'amateurs' left in the game. Precisely. This is how football authorities regard referees: as amateurs, and as such to be treated with less regard than professionals.

One other thing embarrassed me. Throughout the tournament, referees from other countries were able to give away badges, pennants, ashtrays and so on provided by their associations. I could not reciprocate. The FAW had given me nothing.

*   *   *   *   *

The first inkling I had of the possibility of being included for the Argentinian World Cup finals four years later came in May 1977, when the director of Conrad Film, a London company, told me they wished to make a film that would compare the life and times of Clive Thomas with that of a Brazilian referee, Arnaldo Coelho, and that they had permission from FIFA to film us in our respective countries. This did not in itself prove that we were on the list, but I also had it on reasonably good authority that we would be there and as a result agreed to do the film on the one condition that it showed exactly my character, way of life and way of living it.

And so the cameras roved round with me from my promotions office at OCS in Cardiff to Charles Rand at OP Chocolates in Merthyr and to Treorchy where I lived. The biggest problem during the filming came not from the weather, the crew or the locations but from my wife, because the director wished to bring the cameras into our home in Colum Street, Treorchy, to compare it with Arnaldo's spacious flat overlooking the beach at Copacabana. Now Beryl had made it abundantly clear to me that while much of my life could not be private because of my personality and career, the house was sacrosanct: it took days of persuasion for her to allow the camera crew through the door for one hour to show us with our daughters, Caryn and Allyson.

I also asked that the film should include my local – the *Griffin Inn* at Pentre with landlord Gwyn Lewis and his wife Pam – to compare with Arnaldo's hotel in Rio. Obviously, we warned Pam and Gwyn and gave them a few days' notice but asked them to keep quiet and ensure that only the usual regulars were present. When I arrived with my friends Howard Jones and Don Jones I was astonished. I had never seen so many women in the *Griffin* on a Wednesday night before, all apparently having ensured that the hairdressers of Treorchy and Pentre had done good business that day, but we tried to convey the atmosphere of an informal evening as the cameras rolled. All of which was fine until the players of Penygraig Rugby Club turned up. They had been playing up at Treherbert and, as is their habit, called in for a drink on their way home at Gwyn's, because he is a former rugby player of some standing. They took over the show from that point, asking what the hell was going on, making slanderous statements about my parents, my abilities, my friends – and letting it be known generally that I had been fortunate to have one World Cup, let alone look forward to another. The film director let the cameras roll on: if he were seeking unrehearsed, authentic material from unrehearsed, authentic valley folk, then he had it in abundance. It certainly produced a contrast with Copacabana beach.

I was still aware at the end of the filming that there had been no confirmation of any appointment for Argentina. Although I felt it was a near certainty, I would have been one of only a few who had not taken charge of a preliminary round match. But that was rectified in October 1977 when I took the qualifying round game between Iran and Kuwait, a local derby in effect although the two countries are miles apart, and a match regarded in the area as the cup final of Arabia. Because of strikes among air crew at the time, it was decided that linesmen Keith Cooper and Donald Bond and I would travel out on the Monday for the Friday match to ensure our safe arrival, with the result that we had the best part of a week in Iran. The director of the film company, Dereck Conrad, had a further bright idea: he would bring his crew and seek permission from FIFA to attach a microphone to my jersey for me to give a running commentary during the game.

We were met at the start of what was to be a strange week by the representative of the Iran FA, and then at our hotel by the FIFA inspector from Scotland, Jack Mowat, about whom I had heard so much. At one time he was reputed to be one of the strictest referees in the world. He turned out to be an embarrassment. He was in the room next to mine, he tagged along the whole time and, on a visit to a nightclub, insisted on keeping his mackintosh on throughout dinner despite my protests! Apparently he also forgot the rules and regulations of FIFA concerning gifts. Because he knew I had become friendly with the Iranians, and because he learned that they would be presenting us with gentlemen's gold watches, he asked me whether I could tell them that he would prefer a lady's watch for his wife. Keith Cooper and I, as it happened, also wanted ladies' watches and so, when we were contacted by the secretary of the Iranian FA and taken to a luxurious flat for drinks and to see a choice of gold watches, I chose one for Mowat and it was duly placed in a box with his name on it.

Having received his present immediately after the match (Don, Keith and I could scarcely refrain from laughing when he showed it to us so proudly: we had after all been there to choose it) he told me he was reporting the Iranian FA for the below-standard hospitality at the ground. He said an inspector of FIFA should have one of the best seats and the best facilities. He felt he had not. When I asked whether he would reconsider his report, or alternatively hand back the watch, he would have none of it.

The match itself had its fascinations. Mowat tried to prevent the use of the film company's microphone and took great exception at having to travel to the ground in a separate car from the linesmen and myself. There was simply no room: the camera crew wanted to film us three Welshmen in full song as we drove through the crowded streets.

Crowded? We were approximately three hundred yards from the ground when we saw a weird sight. The stadium was, I suppose, as large as Wembley, and it appeared that the walls were covered with ants. As we approached a little closer we could see the 'ants' were actually people climbing in. It was chaos: the ground officially held 100,000 but they were estimating that close to 135,000 would be inside for the kick-off. We were not allowed to kick off until the Shah's son was seated. We then learned that he was so impressed – or worried – at the interest in the game that, five minutes before it was due to start, he decreed that the match should go out live on television. Those looking forward to the local equivalent of *Coronation Street*, or whatever, had to do without.

Nevertheless, the game went well; Iran won and qualified for the cup proper. And, after giving a press conference after the match, against FIFA regulations, Jack Mowat, in fairness and despite our altercations, told me he had given me ten out of ten.

Confirmation arrived from FIFA on 20 February, 1978, in a circular from Helmut Kaser, that I had been chosen for Argentina. With the circular came a contract which included, along with the requirements on mode of travel, visas, vaccinations, insurance and so on, point number five headed 'Reporting'. It stated that: 'I undertake to refrain from giving interviews or writing reports of matches of the final competition without the written consent of the Referees' Committee of FIFA, such consent to be requested before the end of March 1978.'

I replied to Dr Kaser immediately, accepting the contract but with the proviso that I was not prepared to be gagged – I wished to be allowed to speak to the press. His polite reply stated that 'the decision on referees not speaking to the press concerns matches of the final competition only and that you may, therefore, should the case arise, ask for the committee's permission in Buenos Aires'.

A letter also arrived from the Football Association of Wales, congratulating me on my appointment, and offering me badges to take with me. Some good had come from the German experience.

The instructions stated that we were to arrive in Buenos Aires on Thursday, 25 May, and my preparations were complete for me to leave Heathrow in the early hours of Wednesday, 24 May. But, sadly, in the early hours of Tuesday, my very good friend Maisy Jones, wife of Howard, died at Treherbert Hospital. I simply could not fly out the next day and, consequently, I telephoned the FAW at 9.30 that Tuesday morning to explain that I could not now arrive in Buenos Aires on 25 May. Would they please, I asked, contact FIFA to tell them of the change in arrangements? To my astonishment, they said I must go at the time stated and that FIFA would not be prepared to accept a change in plans. I told them nevertheless to telex FIFA that I would not travel until after the funeral on the Friday. The FAW rang me back to say they had sent the telex and, by that time, I was able to give them some new flight times which meant arriving in Argentina at 11.30 on the Saturday morning. What is more, I said, I would not be officiating in Argentina if FIFA rejected my humanitarian request. The FAW agreed to telex FIFA the new date. I heard no more. I attended Maisy's funeral and was taken immediately to Heathrow, by my friend Jack Trembath.

I arrived at midday on Saturday, 27 May. As there was no one at Buenos Aires airport, I made my way by taxi to the Carlton Hotel where in the reception area was no less a person than Friedrich Seipelt, the referees' committee member, along with other members of the committee and some referees all in their tracksuits. 'Where do you think you have been?' Seipelt greeted me. After the funeral of a close friend and after nearly twenty-four hours of travel, I felt like telling him what I thought of him. Instead, I merely explained what had happened, as he did not seem to know. But, he said, you now have to change immediately into your tracksuit because, in half an hour, we are travelling to the stadium to have the physical fitness tests. Which we did. I was determined to complete those tests so that no one could say I was finding excuses, but what reason could the others have? Once more I was shaken by the number of referees who failed the tests. Believe me, no matter what the records show, they failed. But no one was sent home. This was the start of a month of disillusionment with football administration, my colleagues, the organisation of set-pieces, the general politics of the game and the behaviour of some of those at the highest level.

The Carlton Hotel, right in the centre of Buenos Aires, was quite the most unsuitable hotel that FIFA could have chosen for referees. The accommodation was a small room, albeit unshared, with few extras. There was only one entrance to the hotel with a small reception area and a dark and dingy foyer. The hotel is situated in the middle of what is surely the noisiest city in the world, with traffic thundering past day and night. There was no trace of grass on which to train, so no fresh air and nowhere to exercise. The menu was poor and, with only one lift holding no more than four people, one of whom was always a security guard, the stairs provided much of the physical effort. No excursions were arranged, with the result that I was very grateful to the Welsh Rugby Union, with whom I have a very happy relationship, and in particular to George Morgan, who so often acts as liaison officer for touring teams, for arranging with their rugby friends in Argentina to look after me socially.

In order to maintain some kind of fitness Abraham Klein, the Israeli referee, and I found a patch of grass about twenty yards square and some five hundred yards from the hotel, where we went through our calisthenics with traffic sweeping past in all directions and an amused Argentinian public looked on.

During the first few days, there were seminars similar to those in Germany in 1974. They were, I'm afraid, hopelessly chaired. Dr Artemio Franchi, the official chairman, attended as far as I could calculate only two meetings out of twelve, leaving the charming but weak Koe Ewe Teik, of Malaysia, in charge. At times he was laughed at quite openly by Jose Maria Codesal, from Uruguay, and by Seipelt himself. Other members, unfortunately, were also nothing but a laugh: one half-hour lecture by Javier Arriaga, of Mexico, allegedly on the administration duties of the referee and the co-operation between referees and inspectors, was nothing but a situation comedy.

The standards of refereeing in the first round were, in fact, relatively fair. But there was a tremendous drop thereafter and certainly a marked difference from the standards achieved in Germany four years previously. Here in Argentina, the referees lacked the commitment necessary to take disciplinary action against brutal tackling. One of the prime examples of this was apparent to me in Mendoza airport of all places. I had just been a linesman for Pat Partridge in an unexceptional match between Peru and Poland and, while awaiting our flight back to BA, we were watching on television the match between Argentina and Brazil with the FIFA delegate for our game, Rene Courte. The journey to Mendoza had taken more than seventeen hours by train because the airport had been fog-bound. Nor was that the only problem: Jafar Namdar disliked Pat Partridge immensely and therefore I was acting as referee between them while a Dutchman, Charles Corvo, made fun of Namdar's feelings about his status as reserve linesman. Add to all this the fact that the referees' delegate, a Russian called Labyshev, spoke no English, and you will gather that we made up a very happy party.

Partridge was furious with the travel arrangements but kept quiet nevertheless. Not that it did him any good: he had no further matches. In the first two minutes of the Argentina-Brazil game, there were by my reckoning three potential sending-off offences which went unremarked by the Hungarian referee, Palotai, who received no assistance from Linemayr, the Austrian linesman. You cannot expect anything else, commented Rene Courte, because Palotai lets the players do exactly what they like. Yet Palotai was to be appointed linesman in the play-off between Brazil and Italy for third place, while Linemayr was linesman in the final between Argentina and Holland. Perhaps their constant companionship with Seipelt during the stay in Buenos Aires bore fruit?

Throughout the matches, there was little evidence of co-operation between linesmen and referee, possibly because many of them had not run the line in ten or fifteen years and were not therefore correctly positioned to give offside decisions. Nor were they prepared to assist referees in controlling rough play because, in my opinion, they were aware that a low mark for a referee would be beneficial to the linesman who hoped to have future matches as the man in the middle.

There were on duty, though, referees who were simply not experienced enough to officiate in the Welsh League's premier division: they certainly were not up to Football League standard, and I say this despite the fact that some of them became personal friends. No, referees were chosen in some matches for purely political reasons. Seipelt and Codesal were controlling the referees' meetings and, between them, were trying to do an Aston of 1974 but without the ability, the style or the personality.

But even I could not complain about the appointments for the first round. The sixth to be announced at the meeting of referees was Sweden v Brazil at Mar del Plata. Referee, Thomas of Wales, linesmen Namdar of Iran and Alojzy Jarguz from Poland, with Codesal of Uruguay as inspector. I was delighted to have Brazil, especially in view of the fact that in their 1-1 draw with England at Wembley just a few months previously they had used all the tactics that South Americans can use not to lose a game. The Swedish boss, Georg Ericson, was apparently pleased too. He told the press next day, 'I have seen Brazil against France and West Germany before coming to Argentina. They went in for shirt-pulling, they fouled – in front of the referee and when he was not looking. They were a dirty side. Thankfully, we have a strong referee in. Clive Thomas, generally regarded as the best one here.' And the Brazilians were lectured by their manager on the importance of going for the ball alone. He added that the team were pleased with the choice of referee. 'Clive Thomas is a first-class referee and very careful with fouls', said Claudio Coutinho, the manager. So at least I started with the approval of both sides.

Little did I know that it was to be the last match I would referee in the World Cup Finals. Naturally, it was a very keen game with a few yellow cards being necessary, but all was going exactly as I wished. The Brazilians accepted my style of refereeing and quite obviously knew that any trouble with individual players would lead to marching orders. Then came probably the most controversial decision that any referee has ever made, a decision which reverberated round the world and for which in the minds of many supporters of football, the 1978 World Cup will be remembered. And I have to live with it: wherever I go today someone is certain to raise the subject.

The score was 1-1 with ninety minutes already completed on my watch and only injury-time to be played. Brazil, still pressing for a winning goal, earned a corner. I had time therefore to look at my watch while standing near the Swedish goalkeeper, Ronnie Hellstrom, who asked me in broken English how much longer there was to go. 'Not long', I replied.

The Brazilian taking the corner had not put the ball in the arc and the Polish linesman, Jarguz, was explaining that the ball had to be within it. I looked again at my watch and, with just seconds to go in my allotted injury-time, now coming up to thirty-one seconds, the corner was eventually taken.

I blew the whistle after the ball had travelled about ten yards, turned, and pointed to the tunnel to show that the match was over. Behind me there was uproar. There was a roar from the crowd, I saw the Brazilian players jumping for joy and I turned to see the ball in the back of the net, apparently headed in by Zico.

Curiously, and contrary to what Mike Langley stated in the *Sunday People* and what appeared in other Sunday papers, I was not at that stage pelted with coins by furious Brazilian supporters. There were no physical protests from either crowd or players. Indeed, although the Brazilian players protested mildly, which was hardly surprising, they accepted it when I showed them on my watch that time had indeed been up. The problems arose later, with every journalist and television commentator in Argentina wanting to interview me.

Back in the dressing-room, Codesal told me it was a bad decision but could not explain where I was wrong. Even so, I knew that if I did not have a member of the referees' committee to back me for adhering strictly to the laws, then I would have no chance from that moment of any further participation in the World Cup of 1978 or thereafter. Brian James was the first British journalist to talk his way through a police cordon to see me, and his report in the *Daily Mail* of 5 June, 1978, really sums up much of the scene:

'By some misprint, the official list shows the name of that well-known Treorchy referee as Olive Thomas.

'For an hour or so in Mar del Plata on Saturday night, there was a chance he'd have to dress the part ... with wig and woman's clothing to get away alive.

'By bringing Brazil's opening match, against Sweden, to an end about three-tenths of a second before they scored what would have been a winning goal, Clive Thomas made himself a target for about 20,000 potential assassins.

'Zico was in mid-air, coiling himself to meet a corner with his head when Thomas blew, spun on his heels, and walked towards the tunnel. There was a moment's incredulous silence, then every Brazilian in the place exploded in choruses of *Fillio da puta*. Which, even if you did not know the language, you could guess from the gestures, is horribly obscene.

'They then split up into posses, swarming from the stadium to search for the man who, they claim, had seriously jeopardised their chances of a fourth World Cup.

'Before getting a word with Thomas, I had to identify myself as being indisputably British to two very nervy-looking policemen.

'Thomas himself was entirely calm ...'

Interestingly, the great Pele told Steve Richards in the *Sunday People* a little later on 25 June: 'In my view, if it was time, then Thomas had to blow and the Brazilians should have been asking themselves why they delayed the corner kick as long as they did.'

After being taken to the airport under police protection at Mar del Plata, I was informed that Jack Taylor had told television audiences back in Britain that I had made the wrong decision. Inevitably, back in Buenos Aires in the foyer of the hotel, the press were waiting to pounce. I was quite prepared to take them all on but I decided not to and, instead, went to bed. I slept the sleep of the just.

I had a rude awakening. Although it was my day off as I had officiated the day before, Friedrich Seipelt rang me, which had to mean trouble because he never spoke to me unless there was a problem or to tell me I was wrong. You should have allowed the corner to be taken, he said, and awaited the outcome before terminating the game. I told him that would have been dishonest as we would have been over time.

I could scarcely believe him when he said bluntly that I would not have another game in the Argentine. Because I still felt that I had the ability and that this would count in the end, I asked him to bring up my case at the meeting the following day when referees and members of the committee would raise points of interest from the matches. No one, in fact, raised the matter: all the referees were too afraid to voice an opinion and run the risk of being banned. The British press stated that Brazil had reported me to FIFA, that there was a special meeting and, although this was categorically denied, something must have gone on either in private or at an official meeting. Either way, it meant the end of Thomas.

Throughout my stay in Argentina, I received tremendous hospitality from my new rugby friends, both in their clubhouses and at home, while other referees were busy trying to curry favour by taking members of the referees' committee out for dinner. If that is the way to gain further appointments, then let me stay with the rugby folk.

The seminars continued but they were little more than a farce. On one occasion, following a match between Argentina and France when a Swiss referee, Jean Dubach, had awarded the host nation a penalty when the incident was quite clearly outside the area, Seipelt interrogated Dubach disgracefully in front of the other referees. I could not take it any longer – anyone can make a mistake after all – and told Seipelt so. He immediately told me to sit down and be quiet. Dubach afterwards thanked me sincerely and quite a number of colleagues said well done, but not one would say it in front of the committee.

There had also been problems, as in Germany, over the kit. We had been told that we must wear the Adidas referee's outfit despite having been asked in a circular of 31 March to bring our own equipment and, even before that in a circular of 20 February, paragraph twelve, to bring 'personal outfit and stopwatch'. In fact, eighteen referees felt the instruction to wear the Adidas kit was wrong and that they would be more comfortable, surely of great importance, in their normal 'uniform'. Dr Franchi, who had taken me aside at one social gathering to ask whether I could persuade the other referees to fall into line, insisted that the decision was final. What was not known to the referees' committee or to FIFA was that I was in fact already contracted to Adidas. It was the principle that I was against.

I was also against the principle of using a particular make of stopwatch. At a reception given by Seiko, we were presented with watches and asked to wear them for our matches. The referees' committee even gave permission for photographs to be taken for publicity purposes by the company but I had no intention of using the watch – which turned out to be a valuable decision because others took three days at least to master the mechanics. Seiko indeed may have been grateful: it might have been counterproductive to claim that I was using their watch in one of the most controversial incidents of the competition.

But I digress. The poor standards of refereeing in the second round had nothing to do either with kit or with watches. And although I had it 'Seipelt' out to me that I would be taking no further part in the proceedings, I still had the vain hope that ability would out and that I would come back in favour. Rumour said the contrary. By 21 June, the word was so strong about who had been awarded the final and who the third-place play-off that I made my way to British Airways in downtown Buenos Aires and asked them to change the date of my ticket from Monday, 28 June, to 25 June.

I had had enough, even before Jack Mowat told the Scottish referee John Gordon and myself on the evening of 22 June that the officials for the finals and semi-finals had been decided. Dr Franchi had made a casting vote that the final would be refereed by his fellow countryman, Gonella, who sounds like a danceband leader and who to my mind referees like one, with the 'runner-up', Klein of Israel, having the semi-final between Brazil and Italy. This confirmed to me the utter disgrace of the appointments: Gonella, placed in the final by the doubtful wisdom of his friend and countryman, made a comprehensive mess of the game between Argentina and Holland and badly let down the profession of refereeing.

As a postscript to the Argentine finals, though, even I have to admit to being astonished, astounded, shocked and even flabbergasted as, without regret, I left the Carlton Hotel in Buenos Aires that Friday morning before the competition reached its peak with the weekend finals.

Accompanying me to the airport for an early departure were three members of the referees' committee. In my car was Jack Mowat. In another were Friedrich Seipelt and Artemio Franchi. None of them was therefore available for comment on the standard of refereeing in those crucial games.

Gonella, incidentally, did not referee another game, either in Europe or in his own country after this final debacle. Klein was bitterly disappointed but many members of the referees' committee were to visit his homeland, Israel, in the next few months. Strange. Dr Franchi continued as president of the FIFA referees' committee, and chairman of the UEFA referees' committee. In fact, his position in UEFA was strengthened before his death. But Jack Mowat was taken off the committee before the 1982 World Cup. I wonder why?

After all this, I suppose I should not have been surprised to learn two days before the official announcement of the referees appointed for the 1982 series in Spain that I would not be on the list. No, maybe I wasn't surprised really, but that does not mean that I was not bitterly disappointed because I had always hoped that ability would count rather more than politics.

Friends tell me – and it was clear from television – that the preparation and training encountered by the referees was still amateurish; that there were still major language problems leading to misunderstandings between referees and linesmen who were unable to have essential pre-match discussions; and that there were referees who were not from a top category even in their home country.

We saw penalty kicks given instead of free kicks outside the area, we saw blatant hand-balls going unpenalised, we saw referees favouring one particular team. Referees had to be so busy ensuring that a defensive wall was properly placed at free kicks that they frequently failed to signal the restart of the game, leading on one occasion to a goal. Players gesticulated with annoyance at linesmen but no disciplinary action was taken. Others were given yellow cards for offences but were then allowed to commit more serious fouls with impunity.

To me, the 1982 World Cup put back the art of refereeing by about twenty years. Referees did not seem to know what was acceptable, and chaos resulted. Yet Dr Havelange, the President of FIFA, congratulated the referees on their officiating throughout the series. The general secretary, Josef Blatter, made special mention of the referees' committee under the expert and clever chairmanship of Dr Franchi. Well, yes, one has to admit he was clever.

I queried with the Football Association of Wales the omission from the list of referees in Spain any representative from Wales and received a letter from the secretary, Trevor Morris, regretting the fact and sharing my disappointment. He pointed out that I knew full well the politics involved and said the FAW would query the reasons why no Welshman had been chosen. Neither he nor his successor, Alun Evans, have ever informed me of what action the FAW took: if any.

Ah well. Perhaps I should have learned Italian instead of carpentry.

·9·

WORK AND PLAY

Away from football, those days with the Boys' Clubs of Wales in the sixties and seventies were in retrospect a very important period. They helped to shape what became a business career which could run parallel to refereeing. My outlook now was geared towards legal and administrative skills. When I moved to the Boys' Clubs of Wales, where I was to become general secretary, it meant of course a change to the besuited Thomas you meet today, a white-collar operative now surrounded by law books.

And did I have to use my brains! Because the boys' clubs are a voluntary organisation, money is of prime importance. The grant we received from the government paid only twenty-five per cent of the salaries and, believe me, it was very difficult to promote events and to seek covenants from individuals, or indeed organisations, when you were indirectly asking people to pay your wages. But it was tremendous experience: I was one of the first to seek sponsorship from companies for various activities in the organisation – and as I was in charge of 110 clubs, with more than 10,000 boys in membership, there was an enormous number of activities.

Also in my control were two residential centres, one being St Athan Boys' Village, which caters for 120 boys, and the other Abercrave Outdoor Pursuits Centre, which was for the boy who loved the mountains and the outdoor, adventurous life. I also directed week-long Adjustment to Industry courses, during which apprentices sent by companies throughout the principality would acclimatise themselves to industry through lectures by senior management personnel and union leaders as well as being instructed in the use of leisure. It was gratifying for me to see how many boys would turn up on the Monday morning, vastly reluctant to be away from home, their mates and their girlfriends, but who by the Friday would be returning home and joining their local boys' clubs. Mind you, not all was plain sailing: the young people had to be shown that discipline was essential. Most of them reacted well as I could judge from the end-of-week essays they had to write on the course – but I admit, too, that some of the comments were rather worse than those I was to hear over the years on the football field.

One of the highlights of the year was the Junior Boys' Holiday Week, held always in the first week in August at St Athan, when some 120 boys between twelve and fourteen would assemble under twenty leaders. It was a competitive week, during which I directed all types of sport, starting at eight in the morning and inevitably not finishing until past midnight. By the last morning of the week, the lads had to be helped on to their coaches, while the leaders needed the following week off work to recover!

Just about everyone, nevertheless, would feel exhilarated by his involvement. Only once do I recall a specific problem. The boys were out on manoeuvres late at night, and there were complaints from local residents that a boy had been using very bad language. After investigation the following day, I interviewed the boy concerned and felt he had to be sent home, a decision which was not accepted fully by the other leaders or the boys on the course – to such an extent that I thought I might have had a strike on my hands as they waved goodbye and clapped him as he left the village. But there was no further trouble, and the boy concerned – now a man, of course – always acknowledges me when we meet in the Rhondda.

The sad thing for me is that he was a member of Treorchy Boys' Club where, incidentally, the whole of the boys' club movement started during the late twenties through the serious unemployment of the time. The clubs grew to become the focal point of the young community, and spawned such well-known figures in Wales as Huw Weldon, Stanley Baker, Donald Houston and Lyn Davies. Outside Wales, footballers like Bobby Charlton, Terry Venables and Bobby Moore began in the boys' club.

But money was always the problem. It is needed now just as much as in the twenties, as so many young people seek help and advice and encouragement: then the clubs could perhaps be open day and night to make their sporting and social facilities available to the unemployed, both young and old.

During the course of fund-raising operations, under the presidency of Sir Maynard Jenour, the chairmanship of D. E. J. Davies, and with the enormous help of the late Lord Brecon, I had the responsibility of organising three royal visits to Wales – from the Queen Mother, the Duke of Edinburgh and the Duke of Kent. It was all invaluable experience.

On the occasion of the Duke of Edinburgh's visit to St Athan Boys' Village, I was very surprised to see the amount of organisation required. Indeed, I did not at first see eye-to-eye with Don Carsley, now head of CID in South Wales, who was in charge of the arrangements for the first visit, when he went to such lengths as to bring dogs to sniff round the dormitories and so on. But I quickly learned that he was a professional doing a professional job, and we have since become good friends.

One year, the Boys' Clubs of Wales received no increase in grant from the government of the day despite rises in the cost of living and I took this up with the Welsh Office. I even went to the House of Commons where I addressed a meeting of Welsh MPs – tremendous experience again. The Conservatives were in power at the time, with the result that I received great support from the Labour MPs. (It was here that I first met that other 'referee' from the Rhondda, George Thomas MP, later to become Speaker of the House of Commons and then Lord Tonypandy.) But the meeting was to no avail: no increase, said the Welsh Office. I was determined to fight on, and took the matter up next with the Department of Education and Science, who agreed to meet me and my chairman at their offices in Curzon Street. Thomas again put the case forward, stressing exactly those points I had made to the Welsh Office, and was thoroughly grilled by the Minister of the department. Naturally, we were delighted when we were given the increase. The Minister at the time? None other than Mrs Margaret Thatcher.

Money, of course, was also needed at home and, while I was still working with the boys' clubs, I went into a business partnership with a friend, ex-Cardiff rugby player Steve Hughes, to run a sports shop in Treorchy. I stayed in the business for two years but, because I could not give enough time to it and the demands of the two 'jobs' were pulling both ways, it became necessary to decide whether to be a full-time shop-owner or full-time boys' club general secretary. My partner, Steve, continued by himself.

I moved on in due course to join, in January 1977, Lillywhite Frowd Limited, the sports goods manufacturers and a part of the OCS (Office Cleaning Services) Group of Companies. I had been with them for eight months or so as a sales executive when I put forward to the group proposals whereby I could be far more beneficial to the organisation and in which I included suggestions that I should, along with a regional director, host a lunch before any match I was refereeing throughout England for selected clients who would then be guests at the match.

The idea was accepted and extended until I found myself performing the role of chairman at sales meetings, lunches and dinners for staff and clients round the country, events which would include promotional films and business meetings as well as speeches and question-and-answer sessions with leading sports personalities.

I remember one such function at the Savoy Hotel in London when, before the lunch, 150 clients were watching the start of an OCS promotional film when, horror of horrors, at the Savoy of all places, the projector broke down. I immediately had a word with the main board director present and suggested that I should make an impromptu speech about sport. I had been on my feet ten minutes or so when I was aware that the senior staff were waving their arms frantically from the back, presumably to inform me that the film could now continue. No way. Once a Welshman is on his feet, you won't get him to sit down – unless, as happened on this occasion, the chief comes back on stage and almost physically interrupts! So we did get back to the original programme. But it was not the end of the Welsh connection. Chief guest that day was Cliff Morgan, former rugby international, head of BBC Outside Broadcasts and a remarkable speaker as you will hear: there were tears in the eyes of the clients that afternoon.

On another occasion, I had invited Jimmy Hill down as guest speaker at a time when England had failed to qualify for the World Cup finals and it looked odds-on that Wales would win through. From a client came a three-part question to Jimmy, which brought the response that (a) the England manager faced huge problems in bringing together his squad until two days before an international, (b) that the different types of coaching in the Football League made it difficult to blend a national side, and (c) that there were far too many matches being played and this brought staleness. He was applauded, but I could not resist asking why it was that there was another little country, with far fewer players to choose from but where the same pressures and conditions applied, which could qualify. One client clapped. He was from Newport.

Not that these events always went without a hiccough. Lawrie Mc-Menemy and Jackie Charlton were due to speak at a sales dinner in Gosforth just outside Newcastle one evening but at 8.30, an hour and a half later than scheduled, they had not arrived. The clients remained blissfully unaware of this as they were not due to be confronted with the guests until dinner at 9 pm and they were watching the films. Lawrie and Jack turned up just in time. Lawrie tried to explain – they had been to a meeting of managers at Coventry, Jack had taken great exception to some of the comments made and had threatened to walk out, which in Lawrie's opinion would have resulted in neither of them reaching Newcastle, so he had persuaded Jack to stay at the meeting, which then went on much longer than anticipated ...

My title with OCS was eventually changed to Group Executive, primarily to become involved in industrial relations. I worked alongside the industrial relations controller, George Parrott, and attended many courses and conferences. Eventually I came to be responsible for advising the directors of the forty-eight companies within the OCS Group on industrial relations and representing them whenever necessary at tribunals. From my office in Cardiff – I also have facilities at headquarters in London, in Eagle Street, Holborn – I have to travel round Britain, and indeed Ireland, meeting union representatives and leaders, including

Len Murray, Moss Evans, George Wright and the regional officers: in the main, I must say, I have found them very fair and helpful.

I believe that every person, from the MD down, is a salesman for a company, which is easy within OCS insofar as it is very much a family-run concern, where they believe in communicating with everybody and where motivation is so much easier.

Because of my refereeing, I have to keep physically fit and it is not unusual for me to be out training at 6 am and to be in my Cardiff office at 8. On days when I have to be in London, I leave by car at perhaps 4.30 am to be in Eagle Street for a 7.30 start. No one prompts me to do this: it is simply that the OCS main board directors start at 6.30, to give themselves a couple of hours of talk and work without interference from the telephone, and it is also a reflection of the business hours of many of the work staff. The directors are accustomed to this early start because they have all begun on the bottom rung of the ladder – almost literally. Even today, Peter Goodliffe and Chris Cracknell, sons of the managing director and his deputy, are learning the business in exactly this way.

I am fortunate in that the company is so sports-oriented. Every director has played at a fairly high standard of rugby, soccer or golf, and OCS were the first company many years ago to sponsor a sports scholarship in conjunction with Bath University, in the belief that young people with particular sporting attributes should be encouraged to blend their natural ability with education.

While all this was going on, of course, I was also enjoying a happy family life. As I have two daughters, Caryn and Allyson – and neither is all that keen on football, along with my wife Beryl – you might think that I would have liked a son. On the contrary: while trying not to be selfish, I would say I would almost certainly have had to give more time to a son with regard to sporting interests and involvement. I would have had to take him to matches (and would have wanted to probably) with the result that I might have become more concerned with his welfare at games rather than the important job at hand. I have never had that sort of pressure, which I have seen affect other referees; consequently I can travel with a free mind the night before a match. Without a doubt this has also had an effect on my international career and I am very grateful.

I do accept, however, that there has been pressure on my family. Indeed, my greatest family critic – if that is the right word – is my father-in-law, Evan Mars, who used to travel to matches with me before he had a stroke. He keeps my feet on the ground, even when he has merely heard about a game from radio or seen a televised game. If I ever needed someone to prevent my head disappearing into the clouds, Evan would be there.

The two girls have had to put up with a great deal, because their friends have seen me on television or because in restaurants and hotels strangers occasionally stop us to speak to me. Caryn and Beryl were particularly upset on one occasion, as we were travelling along the M4 to Cardiff, when Beryl read out to me an article by a former referee, Kevin McNally. We stopped the car and, for the first time, they wanted to reply, to explain what I was really like as a husband and father. While I could not understand why a former referee had written these particular things, I tried to point out – successfully, I think – that this was sadly the price you had to pay if you were at the top of any profession.

Caryn, who was born in 1959, took the early pressure at school and yet it might have been Allyson who was the more interested in the game. She was born at 2 am in the morning on Wednesday, 25 October, 1967. I was due to referee a match that evening and, although I had notified the League that the baby was imminent, I had not cancelled. I checked after the birth that all was well, Beryl saw no reason why I should not go ahead and the midwife commented laconically that I had concluded my part of the proceedings some time previously and that I could do nothing further.

The result was that that evening I refereed a highly romantic game, between Exeter City and Workington Town, during which I cautioned two players. I remember they announced the news of Allyson's arrival over the loudspeakers at half-time, but I honestly cannot recall whether I allowed those two particular players to remain on the field because of my happiness or because their offences were not particularly serious.

Allyson's second name, by the way, is Gaynor. She was named after my sister-in-law, who died so tragically from tuberculosis at the young age of twenty-one. Gaynor, had she lived, would have been my greatest supporter, she would have wanted to travel to matches and she would have kept my scrapbook. A tragic, tragic loss.

The family may not be in a position to criticise my footballing decisions but they are not slow to tell me of other errors. They have seen me judge beauty competitions, for example, and they have no respect for their father's ability to read the game here ... But in general terms I try not to let the refereeing, or business for that matter, interfere with my home life. Neither have the family in any way attempted to step into the limelight: on the contrary, they dislike any VIP treatment. Bless them, though, they do become a little uptight at some of the harsh things that are said about me, when they know just a few of the good things I have done without publicity.

My lifestyle, then, is very straightforward really. Because of my two jobs I have had some of the freedom and the travel which others may yearn. The result is that I have never since the boys' club days had to seek companionship and relaxation in pubs or clubs. Indeed, I have never been a member of any club, other than to become a patron of Blaenrhondda Football Club, nor have I ever been refused admission into any valley club although I would never take entry for granted. I have been asked to become a member by many organisations and I am always happy to speak at functions both in Wales and around England.

I am as content to be in the warmth and privacy of my own home as I am to be in the public eye. Perhaps one little incident may sum up what I mean. One Saturday night when Caryn was about twelve or thirteen, we were sitting at home when I was due on *Match of the Day*. Caryn wanted to watch another channel and Beryl gave in to her. Well, well, I thought, you've been in charge of a game with 40,000 watching. There are millions more sitting in front of their television sets at this moment awaiting your match. But the referee had been overruled by the most important linesman in his life. Yes, we live a private life behind our front door in Porthcawl.

The good people of the Rhondda took a dim view of it, in fact, when I moved from Treorchy six or more years ago now, to the coastal town. Once from the Rhondda, always from the Rhondda – to such an extent that I asked television producers and programme-note writers to say it was Clive Thomas of Mid-Glamorgan (as that would include Treorchy and Porthcawl) rather than commit myself fully to the emotive move.

But Porthcawl, in my very young days, was like the Bahamas: anyone who went there for his holiday was very much of the *crachach* – the Welsh hierarchy. The chapel outing was inevitably to Aberavon or Barry Island with Porthcawl once every five years if you were lucky.

We had to look to the future, and we are lucky to be able to afford a nice house on the coast, but who knows where the ultimate future may lie.

It has other advantages, too. As I train now, running along the top of the cliffs along Rest Bay out towards the famous Royal Porthcawl Golf Club, I reflect that it is easier and flatter than the gruelling mountainside training runs around Treorchy.

Thomas, me boy, you must be growing older . . .

·10·
A FAIRY TALE
OR SWEET FAW

A fairy tale, according to my dictionary, is a folk-tale, a romantic tale, an incredible tale or, euphemistically, a lie. A fairy is an imaginary being capable of kindly or unkindly acts towards man. In view of these snippets of information and those which follow, it will come as no surprise to the discerning that the headquarters of the Football Association of Wales (hereinafter, as the lawyers say, referred to as the FAW) is in, guess where, Fairy Road, Wrexham.

From where else could an official tell a linesman who has just disallowed a goal to the home team – when the score was 2–1 to the visitors, in the first leg of a cup final which provides entry into Europe – 'Thank you very much. You have just lost the FAW a lot of money.' He was referring, of course, to the fact that the attendance at the next match would be small, which it was. The linesman and his referee apparently stood stock-still in amazement. The official is very fortunate that I was not referee that day: I would not only have thrown him out of the dressing-room but would also certainly have reported him to the Association, for what that would have been worth.

Where else would there be thirty-six referees' instructors, only two of whom had ever refereed in the Football League?

Where else would a linesman be chosen for an international immediately after receiving a letter from the Welsh League saying he would be removed from their list unless he bucked up his ideas?

Isn't it totally absurd, too, that I was automatically taken off the Welsh League list once I became a Football League referee? The result is that you sit on your backside, or help with the shopping, on those Saturdays – and there are plenty, as we shall see – when you don't have a match. Fairy Road-land, indeed.

Let us consider first the vexed question of the training and instruction of referees. I had become so appalled at my experience of the way in which the FAW were coaching their referees that I applied to FIFA and UEFA to forward details of how I could become an instructor, because it seemed clear to me that my knowledge and experience should be of value to someone, but that a proper title would be a positive and probably necessary advantage. Rene Courte, senior assistant secretary of FIFA, replied to me on 15 February, 1979, to say how pleased they were that I

74

wished to become an instructor, but pointing out that this had to be achieved at national association level first. Only if a referee is a successful instructor in his own country is he then recommended by his national FA for international courses. FIFA would then take advantage of these courses to assess the referee, but only after that could he be included on the FIFA list of instructors and lecturers. A further letter, from Gerhard Aigner of UEFA, to the FAW on 28 March said that the task at UEFA level was fulfilled by the referees' committee and stated that the FAW should request me to communicate with them direct.

After contacting Trevor Morris, then secretary of the FAW, who told me that there were thirty-six referees' instructors in Wales appointed by the area associations (but that only two of them had refereed in the Football League), I wrote to him with my views on refereeing under his association. I pointed out in my letter of 30 March that, in the past eight years, six referees from South Wales had gone forward to the Football League from the Welsh League and had failed to make the grade. One would have to look very closely, I said, at the reasons for this failure.

Was it (a) an incorrect choice being made from the Welsh League, or (b) the marking system in the Welsh League? Was our standard of refereeing in the Welsh League as high as it should be? And how could we help those referees who were promoted because the gap appeared too wide for them to jump? I recommended that one-day training courses should be held monthly, bringing in all aspects of refereeing and lining and other points, to promote the profession in the principality.

The reply was astonishing. Firstly, it did not come for seven months until 2 November, apparently following a referees' and coaching committee meeting held in Birmingham on 26 October, which suggests that they meet only infrequently; secondly, the committee felt that my comments should have been addressed to the Welsh League secretary, Tony Griffiths. The committee did, however, note with interest my concern regarding the coaching of referees and said the South Wales FA would be happy to avail themselves of my services. Would I contact Mr E.M. Danter, the South Wales FA secretary, or Terry Stewart, South Wales referees' section? In fact, because a copy of the letter had been sent to Mr Danter, I contacted neither. Nor did they contact me. I was aiming higher than them because, for example, my linesmen for European Cup matches could not possibly be up to standard if some of them were Football League rejects, and my concern was with the reputation of Wales.

Between the letters, in fact, I did have the chance to open the FAW Instructors' Conference in Cardiff and received a letter later from Mike Smith, the Welsh team manager at the time and director of coaching, in which he thanked me sincerely, 'for setting the scene of the conference and bringing home forcibly that people have to be of the right standards and calibre in order to demand standards from others'.

I admit I pulled no punches, for although I saw in many of the instructors people with big hearts and a feeling for the game, they had not attained even Welsh League status. With them were Welsh League referees' assessors who had never reached Football League lining level. After I had spoken, I said I was prepared to answer all types of queries but when a North Wales instructor started to raise a point he was told by the chairman, ex-FA Cup Final referee Leo Callaghan, that I would answer questions on my talk and on nothing else. I intervened and said I would answer questions on any point relevant to refereeing, and that therefore the questioner should continue. I sensed that this was almost certainly a North–South confrontation, which bugs FAW Council meetings but which I did not expect to find in refereeing. My points hurt them, but when I was invited to open the same conference in 1983, the same faces were peering up at me. Only two ex-Football League referees were in attendance.

Talking of Leo Callaghan, Wales is one of the few countries in which referees do not receive the assessors' reports from European matches. UEFA send the assessor's report to the FAW; they, in turn, send the report to Mr Callaghan, the Welsh National Referees' Instructor, with a letter which says, 'Enclosed copies of referees' inspector's (assessor's) reports relating to C. Thomas. I shall be obliged if you will discuss the reports with each official in the normal manner.' The referee receives a copy of the letter without the reports. I grew so bored with this stencilled letter that I wrote to Trevor Morris on 3 November, 1980, pointing out that Callaghan had spoken to me only once concerning the reports in the last ten years. (That was only because he attended a fitness test at Newport which ensured that the five FIFA referees were present and at which he took me to one side and said, 'Do you want to read this report? There's no point really as he has given you four out of four.' This was the first I knew that the maximum marking was four, as opposed to the Football League's ten.) However, I said in my letter to Mr Morris that it would be more convenient if the FAW followed the system operating in most countries by sending the reports direct to the referees. If referees wanted to discuss the assessment with Leo Callaghan, they would still be free so to do.

Trevor Morris replied that it was the FAW's policy to continue with the assessments being sent to Callaghan as it was not considered appropriate to send them to the referees. I simply could not understand any reason behind this other than to keep referees in the dark: if a German assessor, say, in a match in France sent his report on me (in English) to Leo Callaghan, any queries would still have to come back to the German.

If I had a query Callaghan clearly could not answer it anyhow because he had not been at the match.

As Trevor Morris retired, I then had a similar letter from Alun Evans, the new secretary, regarding assessors' reports. I pointed out to him as a newcomer that Callaghan would not discuss the reports as he never did and, in a letter of 15 October, 1982, again outlined my reasons as to why the reports should go to the referee concerned. On 2 November he informed me that the present practice would continue and he had been assured by UEFA that this was the correct course but that he would nevertheless place the matter in front of his referees' committee when they met in the spring of 1983.

Alun Evans also said in his letter that he regretted that I felt that there was no value in discussing the reports with Leo Callaghan. He simply had not read my letter correctly: I replied immediately on 8 November to point out that there was value in seeing the report, but not in discussing it with a national referees' instructor who had not even seen the game in question. However, as he was placing the matter before the referees' committee and to strengthen my case, I wrote that I would be pleased to meet Mr Callaghan with a view to discussing matches at which I had officiated in Europe.

Accordingly, I wrote to Leo Callaghan on 30 November, Alun Evans again on 15 December and Callaghan again on 25 January. I did receive a letter on 28 January from Leo Callaghan to say that he was going to Kuwait but would send a summary of the assessment of my game on 29 September (Werder Bremen v Vorwarts Frankfurt) and on Anderlecht v Oporto on 20 October. In fact, I received but one assessment from UEFA, and that was one sent to the FA in London by mistake and of which the FAW and Mr Callaghan probably remain in ignorance.

I heard no more about the spring meeting of the referees' committee. I don't know even if they did meet at all, or whether they discussed the matter. Nobody has bothered to let me know. A leading UEFA administrator was later to tell me he had no knowledge of any approach by the FAW on assessors' reports.

In view of this, I might have realised that further problems would lie in store in a European context.

Before 1983, I had generally had a first-round match either at the request of UEFA or, as the senior referee in Wales, by FAW appointment. But on 11 August, 1983, at a six-a-side football tournament at Newtown in mid-Wales, Ron Bridges, the referee from the north, told me he had been appointed for a European Cup match. I telephoned the FAW on 17 August to enquire whether I had a game, as I was due to fly to Portugal on holiday and would therefore be unavailable.

I spoke to Eddie Harrison, who normally looks after such matters, and he replied no, no appointment. I said I had spoken to Bridges and wondered if there were any other games. He confirmed that there were two, for one of which UEFA had named the referee; when I asked why the FAW had not appointed me, as senior referee, for the other, he suggested that the secretary, Alun Evans, could answer. When I was transferred to Alun after a few minutes delay, he told me that the referees were appointed by UEFA.

I repeated to him what Harrison had told me, and he then said that he did not know how the appointments were made, and that if that was what Harrison had said, then it was so, and he would transfer me back. Three minutes later, Harrison came back on the line and I asked him to confirm what he had told me. He confirmed that the other referee was to be Howard King and said that the FAW were trying to give him experience. At that stage I asked him whether he would repeat everything while I wrote it down, and he immediately asked, is this for the press again? He told me that the appointments had the full backing of the FAW and that no individual referee was entitled to an explanation. I was incensed. 'Are you insinuating that I will tell the press?' I demanded. He then withdrew the comment about the referee's experience.

I was left somewhat baffled by the selection procedure. Quite honestly, I have no idea, despite all my experience, as to who makes the appointments and how. Although the FAW has a referees' committee, under the chairmanship of Leo Callaghan, they meet only to discuss promotion, training and recruitment. I assume, therefore, that the decisions are made by somebody at 3, Fairy Road, Wrexham. If there is a rota for linesmen, for example, it is a random rota. There are linesmen who, after one season on the FL list, go out to line European Cup matches, while others below the referees' retained mark in the Senior Welsh League, are told to buck their ideas up and yet at the same time are appointed by the FAW to international matches. Even if it means having four matches on the run, in my opinion the best men should have the appointments. But as usual, and not just with the FAW, ability is not necessarily a priority.

Finance is clearly a major worry for the FAW and the arrogant decision of England and Scotland to break up the home international championship may do irreparable harm, insofar as the revenue from those matches is so crucial. Worse, just four days before Christmas 1983, Yugoslavia scored an injury-time goal to beat Bulgaria and thus prevented Wales from being the lone British representative in the 1984 European Championships following the summary departure of England and Scotland. In view of this, and along with the fact that Northern Ireland were the most successful British qualifiers for the World Cup in Spain, I think that the English and Scottish associations frankly have a nerve.

Two examples of financial problems emerged during one Welsh Cup quarter-final between Wrexham and Swansea City. As usual, there were problems over hotel allowances even for an evening match in bad weather and the Wrexham ground, when I arrived at about 4 pm with my colleague Don Jones, was a mess. John Neal, Wrexham's manager at that time, suggested a look at the pitch before going off for a cup of tea. 'But don't put your boots on', he said, 'I've got wellingtons for you. It's that bad.' No way could the match be played, so I telephoned the Swansea manager, Harry Griffiths, at the Crest Hotel and explained the predicament.

Harry arrived with his chairman, Malcolm Struel, but, though he quickly realised the pitch was in a mess, he did not explain this strongly enough to Malcolm Struel. Harry and I were in John Neal's office arranging another date when Struel came in, highly annoyed that the game was off in view of the travelling expenses of his club and their supporters. He suggested that we ring Trevor Morris at the FAW headquarters for him to make a decision.

'By all means', I said, 'but when you phone him, tell him to bring a referee with him because I won't do the match now'. I was delighted, even if it was just what I would have expected of him, when John Neal said, 'We shall not be playing with another referee. Clive Thomas's decision is final. We are now looking for an alternative date.'

Another Swansea quarter-final match I had to cancel caused the FAW problems. Swansea were due to play Merthyr Tydfil at Penydarren Park on a Wednesday evening, and the match was expected to be a real crowd-puller. Alas, frost made the ground unplayable in my opinion. Both managers – with John Toshack there for Swansea – were surprised when I asked their views, for this was contrary to FAW instructions.

'Would you be prepared to play on it?' I asked. 'If not, then you should not expect your players to go out there.'

I always maintain that if the two managers agree to a decision on a pitch, then everyone is happy. The referee need only make a casting vote. In this case, they both agreed with me, and I phoned the FAW to tell them of the postponement and that an alternative date had been found. 'But', I said, 'I have a match for the Football League on that particular day.' Because of the importance of the Welsh Cup match, the FAW said they would seek my release, and asked if I minded. 'It is your decision', I said. 'Not mine.' During the course of the conversation, I told them the League appointment was for a Liverpool–Everton match. There was a pause – and the FAW then had the audacity to pass the responsibility to me, asking which game *I* would choose. I repeated that it was up to them to decide. They did, finally: and I refereed at Anfield.

On another occasion, the first I knew of an appointment to referee a Colwyn Bay–Swansea semi-final was when I received a call from Radio

Manx, in the Isle of Man, asking if I would be prepared to give an interview because they were sponsoring the match. I said I would let them know when I had confirmed their news, but an office clerk at Fairy Road insisted no decision had yet been taken. It was forty-eight hours before I finally told Radio Manx that we could go ahead. Even then, no administrator from Wrexham was present for the game, nor any South Wales member of the FAW – and this is allegedly the most important competition in Wales, with entry into Europe for the victors.

The FAW do attempt to run on a small budget, although even that does not really excuse their low rate of expenses and their fees to referees. Their reaction is that it should be an honour to officiate at these games. I would accept this so long as too many officials of the FAW do not spend the profit from the finals in gallivanting around Europe.

Of all people, perhaps, I was in a position to compare the differences not only in payment and expenses but in awards (a gold medal to a tankard) and general splendour between the FA Cup Final and the Welsh Cup Final. In 1976 I did them both, within the space of four days: Cardiff City v Hereford United on the Wednesday, and Manchester United v Southampton on the Saturday. The FA at one stage asked me to reconsider my availability for the Welsh game; the FAW were, I would think, aware of the Wembley invitation. But they would never go against that ancient and worthy institution, the Football Association.

·11·

LANCASTER GATE AND ALL THAT

*'Mediocrity knows nothing higher than itself
but talent instantly recognises genius'*

Sir Arthur Conan Doyle

Once upon a time, there was a Football Association that was a power in the world. No, not simply a Football Association but *the* Football Association, without the name of a country attached but which was nevertheless known by everyone. When the FA said 'We do it this way', the world did it this way.

Even with the decline of the British Empire, the Football Association maintained its credibility and charisma in the world game. Until, that is, in 1974, when Sir Stanley Rous had to relinquish his hold on FIFA. By then, the standard of English football was accelerating rapidly downhill. No longer could we claim disarmingly and dishonestly that other countries were merely catching us up. They were doing that all right – but we were passing them on our way down. Today, we have an out-of-date administrative structure that leads only to mediocrity, reflecting a lack of leadership from the top and the absolute division of interests between the Football Association and the Football League.

I lay the blame for this firmly at those elegant doors in Lancaster Gate, for behind them are people reneging on their duties as the governing body of football in England and Wales, allowing Europe and South America to dictate to them. They renege by failing to modernise the game in changing the laws; they renege by failing to maintain discipline over their supporters; they renege by accepting edicts from FIFA apparently unquestioningly; and they renege by allowing the ham-handed professionals, who live 250 miles away in an obscure Lancashire coastal town, the Football League, to dominate them.

Neither of those once august bodies apparently has any pride in the country any more, as the League stumbles along its clumsy course towards crisis. (This I discuss much more fully in the final chapter.) In just about every country I can think of, for example, national requirements are placed well in front of those of the clubs; league matches on the Saturday or Saturdays before internationals are cancelled, in order to allow proper preparation of the national side and to reduce the likelihood of injuries. Think also of the problems of Wales, Scotland, Northern Ireland and the Republic who are never sure that their players will be released at all.

The clubs rule the roost, so that there must be as many fixtures in as many competitions as possible to fill the coffers or, at least, not to leave them empty. Therefore they must win and to hell with entertainment, to hell with skills, to hell with flair. Inevitably this attitude permeates right down to schools level with the consequent disenchantment all the way through. The FA simply must halt this sad decline.

Disenchantment in my case reached its peak when I was not appointed to referee a single FA cup-tie for the 1982–83 season. I do not know the reason for this insult, although I suspect that I may have been 'disciplined' for one of two reasons: either the furore over West Ham manager John Lyall's alleged comments at Wembley after the 1981 League Cup Final, or because of what I said at the annual conference of the Association of Football League Referees and Linesmen in Birmingham during the summer. As chairman of one of the groups I asserted that referees should not be concerned with whatever directive might be given by the Football Association, the Football League, UEFA and FIFA on the professional foul and its punishment.

Yet I could not have been all that unpopular. One evening at Southampton in October 1982, after a League Cup match with Manchester City, into my dressing-room – against Football League instructions – came a gentleman who said I had given the finest display of refereeing he had seen in years. That man was Mr Lionel Smart, chairman of the FA Challenge Cup Committee. I had also been congratulated earlier in the year after an FA Cup match between Luton, top of Division Two, and Ipswich Town, top of Division One, by Mr A.D. McMullen. Now Mr McMullen is not my favourite man. We have had our difficulties because he is on the Referees' Committee of UEFA despite the fact that the most senior league in which he officiated was the Metropolitan League (below the standard of the Southern League). A schoolmaster, he worked his way through Bedfordshire Schools Association and Bedford County FA to his seat on the FA Council. But he is also chairman of the FA Referees' Committee and might, therefore, be another voice in court to suggest that I was capable of taking some FA Cup match.

But no. Even though the Football League informed me that they had given me certain clear dates in order to leave me available for the FA Cup rounds in 1983, I was still sufficiently worried by 7 February, having tried in vain to contact Reg Payne, who is always introduced as appointments secretary of the FA but who did not return my call, to write to the general secretary, E.A. Croker, otherwise known as Ted.

'Dear Ted', I said. 'I would like to express my concern that I have not yet received an FA Cup appointment for the current 1982–83 season and wondered if you could give me a reason for my exclusion.' All very friendly like.

Ted replied in likewise friendly fashion.

'Dear Clive' he began, then said he was sure I would appreciate that 'with only 123 matches to allocate and almost 90 referees available it is inevitable that every season several referees do not receive an appointment from the committee'. Just work out those statistics again, Ted.

On 16 February, I wrote to 'Dear Ted' asking 'respectfully how your committee selects the referees for the FA Cup competition'.

On 24 February, back came his reply: 'Many criteria are studied concerning all aspects of a referee's suitability, and the members responsible make appropriate appointments according to their opinions, which are the final deciding factor.'

It was still a Ted and Clive affair, even when I wrote again on 8 March. 'I certainly do not wish my exclusion from the FA Cup appointments for season 1982–83 to be a continued saga but in view of the last letter my concern deepens. I therefore would like you to clarify what aspects (if any) of my refereeing are not suitable or is it the members' opinions, or is it both?'

On 14 March Ted replies: 'Dear Clive, I acknowledge receipt of your letter of 8 March, but I cannot enlarge on the information in my previous replies.'

Our correspondence may have died a death at that stage. But then John Sadler, in *The Sun* of 2 April, without any approach by me, really stirred things up. He had been querying my absence from the competition since January and, with the semi-final appointments made, could now confirm I had not one single appointment.

'(Clive Thomas) has not been allocated an FA Cup tie all season – for the first time in seventeen years', wrote Sadler. 'Officials at Lancaster Gate attempt to throw a cloak of secrecy over the issue.'

Ted Croker eventually issued the curt statement: 'The appointment of referees to FA Cup matches is a private matter within the Association and is not discussed with outside bodies.' Dick Speake, a member of the Referees' Committee, was quoted as saying: 'He has been a bit unlucky.' But Sadler concluded: 'And the FA should be duty bound to explain why the name of their most famous referee has been missing from the Cup all season.'

Mr Speake had said in the article that 'we take into account the marks received by referees in League games they have handled prior to the Cup as well as geographical considerations'.

This angered me so much that I resumed the correspondence with the FA. On 6 April, I wrote to tell Croker – it was 'Dear Mr Croker' by now

– that I was baffled by Mr Speake's comments which were more explicit than those stated in the FA's letters but which were still unsatisfactory.

'In view of the reasons stated by Mr Speake, I now feel that an injustice has been committed in my exclusion of an FA Cup appointment and can prove it by facts and figures. I, therefore, respectfully ask you to consider this letter as an application to attend an FA Council Meeting for members to hear my side of the case, or alternatively to receive the contents of my case in writing for you to place before the Council.'

Croker replied on 12 April to tell me the matter would be put before the Referees' Committee on 3 May. On 12 May, I wrote again to ask whether he could give me information from that meeting. The response was that my letter had been placed before the committee and its contents noted.

Not good enough. On 17 May, a letter to Mr Croker: 'Please would you confirm what your committee decided and what action was taken in response to my letter dated 8 April, bearing in mind that this letter was only an application to attend an FA Council Meeting or alternatively to convey to you the comments of my case in writing to be placed before the Council.' On 19 May, a letter from Croker: 'Dear Mr Thomas, With reference to your letter dated 17 May, the decision of the committee was that your letter should be noted only and, therefore, that no other action should be taken. We cannot add to the comments previously made.'

My turn again. On 26 May, a letter to Croker: 'I am totally dissatisfied not only with the decision, if a decision has been made, but also with the inept answers given to my questions raised in my letters as far back as 7 February, 1983.

'I now charge the Challenge Cup Committee and/or the Referees' Committee of the Football Association Ltd with using improper methods in my exclusion of an appointment in the FA Challenge Cup Competition in the season of 1982–83.

'In view of the seriousness of the charge, I would make myself available at any time to meet the Football Association Council to substantiate my charge with necessary evidence.'

I was thanked for the letter, but the FA failed to take up the challenge. 'I regret that you are still dissatisfied', wrote Croker on 31 May, 'and confirm that as far as we are concerned this matter is now closed. We are sending copies of the correspondence to the Football Association of Wales, so that they are aware of the situation', he concluded. For what reason? At no point in the earlier correspondence did Croker say he was going to involve the FAW. So why now?

There are still a number of issues which I believe should be answered publicly by the FA because the Challenge Cup is followed by millions of people who, like me, are under the impression that top referees are appointed to the games. I put it again to the FA that for some reason they have connived to exclude me. I have already charged the Challenge Cup/Referees' Committees with using improper methods in my exclusion – a very, very serious charge which, unless proved, could lead to a countercharge against me for bringing the game into disrepute. Yet all the FA does is to regret that I am dissatisfied.

I charge the two committees because, throughout the correspondence from 10 February to 31 May, I am not certain which of them actually makes the appointments for the FA Cup. The FA Handbook states quite categorically that the Challenge Cup Committee's duties include accepting entries, making the draw and appointing officials to matches. The Referees' Committee, on the other hand, deals with matters arising under the regulations for the control of referees, recommendations on the laws of the game and also recommendations on referees for FIFA. Because my grouse was simply about lack of appointments, I would assume that the Challenge Cup Committee should have dealt with the complaint. Why then, Ted, did you place the matter before the Referees' Committee? Why did you not allow me to meet your Council?

One final question on the subject: is Reg Payne, the referees' appointments secretary, merely an administrator or is he able to authorise appointments, as is the impression given when he is introduced at conference? If he has such authority, may I respectfully suggest you ask him for his assessment of my ability in the game on 23 April, 1983, between West Ham and Aston Villa. 'Finally', he wrote, 'may I say that your performance from first to last whistle showed how a referee should command the players and control the match on the field'.

It is still not too late to hold a full inquiry, to reveal the truth and to explain to referees throughout the country just how referees are appointed to FA Cup matches.

After all that, I simply could not resist having a go at the Football Association in July 1983 when I received from them the annual form RAP/GEC seeking personal details and career facts to acknowledge availability for FA Cup matches in 1983–84.

I wrote to Mr Croker: 'Unless there is a change in the Challenge Cup Committee/Referees' Committee policy in appointing referees for FA Cup matches, this form is superfluous. I therefore can only assume that because the form has been sent to me there will be a change of policy for the season 1983–84 and it is only for that reason that I have completed the form.'

As you can judge, I was thoroughly disenchanted with the activities of the FA. And, indeed, the inactivity, for what the FA does not do is sometimes more important that what it does do.

Take the case of Reading striker Ken Price, who was reported by

Graham Baker, in the *Daily Mirror* on 4 April 1983, to have called me a cheat after I had awarded Portsmouth two penalties (from which Kevin Dillon scored) in a 2–2 draw. Accordingly, on 5 April I wrote to the FA to ask if they would be taking action over what I regarded as a serious accusation. They wrote back the following day to say they would 'certainly write to Ken Price in respect of his alleged remarks'.

More than a month later, on 12 May, I again wrote to the FA asking to be brought up to date and, a week later, I had a reply (from Mr E. Dinnie on behalf of the general secretary) to say that the relevant newspaper reports were referred to the members of a disciplinary commission together with a letter from Price. 'What was considered to be appropriate action was taken by the members', said the letter. Not unnaturally, I then wrote to discover what constituted 'appropriate action'.

The FA replied on 7 June, again through Mr Dinnie, who dealt with all the early correspondence in this affair, that the player 'denies that he called you a cheat and says that he was misquoted in the press. He apologised for the remarks he made and the commission warned him as to his future conduct.' Consequently I wrote to the *Daily Mirror* to point out that the player claimed he had been misquoted but the *Mirror*, in turn, informed me that the reporter, Graham Baker, stood by his story and that a colleague, Peter Oakes from *The Star*, had also heard the comment although he had refrained from using it in his paper.

Accordingly I wrote again to the FA for clarification. 'I cannot understand why Price has apologised for something on which he says he was misquoted.' Should not the committee have notified me if the press were to blame? Were any witnesses called to justify whether Price did or did not make the comment? You see, Mr Dinnie and the members of the FA, those millions who read the *Daily Mirror* still believe that Price called me a cheat.

Ted Croker himself finally wrote to me on 29 June. 'The facts are that you did not hear Mr Price call you "a cheat" and Mr Price emphatically denies having done so. We do not take action on the basis of unconfirmed newspaper reports. The commission warned Mr Price about his future conduct after considering the correspondence with the player and the club.'

Unconfirmed? They really do support their referees, don't they? If I hadn't pursued the matter, would it have been swept under the carpet at 16 Lancaster Gate, where so many complaints end?

By then, though, I was thoroughly disillusioned with the FA and its disciplinary hearings. Indeed, many years before when I met the late and capable secretary, Sir Dennis Follows, at Lancaster Gate one morning, he said: 'You know where to go better than I do. I'll see you later.' And Bert Millichip, now chairman of the FA, referred to me as 'my learned friend' at another commission, a compliment as he himself is a solicitor. Mind you, at the time I was trying to argue that such commissions were illegal because they should not be in a position to charge a player with an offence and then act as judge and jury.

There have been times when the FA have reneged on other responsibilities, too. I remember that 1982 Tottenham–Wolves semi-final at the Sheffield Wednesday ground for reasons other than the Hibbitt-Hoddle penalty. Some of the points were small but I feel that the FA might have taken a lead.

When I arrived at the ground, I was asked by the Sheffield Wednesday staff if I had any objection to the national anthem being played before the match. I had no objection but it was, as it were, a 'home' match for the FA and so I said they would have to sanction it. Threequarters of an hour before the kick-off, Mr Hawes, an official of the FA and one of nature's gentlemen, came into the dressing-room – the first FA representative I had seen – and I told him about the request. 'I leave it to you', he said.

That was one of the small points but perhaps it was symptomatic. In the twenty-fourth minute, I noticed that the police were allowing supporters from one of the terraces to sit on the touchline behind the goal in front of Spion Kop. I ran over and asked the substitute linesman to supervise the encroachment. All was well for a time but, when I had rung the bell for the teams to return after half-time, I heard noises off and the reserve linesman reported that there were about a thousand supporters on the pitch. I told the teams we would not go out until I had inspected the pitch. I spoke with the police in charge and asked how the crowd could be dispersed but, after a few minutes, it seemed clear that they would not leave the pitch until the players were brought on. The police chief was not in favour: I understood his feelings but asked whether he minded if I made that decision. Despite being responsible for the ground, the FA were conspicuous by their absence and it was not until I returned to bring back the teams that I met Mr McMullen and Mr Hawes, who disappeared again when I told them what was happening.

After the match I sent for Eric England, the Wednesday secretary, and the police chief so that we could talk the matter over. Just before they arrived, Mr McMullen came in to discuss the match and I asked him whether he would stay but he declined. On the following Monday morning, I spoke to the FA about the crowd problems but they told me politely that they did not need a report.

In short, the Football Association does not appear to be over-interested in discipline, either of players or followers, in supporting its referees (for no referee is permitted to officiate in any league unless he is affiliated to his local FA), nor in its influence in the game at international level.

I mention the supporters because the FA has little or no chance of controlling the game totally if it cannot put parts of its own house in order. Hooliganism may be a social problem, but make no mistake, the FA should take more responsibility for those wayward supporters who ruin everyone's enjoyment. I suggest ways in which they could do this later in the book.

Those bewhiskered gentlemen of olden days may have ruled the FA in an autocratic manner but they did so with discipline and with the betterment of the game at heart. Today, the officials still try to be autocratic but apparently without the authority, knowledge, understanding or the personalities to carry it through.

No wonder the game in Britain has been in decline and no wonder authority has moved to Zurich and beyond.

·12·

AN UNHOLY LEAGUE

I have always maintained that the Football League is the strongest in the world not only in the sheer numbers of clubs and players participating but also in the football it provides. Its strength can also be its weakness as we have seen in the previous chapter, so that problems can occur at international level. The number of matches during the season is absurd with the FA Cup, the Milk Cup, European competitions, internationals and sundry other tournaments to be accommodated along with seasonal fluctuations. There are more professional players in England than anywhere in the world and more people fully employed in administration at club and League levels.

There is also therefore a great need for strong referees and the pressures on them are, I believe, even greater than in any other country – although my colleagues in Brazil and Italy disagree on the grounds that they have to contend with the so-called 'mafia of football' and the accompanying bribery and corruption. Most recently, as we have heard, this is even the case in Hungary.

The net result of this vastness is that there is a great capacity for trouble among the strong personalities around.

But none of this occurred to me, even after my preliminary skirmishes in Wales, when, after two seasons as a linesman, I was invited in 1966 with Iorrie Jones from Trelewis to an interview with members of the Football League Management Committee and Referees' Committee at the Great Western Hotel at London's Paddington Station. We were waiting in an anteroom when in walked John Homewood, a London linesman who was also up for interview and who later became a close friend. He was in no doubt. 'Don't worry, Thomas', he said. 'You'll be on the list.' I assumed he meant on ability though I learned later that he knew two referees were needed from the Welsh area. But really, how could I fail? I was a linesman and a top-marked referee from Wales. The questions asked were superfluous: could I officiate at short notice, and how would I react to press queries? Basically they were seeking someone who did not require a white stick.

That was the first time I had come face to face with Alan Hardaker, the Football League secretary who ruled from his Lytham St Annes office with stern benevolence and with whom I was to have the most stormy of relationships over the next few years. Lytham St Annes? Well, look it up on the map of England and tell me if it is the best place from which to run the Football League.

I passed the interview and was invited on to the supplementary list. In my heart I knew it was the start of a career that would take me to the top. Not so easy: I had to prove myself in ten matches in that first season of 1966–67 and did this, as we have seen, only after a severe warning from Alan Hardaker and then a reversion to style.

Outbreak of war, then, was delayed for a year or two until 8 November, 1969, at Gillingham, who were playing Walsall. I left my Treorchy home at 7 am to arrive at Cardiff General at 8.10 to catch the 8.30 for Paddington and finally to reach Gillingham at 12.26: in ample time for the 3 pm kick-off and also adhering to the Football League rules of arriving an hour before the start.

I reckoned without British Rail. The 8.30 had broken down, the 9.30 was cancelled and eventually I caught a relief train at 10.20. The stationmaster 'phoned Gillingham to tell them of the difficulties and I reached the ground at 2.15, scarcely after the gates had opened. Then I made my mistake. As a new boy, I felt it proper to notify the League of my predicament and pointed out that the stationmaster could verify the details. Honesty was not the best policy for, on 15 December, I received a letter from Hardaker to tell me that the management committee did not consider that I had allowed for all eventualities and fined me ten guineas. I was appalled because Hardaker had told referees at the 1968 conference that we were to cut down on expenses. By leaving home at 7 am I had therefore avoided an overnight hotel stay, but paid the penalty – never again.

I was so angry that I phoned the League and demanded to speak to Hardaker to tell him what I thought. I was warned off by his henchman, Lee Walker, who suggested that I should leave the matter well alone, such was his boss's mood. When I pressed the matter, he thought it might be better to ring again in the afternoon. I did, whereupon Walker politely told me that if I did not accept the decision, I would probably be off the list. 'There is', he added, 'no room for appeal'. From that moment, it was clear, I had to be clever – not only on the field but even more so off it in all communications with the Football League. I was to find that they would commit themselves to paper only if there were no possible come-backs for them.

Four months after the Gillingham incident I was in trouble again. Because the players in a Coventry City-Sheffield Wednesday match in March 1970 were apparently not willing to take into account the water-logged ground, I went into the dressing-rooms at half-time to tell them that I was not prepared to accept some of the tackling. 'We need the points, ref', argued some of the Wednesday players and yet, in the second half, it was Coventry who offended most. I cautioned a Wednesday player and three from Coventry, including their big centre-half, Roy Barry, while he was lying on a stretcher with a broken leg – a case of the biter being well and truly bit.

The players appealed. At the FA commission the case against Lawson (Wednesday) was dismissed, those against Cattlin and Barry were 'not proved' and only against Blockley did the caution stand. If ever there was a mockery of a hearing, this was one. I told the commission what I thought of the way it had been handled, I attempted to point out that it was illegal and said that I wondered at the end whether I was on trial or the players.

I suppose, then, I should have expected the letter from Hardaker summoning me to a meeting concerning the matter. I was to make myself available at 3 pm on 14 August. His management committee had instructed him, he said, although I find it hard to believe that anyone actually instructed Alan Hardaker.

He really tore a strip off me. I was to behave myself at disciplinary hearings in future, I was to answer the questions put to me by the members of the commission and the players' representatives, and I was to referee matches and not to try to change the FA and the Football League in one fell swoop. He had been in the game for many years, I was just a newcomer and so on. But, after winding down from his wrath, he commented for the first time on my ability and told me that the League accepted that I was already one of the best referees in the country and that there was the probability of greater things if only I would calm down. Over a cup of coffee, he offered to have a chat with me on the phone in future about any problems I felt were in the game. I left Lytham on amicable terms with Hardaker; here was someone I could understand and for whom I could feel respect. Indeed, his next act was in my defence.

The Football League received a letter from a Mr Charles Edwards, of New Southgate, complaining that at the end of a match between Tottenham and Coventry on Wednesday, 18 November, I was seen to answer spectators by raising two fingers of each hand. 'This gesture', wrote Mr Edwards, 'has been used by players in the past and they have been rightly punished for it'.

Alan Hardaker replied to Mr Edwards that the complaint would be investigated but said 'from our knowledge of Mr Thomas we would be surprised if he did in fact make the gesture to which you refer' and warned that 'it may be that (Mr Thomas) may wish to take legal advice on the matter'. Too true he did. My lawyers believed that the allegation was libellous, but we wrote simply to say that we would take no further action unless anything of a similar nature followed. It didn't.

It is perhaps symptomatic of my relationship with the League at this time that the two subjects which occupied my thoughts for a year or two were players' studs and an experiment with referees and linesmen. The first subject had its hilarious moments, the second was more serious.

The League, to take the stud issue first, instructed referees and linesmen in 1971 that the studs on players' boots should be checked in the dressing-rooms before a match – a somewhat farcical suggestion, I told Mr Hardaker, as players could change studs, or, indeed, boots, after the referee had left the room. He agreed, with the result that the referees' committee countermanded the instruction. Yet they later went on to state that a linesman should check only the substitute's boots when he came on to the pitch. The latest instruction is that it is left to the referee. But in season 1972–73, each referee and linesman was sent a gauge to measure the studs, which must be changed if they did not conform. But no one had checked with the manufacturers: the result was that a circular of 19 November, 1972, cancelled the use of gauges because very few studs were being manufactured which complied with the laws of the game. The League therefore had to accept illegal studs for a while.

I was more than happy to take part in the experiment whereby in the season 1972–73 the Football League Referees' Committee, after many private discussions, invited five referees to have with them the same linesmen, chosen for geographical reasons, throughout the season. In the past you would have different linesmen for each match, but now, for example, I had Colin Wade and Joe Wright for northern matches, and the brilliant Jim Sims and Gerry Faulkner in the south. The object of the exercise was to achieve better co-operation between referees and linesmen, to work together as a team. To my mind, it worked very well. I was able to introduce many innovations, like introducing the linesmen to the captains before the toss-up, which are still in use today, and we reached the stage of having almost telepathic communication and understanding.

Accordingly, I sent a glowing two-page report to the League at the end of the season; it really annoyed me when the League said it was unlikely for administrative reasons that the scheme could continue. They did implement the points I had recommended: the introduction of linesmen to captains, linesmen standing at corner-flags when corner-kicks are taken, and offside to be the total responsibility of the linesmen. And, in August 1973, they also asked me to speak on the subject to a pre-season meeting of referees, linesmen and assessors. What is more, they did not have an advance copy of my speech. They did ask for one but I said I spoke only off-the-cuff. They accepted this: they trusted me in 1973.

But I was surprised nevertheless when a meeting held at Bowden, near Manchester, in November decided that the scheme would be resumed. I was the only referee from the previous season to be retained on the

The family man, at home in Porthcawl with wife Beryl framed by daughters Caryn. (left) and Allyson

Eric Rees, Neath

Meeting people has always been a pleasure and, despite official warnings, I have always felt that it is to the benefit of the game for me to get out and about.

Left; Here I'm deep in discussion in the Plymouth Argyle Supporters Club after sending off two players in a match against Reading in October 1980.

Below; A different type of get-together, this time with children at the Ashgrove School for the Deaf in Penarth.

Photograph left: by courtesy of Plymouth Argyle FC

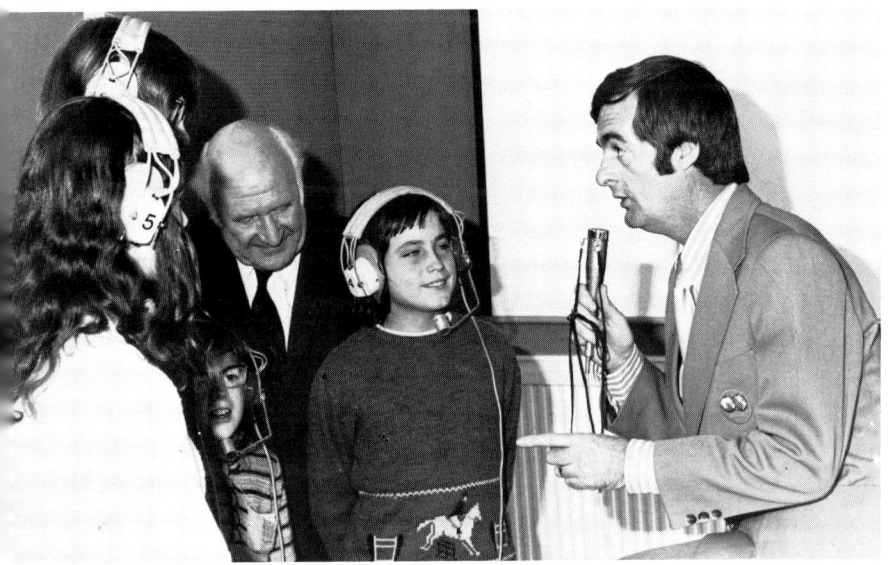

Control is not just about players — or
what might have been. Ball-skills did
not disappear when Clive Thomas had
to give up playing through injury:
there's immaculate style and technique
on view as Reg Lancaster of the *Daily
Express* catches me passing back to a
goalkeeper. By the way, the ball was
'dead' at the time…

ose friends all as Frankie Vaughan and Lawrie McMenemy inspect an engraved plaque
sented to me by the Rhondda Recognition Committee at Drisoll's in Porth in October 1978,
tched by the chairman of the committee, Bill Jones. And close friends for once, *(below)* as
bby Robson, no less, puts an arm round me at the Anfield testimonial for Phil Thompson,
o makes up the front row with Bob Paisley. Others in the picture include Gary Owen, Paul
riner, Phil Neal, Craig Johnston and Alan Kennedy.

Above: Clive Thomas shaking hands with the Queen after the 1976 FA Cup Final at Wembley, in which Southampton beat Manchester United.

As one referee to another... or simply a get-together of two Thomases from the Rhondda. Viscount Tonypandy, alias the former Speaker (and self-described referee) of the House of Commons George Thomas, invited me to his beautiful Westminster residence for a memorable meeting.

Another famous referee who became president of the FA and FIFA, and whose departure led to the decline in British influence in world soccer, was Sir Stanley Rous, with whom I was photographed at the controversial eve-of-Cup-Final dinner at Alexandra Palace in 1976.

Brian Clough would always help with fund-raising for the Boys' Clubs. Here, at Ninian Park, Cardiff, Brian had brought the full Nottingham Forest side for a charity match organised by my old friend Des Thomas, President of Margam Boys' Club.

Below: I was there... to caution Max Boyce at a charity match at Tonyrefail. Any more looks like that and he'll be off.

Above: Typical Thomas? I maintain there is nothing wrong in a referee expressing himself on the pitch. Photographer Owen Barnes captures the ups and downs in a referee's life.

EH/BGW/899

THE FOOTBALL LEAGUE LIMITED

SECRETARY:
ALAN HARDAKER

MY REPLY TO THIS LETTER
SHOULD BE ADDRESSED TO THE
SECRETARY AND THE FOLLOWING
REFERENCE QUOTED

LYTHAM ST. ANNES
LANCS.

TELEPHONE:
ST. ANNES 22161-2
TELEX
87878
TELEGRAMS
'LEAGUE' ST. ANNES

C. Thomas, Esq.,
68, Conway Road,
Treorchy,
RHONDDA,
Glamorgan.

9 February, 1967

Dear Mr. Thomas,

The Management Committee have been considering the averages of Match Officials up to date, and they note that your average is below the accepted minimum of 2.5.

They appreciate that this is your first year on the List, and have asked me to draw your attention to the points which have drawn comment from the Clubs, which are as follows:-

(1) Allowed far too much rough play;
(2) Hesitant and indecisive in control;
(3) Did not inspire confidence in his decisions.

In drawing your attention to these points, I may say that it is not unusual in the case of Officials who are new to The Football League List, but the Committee hope that now that the matter has been drawn to your attention, your record will improve in the knowledge that, so long as you control the players firmly and fairly, the Management Committee will give you their unqualified support.

Yours sincerely,

Secretary.

The route to the top was not without its potholes as can be seen from this example of official views on the early standards of my refereeing — a letter to which I would refer at least once a year to keep my feet on the ground.

he beginning, there was a rugby player: first on the list, too... The fledgling Thomas is on the reme left of the back row in this Treorchy County Secondary School team picture of season 9-50. Others in the back row are Brian Merriman, John Loney and Arthur Thomas. Middle v: Malcolm North, Kenneth Tomkinson, Malcolm Evans, Maldwyn Barfoot, David Trott, rvyn Pierce. Front row: Percy Griffiths (headmaster), John I Evans, Terry Carpenter, John mingham, Colin Jones, Elwyn Woolson and Haydn Williams (trainer and coach).

e declared, I'm now with the Treorchy Boys' Club which won a local championship and knock-out cups. In the back row, from the left, are Tom Grant (trainer), Dennis Rose, Arwel gan, John Jones, Len Davies, Ken Scane, Lyn Clark (secretary). Seated: Tony Rees, Clive mas, David Parry, Gwyn Evans, Gareth Evans, David Herbert, Ken Mathews.

Taking the field at Mar del Plata, on June 3, 1978, for the notorious World Cup match between Brazil and Sweden — and I've already been offered protection, albeit from the elements! Jafar Namdar, the linesman on the left, is clearly amused although Alojzy Jarguz, my other colleague from Poland, is in two minds. More protection of a serious nature was required after I had blown for time as the Brazilians were in the act of scoring although the players *(below)* were not too vehement in their protests as I headed from the field. The incident, nevertheless, killed my World Cup career.

experiment but I had new linesmen, Gary Cooke and Gerald Atkinson from the north and Colin Boswell and Ray Bartlett in the south. Further, the linesmen could be asked to report to the ground a few hours before the match to discuss the teams and plans, with the Football League accepting that this could mean increased expense allowances. However, at the end of the season the League cancelled the experiment. I told them in no uncertain terms that this was a backward step. I was pleased, though, when Colin Wade, who was in the first experiment, was chosen as reserve linesman for the League Cup Final.

Before heading off for Germany in the World Cup, I had achieved a minor victory over the League. I was refereeing in London on 12 January, 1974, and stayed at the Great Western on the Friday evening. Who should I bump into quite accidentally at the hotel, but Alan Hardaker and his entourage, the FL management committee. Aha, I thought, further proof that the referee is a second-class citizen – for I was allowed at that time only a £6 hotel allowance and the cost for me was £7.25. When I confronted Mr Hardaker, he said he did not think I would stay in such hotels. What is good enough for the management committee, I told him, is good enough for Clive Thomas, and I would therefore expect a reimbursement of £1.25, which was sent on to me immediately I sent in my expenses. I tested the water still further on 22 February for a match between West Ham and Birmingham, staying in an even better hotel which cost £8.15, which was also duly reimbursed. I considered the Hilton and the Dorchester but decided not to push my luck.

Once back from the World Cup, though, the long-running battle which pursued me to the end of my career really took off.

It started with a phone call on 27 November from Peter Jackson of the *Daily Mail*, ostensibly to ask whether I had any comments on a disciplinary hearing I had attended that day. But he was able to tell me what appointments I had received from the Football League during the first four or five months of the season and asked whether I was satisfied with the matches I had been allocated. I pointed out to Peter that I would give a hundred per cent effort in any match, but still he took the matter up with the League. 'No room at the top for ref Thomas' said the *Mail*'s headline on 29 November, emphasising that my marks in their ratings had never fallen below seven out of ten. Jackson continued to pressurise both me and the FL. 'Baffling as ref Thomas stays in the wilderness' said another headline, over an article which stated that the 'mystery of his relegation to the lower divisions deepened with the appointments for January. Thomas will take two third division games.' It went on to say that I would not have refereed a first or second division match for four months. The League secretary was unavailable for comment but an official said 'he does not want to talk about Clive Thomas'.

The very next day, I had a telephone call from Lee Walker of the League, which started with him saying that the ice had been broken and that Alan Hardaker said I could now be given matches in the top leagues. I took notes at the time and the conversation went like this:

'Thank you, but I would be more pleased if I was told what I have done wrong to have been put on third and fourth division games.'

'Well, you know there are things I just can't say but I hope you'll be pleased it is over.'

'I suppose I am but I am still very worried.'

'About what?'

'Well, Lee, I am a professional man and this is the 1970s and Britain is a democratic country, yet an establishment can do this sort of thing without saying anything.'

'Clive, you must be laughing because you have beaten the Football League with the way you have gone about it.'

'I am professional and I have done what I think was the best for Clive Thomas. I have refereed better than ever in the third and fourth division matches to ensure you couldn't get me on marks.'

'You know you are the top as far as marks are concerned, which made it difficult for the League but my job is to make sure I am a friend of all referees and I am wondering if you will forget what has happened.'

'Lee, I could tell you "yes, as far as I am concerned all is forgotten" but if I did tell you that I would be a bloody liar.'

Walker made a point about using the story in my memoirs (cheers, Lee) but I told him that I would do the top matches in the same way and would therefore presumably continue to do whatever I had been doing wrong.

'You know it is not your refereeing ability', he concluded.

On 13 January, I notified Lee Walker by telephone that I had received another call from Peter Jackson to say he had received a list of referees for the February matches and I still did not have a first division game. That was the first of many similar rows over appointments but I could not yet have been too unpopular because I was appointed reserve referee to Jack Taylor for the Football League Cup Final. George Readle, the assistant secretary, had 'phoned to ask whether I would accept the appointment and I told him I would be reserve only to Jack Taylor (who of course had done so well in the World Cup Final), but to no one else. It was the first time the League had experimented with a reserve referee: it meant that if Jack Taylor were injured, I would take over and not a linesman.

In October 1975, there was another minor altercation over expenses when I charged £33.50 for travelling by car, plus taxi, plus car park fees, to an evening match between Luton Town and Plymouth. Was it necessary, asked Mr Hardaker, for me to travel by car when rail services were quite suitable? In my reply, I said that the League had of course every right to query my expenses but hoped that my integrity was not in question. I pointed out that ninety-five per cent of my travel to matches was by car, that I stayed at the Strathmore Hotel, Luton, where there is no car park and I therefore had had to use public facilities and took a taxi to reach the ground and return. I understood that the League were having a purge on referees who travelled by car but it was far more convenient, it got me back to work or to my home and family more quickly, and that I intended to continue doing so. No reply was received and at the end of the season I refereed the FA Cup Final which suggested that all was still well.

Yet, on 8 October, 1976, I was writing to Alan Hardaker pointing out that in view of the appointments I would by the end of November have officiated in only ten matches. 'I am finding it extremely difficult to motivate myself and show continuity', I complained. The diary of the affair goes on like this:

15 OCTOBER. Letter from me to Football League: 'I wish to confirm a telephone conversation with Mr George Readle today that Hugh Johns of the *Sunday People* telephoned me stating that he had heard I had complained to Mr Readle regarding the number of matches ... I asked him who had told him and he stated he would not divulge his source. I thought it right to let you know about this and I would like to make it absolutely clear that I have not at any time spoken to any journalist concerning appointments (and) I am quite prepared to take legal action against any journalist or any other individual who states contrary to this.'

17 OCTOBER. Hugh Johns, in the *Sunday People*, pointed out that I was going out shopping on Saturdays because of being unemployed by the FL. He wrote that on ten Saturdays out of sixteen, the League could not find a game for one of the best referees in the world. Does that make sense, he asked?

18 OCTOBER. Letter from Alan Hardaker: 'I have to acknowledge receipt of your two letters of 8 and 15 October. It does seem a pity that every time there is correspondence between this office and yourself the press seem to get hold of it ... I have checked the appointments and, partly due to the fact that there have not been the same number of midweek matches available this season as last, the appointments have not been easy. Nevertheless by the end of December you will have had practically the same number ... I would remind you that you refused two appointments last season, which is your prerogative if business and other commitments arise, and I do not recollect the Football League took any objection ...'

18 OCTOBER. Jim Hill (no relation) asks in the *Daily Express* why Clive Thomas is getting so few games after a recent *Daily Express* poll in which league players voted him the best. Emlyn Hughes is quoted as saying: 'At one time Clive thought he was more important than the game. Now he is very good, always making the right decision.' And Brian Clough: 'Thomas can control any type of game, the hallmark of a good referee. He is brave, especially when giving decisions around the penalty area.'

19 OCTOBER. I receive a letter from a secretary of a prominent league club – he's still with them – saying: 'I note by the national press that you are getting very few games in the league and it would seem that you have by your outspokenness upset a few people in high places. Notably, George Readle. It does seem ridiculous . . .'

19 OCTOBER. Peter Batt in the London *Evening News* 'investigates the problem of England's number one man in the middle'. Under the head-line 'Why has Mr Hardaker stuck Referee Thomas up a mountain?' (this was a reference to my training in the valleys on three Saturdays), he wrote: 'When we questioned secretary Alan Hardaker on his behalf, we ran into the customary barbed wire verbal fence which seems to surround that singularly sensitive official. "As far as I am concerned the appoint-ment of referees has nothing to do with Clive Thomas or the press", he scolded us. "In any case, it is not true. He has not written to us complain-ing." Recognising a split-hair when we hear one, we reminded: "No, not complaining, just asking." And with his voice rising to full-pitched authoritative resonance, he added, "There are ninety referees. There is no system which guarantees any referee matches." Well, there damned well should be for a man like Clive Thomas.'

25 OCTOBER. Letter to Alan Hardaker: 'I agree it is a pity that within a few days of my writing confidential letters to your office I am telephoned by pressmen . . . I could not understand quite the necessity for you to point out that I had refused two appointments. I feel I must write to you to state how concerned I am, although I accept your explanation as to the low number of matches I am refereeing . . .'

3 NOVEMBER. Another newspaper, under the heading 'Thomas leads a revolt', carries a story saying I had complained about the new system of keeping referees in their own areas to cut expenditure, which has resulted in top referees having appointments cut by half. Alan Hardaker says he has asked the referees' committee to investigate. Thomas states: 'I would like the chance to submit my views in person.'

8 NOVEMBER. My Welsh referee colleague, Tom Reynolds, complains in the *Daily Mail:* 'It would be wrong to think that Clive was the only one suffering in this way. We are all in the same boat.' Where there were eighty-three Football League referees ten years ago, reports the *Mail*, there are now one hundred and eight.

6 DECEMBER. Letter to Alan Hardaker: 'With reference to my telephone conversation of 3 December 1976, with Lee Walker, I pointed out to him that I was rather surprised that I have for many Saturdays not had matches but now I see that I have three games between 29 December and 3 January. I honestly feel that consideration has not been taken in these appointments in so much that I travel to Torquay on the morning of 29 December, stay the night and then travel back on Thursday 30 December to arrive home at approximately 3.30 pm. On 31 December I travel to Plymouth and return (weather permitting) late on 1 January, then on 2 January I travel to London to officiate at Fulham on the 3rd and shall be returning at approximately 10.30 that night. I wonder whether you feel that this period of intensified fixtures after many Saturdays without matches is fair.'

7 DECEMBER. Letter from Alan Hardaker: 'We do seem to have trouble in finding appointments which satisfy you. Looking at the appointments, however, I feel that perhaps there is too much travel involved and I propose to make it easier for you by appointing another referee to the match at Fulham on 3 January.'

9 DECEMBER. I take notes of a 'phone call made to George Readle at the Football League at 9.25 am.

'Readle here.'

'How are things, George?'

'Busy.'

'What's the matter with you? I have received this letter (from Hardaker) ...' ,

'You asked me and I said "busy". Will you ring me back some time?'

'Your public relations is b. awful. No, I'm not ringing you back.'

CT and GR rap respective telephones down. End of conversation.

Six minutes later, at 9.31, he 'phoned back. I told him that he and Hardaker were not helping the bad state of refereeing and were not acting in the best interests of football. Other referees might be afraid of them but I would continue to fight for what was right. He claimed that I was the only one complaining.

I had to accept the idiotic decision by the Football League to take me off the Fulham game and not the Plymouth game on the first of the month, knowing that I would have travelled back from Torquay on 30 December.

14 DECEMBER. Telephone call from John Parsons of the *Daily Mail*. The Fulham club had confirmed that I was not going to their game with Bolton on 3 January and, said Parsons, the League had told him I had complained about the number of matches in too short a period. I said that was laughable and that I would make a statement if he printed that the following day.

15 DECEMBER. 'Thomas raps League again', says the *Daily Mail* headline, with a sub-heading, 'Holiday fixture plans laughable'. I said in the story that it was nothing to do with the number of matches and that 'I will do five in five days if necessary'. It was simply the travelling getting to each of them.

16 DECEMBER. Letter from Alan Hardaker: 'I am writing this letter purely personally and what I have to say does not have any relation to whatever action the Football League Management Committee may wish to take.

'In future, therefore, I do not intend to correspond with you any further, except when it is necessary officially, and I certainly do not intend to have any further discussions with you, either personally or on the telephone.'

And a happy Christmas to all our readers, I thought.

The letter I had been expecting and, indeed, awaiting for more than two years, arrived late in January 1977. Dated 27 January, it was from Alan Hardaker to say that he had been instructed by the referees' sub-committee to ask me to attend their next meeting at the Great Western Hotel, Paddington, at 10.30 on Wednesday, 9 February. His last paragraph said: 'I do not propose to acquaint the press that you are meeting the management committee and I shall be obliged if you will treat this matter as confidential.' I do not know, in fact, which of the two committees that he mentioned I did meet.

I made my appearance at the hotel at 10.29 to be met by Graham Kelly who, as we walked up the stairs to the meeting, warned me that Bob Lord was the chairman, and that I should listen and not become too involved or they might have to take a far-reaching decision on me. 'Look' I told him, 'you don't worry me and neither do they'.

The autocratic Lord, master butcher, chairman of Burnley and a leading figure in the game, introduced me to the other members of the committee present – Matt Busby, Brian Mears, Jack Wiseman, Dick Wragg, Hardaker, Readle and Kelly, some of them also FA Council members.

What went on at that meeting should, I believe, be known because I would not myself have believed, if I had not been present, that people responsible for association football in England could behave in the way they did. I was so deeply disturbed that on leaving I wrote down immediately my memories of the conversation that took place.

Bob Lord did nearly all the talking. He opened by expressing his concern over the letters and telephone calls I had had with Football League headquarters, and said that this must stop. Thomas was having his share of fixtures and more than many. In future, complaints would have to go through the Association of Football League Referees and

Linesmen. Thomas was just one of ninety referees and, although one of the best, he must accept the system.

'You thought you would be able to do things yourself' he said. 'Well, you can't. And I am not going to allow power from one man to change things. We have also received copies of letters regarding press statements. This has to stop.'

Thomas: 'I am astounded to hear you say that one cannot communicate with the establishment. You wanted me to do it when I was on the experiment two years ago. Also when I was doing the Anglo-Italian Cup. You know my association will not fight for things because they are afraid of all of you. The feeling of referees today is not very good. And the standard has gone back but no one is doing anything about it. The referees have not the guts to put their names to articles. I have. You talk about the press' (I gave details of letters etcetera) 'and I say I have never given a story to the press. I have answered their questions. But why was I left in the low divisions? Something was going on at Football League headquarters.'

Hardaker: 'You are a liar. What about the *Daily Mail* on 15 December? And don't you say something was going on at Football League headquarters.'

Thomas: 'Don't you call me a liar and you had better apologise now or I go.'

Chairman Lord tried to pacify Hardaker and myself but I got up as if to walk out.

Chairman: 'Mr Thomas, if you will disregard what you said about headquarters, Mr Hardaker will withdraw what he said.'

Thomas: 'Very well, but all I'm doing and why I am here is because I feel for the game and something must be done.'

Chairman: 'You will not do it yourself and if you are a man, you will accept what we are telling you, otherwise something else will happen.'

Thomas: 'What?'

Chairman: 'Look, Mr Thomas, you are one of the best referees in the world. We want you on the League but don't let us do something we would all regret. Also, we do not feel it is right for you to discuss the game in the guest room after a match. You also drew a ticket out of a drum before a match. This is wrong and not in the best interests of refereeing.'

Thomas: 'I did not pull a ticket out of a drum.'

The Chairman then showed me a Plymouth programme and every member had a copy of a photograph of Brian Hall and myself with a tombola drum.

Thomas: 'I repeat that I was not pulling the ticket out but witnessed Brian Hall of Plymouth doing it and this was for a management committee member.' (Bob Daniel, then chairman of Plymouth.) 'Also, Mr Hardaker had better get his facts right.'

Wiseman: 'Clive, no one here today questions your ability as a referee. You are one of the best but I have to agree with the chairman and also yourself. I know after the match you speak to anyone because you feel for the game but we have told all referees not to do this. You are the only one we have allowed. For you own interests it would be better not to speak and to try to get your own association going.'

Wragg: 'Mr Thomas, your refereeing is wonderful and that is not in question today but we must back our officials although we see your point of view. I hope we can agree on something today, because it can affect your UEFA career.'

Busby: 'You are a fine referee and there are not many about now. I hope you'll accept what we are saying because I accept what you are saying.'

Mears: 'I agree with what has been said.'

Chairman: 'Mr Thomas, we have had a good discussion. We have all said something. Now I hope you'll accept as a man a democratic decision and no more arguments and thank you for coming today.'

Thomas: 'I will ring my secretary (AFLRL) this evening and tell him I will not get involved. I am telling you here and now that I will never write or telephone the League about anything regarding the game or refereeing again. It it the end of my contact with you. It will take a very long time for me to accept Hardaker. Now, about the press regarding this meeting and them asking me about it?'

Chairman: 'I suggest nothing for the press.'

Hardaker (to me): 'No, you can't lie. Just say you had a meeting.'

Chairman (and others): 'All the best and thank you.'

Readle and Kelly had said not a word.

There were no doubts in my mind that the committee had tried to take me on and, if I was not prepared to toe the line, they intended to strike me off the list. But they had been on sticky ground and some of the points raised were totally spurious.

Take that Plymouth incident as an example. Although I understand that programmes of most Football League matches are sent to Lytham headquarters, I am astonished that someone up there should read them in such detail as to pick out what was in fact an innocent photograph of my attending a prize draw. I had done them a favour in fact by coming out of the dressing-room threequarters of an hour early to witness the draw being made by Brian Hall, because I was not allowed to make such a draw myself. Fair enough, but for someone to insinuate that I had broken Football League regulations is unforgivable. By writing this, I would in no way wish to mar the happy relationship I have with both the Argyle supporters and many of their leading officials, especially secretary Graham Little. But I still wonder to this day whether someone drew the photograph to the attention of the League in order to embarrass me.

One mistake I did make at the meeting. Although I had assured them I would never trouble them by telephone or on notepaper again, my heart was for once temporarily ruling my tongue. With the inefficient way in which they were administering appointments and other subjects relating to referees, I still had to take them on again without going through the AFLRL.

*   *   *   *   *

I believe the League – and Hardaker – took another backward step in March 1979 when Bristol City and Bristol Rovers thought it might be a fine idea to have a better liaison with referees. It appeared on the surface to be a splendid thought. I was duly invited, with referees in the southern part of England, to a regional meeting where we could talk through the idea. The Football League, alas, were informed of the move by someone, and immediately put a block on it with a circular, sent out by Hardaker on St Valentine's Day, which said that linesmen and referees must not accept invitations to such meetings.

It seemed to me that in vetoing the Bristol clubs' idea they were showing their fear of losing a little authority from Lytham St Annes because they had not thought of it themselves. Would it not have been a fine public relations exercise, as well as of educational benefit to clubs and officials, for such an operation to be carried out in all the regions of England and Wales? I was not to know it at the time but that was the last direct contact I had with the authoritarian Alan Hardaker. From that time until his death he was titled Director-General with Graham Kelly as secretary of the Football League.

The death of Alan Hardaker, and I say this quite sincerely, was a blow to football. I had my rows with him, as you have read, but I also had a healthy respect for him because he was his own man and he was prepared to tell you exactly what he thought (of you, as well as of any other subject). I was prepared to accept that we could never become personal friends but, at the very least, there was some personal regard. Lytham St Annes has since had neither the character, the efficiency and certainly not the leadership in my estimation.

Within the refereeing fraternity, there was some surprise at Graham Kelly's appointment. From the day that George Readle had been moved to the Football League from his position as secretary of the Association of Football League Referees and Linesmen some ten years previously, we had thought he might become, firstly, a referees' supremo, which would have been typical in that he had never been a Football League referee, and then take over from Alan Hardaker himself. Either way, Readle had become Alan Hardaker's right-hand man, with the appointment of referees being taken over by Lee Walker, another non-Football League referee, and, more recently, by Miss Pat Callon, who has never refereed a League match either. Pat is a very pleasant lady and may well be a highly efficient administrator: that I would never question but to me her appointment shows a lack of professionalism and respect for the humble referee – and possibly for the players also, because Pat cannot necessarily think of the importance of particular matches as referees are not chosen for their ability but because of their domestic location. Indeed, the League does not think, for example, that First Division matches should have the best referees, as these are chosen on largely geographical grounds, literally and figuratively. I will never be able to accept this, as the First Division should be the showground for top players and referees as seen on television.

Mind you, the first circular under the name of Secretary Graham Kelly was in my view a great start. The management committee had decided as an experiment to raise the maximum age of Football League referees from forty-seven to forty-eight. The experiment is still in operation as I write just before my days are up, but it is entirely without sour grapes when I suggest that the stupidity of the circular was in stating that with the introduction of the fitness test which had been in operation for two seasons, 'the time is ripe to make this experiment which would avoid the necessity to lose experienced officials when, subject to a fitness test, their value is most felt by the clubs'. Pressure from managers may be changing this as I put typewriter to paper. Most European countries have a maximum age of fifty and FIFA likewise. I'm not certain that even fifty should be the break point: it depends on the ability and fitness of the individual.

I digress again slightly. But the mention of fitness brings up an early point in Graham Kelly's career which made me doubt his awareness of public relations. I pulled a calf muscle after only two minutes and forty seconds of a game on 15 September, 1979, between Bristol City and Stoke City. After half a minute's treatment, I was able to continue but only as linesman for the first half with the senior linesman taking over as referee. By the interval the Bristol club had found a replacement for me, a first-class effort which ensured as smooth a takeover as possible. I wrote to both Kelly, to explain the circumstances, and to Tony Rance, the Bristol City secretary, to thank him. Kelly never answered: you would think that he might have said something to me about my injury or to Bristol City about their efficiency.

But I did not really run into trouble again until January 1980. Terry

Neill, then Arsenal manager, took a dim view of my declaration that his club's New Year's Day match at Southampton should be played despite difficult, icy ground conditions. Because some matches had been cancelled and with managers commenting on the pitches (Neill commented before the game which Arsenal then won) I was interviewed by the press. I told the *Daily Mail* that, despite the grim experience of the previous winter, ninety-five per cent of our League clubs had nothing to protect their pitches and there would be much more fixture disruption before every club learned its lesson and did something for the public and for the game. My criticism was not levelled at groundsmen and their staff but at the management of clubs. Hundreds of thousands of pounds were spent on the transfer market, I said, and yet only a handful of clubs were prepared to pay the comparatively modest investment of £40-50,000 on undersoil heating. Might it not, I asked, be a condition of affiliation for every club to have such facilities?

The League were not amused. I can assume only that the management committee had a meeting the very day the article appeared (3 January) because a letter from Graham Kelly dated 4 January said the committee were concerned at my criticisms and summoned me on Monday, 14 January, to yet another meeting at the Great Western. (I have to ask whether Paddington is the most central and therefore least expensive location when the League is always questioning expenditure. Would it not be sensible, on both financial and communication grounds, to house both football bodies under one roof?)

Bob Lord, in the chair once more, pointed out that I had no right to comment on such matters and, before I could reply, gave me a lecture on football finances. 'Do not believe everything you read in the papers', he told me. 'Clubs don't pay that amount of money in transfer fees and, if they do, it's not in a lump sum but on a hire purchase scheme.' Not many clubs, therefore, could afford undersoil heating.

I could not accept this and said that my concern was for supporters in having to watch matches that should never be played. I proposed a change in rules whereby the managers would decide if a game should be played or not, with the referee to make a casting vote instead of being the lone arbiter. He said in his diplomatic way – i.e. nearly standing on the chair – that it would never happen so long as he was with the League. He then proceeded to harangue me about the integrity, and lack of, of managers. We got nowhere.

Much later in the year, on 14 December, I was invited to Lytham by Mr Lord who surprised me by saying he was actually pleased to see me to discuss my views on referees and linesmen. He said, 'Clive, the Football League can learn a lot from you. Be free to say what you like, although it is the first time we have allowed one referee to meet us and there will no doubt be a row in your association but I can handle them and my own committee.' Graham Kelly and George Readle were the only two others present at the meeting.

On the subject of numbers, I showed that there were ninety referees on the list for forty-six matches, requiring ninety-two linesmen when there were two hundred and fifty-two on the list, and that between 16 August and 1 November that season, I shopped with my wife on eight Saturdays, while fifty per cent of my matches were in the third and fourth divisions. On regionalisation, I said that there had been no official communication but I had not refereed in the Liverpool or Manchester areas for a few years because, it appeared, they were more than two hundred miles from my home whereas I am sent to Brighton which is two hundred and twenty miles away. (In season 1983–84, by the way, there were eighty-five referees and two hundred and fifty-nine linesmen on the list.)

As briefly as possible, then, I report now on the points I raised, with Lord's replies, and a promise that the report would be discussed at the Football League Referees' Committee with certain recommendations.

1. Visit to ground: referee and linesmen to meet two hours before kick-off. *Agreed.*
2. Regional training: referees and linesmen to attend FL training sessions at least three times a season. *Agreed to look at possibility of scheme.*
3. Appointment of referees: 'that all appointments are subject to change at short notice, all appointments should be scrutinised prior to notification. Referees to be appointed on their ability to the individual matches.' *Agreed, but with certain reservations.*
4. Number of referees for season 1981–82 to be (a) cut from ninety to fifty-six with (b) a supplemenatary list of twenty-four but these to officiate in the Alliance League and to be on call for the FL in case of extreme urgency. They will also officiate as linesmen in the FL. By the end of season 1981–82 those who have not attained the standard in the FL to be replaced by the top feeder leagues. *Agreed, but list to be cut to seventy-five in first year and seventy in second.*
5. Assessors:
   (a) we would go back to the system of club marking, with
   (b) the assessors only to assess a referee with three consecutive low-marking matches;
   (c) assessors to assess every Alliance League match. *No to all three.*
   Alternatively,
   (a) all FL matches to be assessed with no club marking but the assessment made on a less detailed form, including application of laws and control and co-operation of linesmen;
   (b) and all Alliance League games to be assessed. *Agreed.*

6. Linesmen's list for 1981–82 to be cut to two hundred. *Agreed.*
7. Suggested new laws on goalkeeper's steps, offside, encroachment on free kicks, advantage. *Agreed.*
8. Official time: the completion of a match should be when the referee has played the stated time and the ball is out of play. *No.*
9. Free penalty after professional foul. *More time required to consider.*

I have to admit that I left the meeting feeling elated, thinking that something would now be done. I felt that the day I had given – without a penny in expenses, incidentally, for the five-hundred-mile round trip – was subsidising the League for the benefit of referees and linesmen in the eighties.

Most of the points, in fact, were a refinement of a lecture I had made at the summer conference of the Association of Football League Referees and Linesmen, referred to also in a later chapter. But whether Mr Lord ever had his meeting with the FL Referees' Committee I do not know.

He must, however, have been impressed with something because 1981 was the year I had the Football League Cup Final between Liverpool and West Ham. But even that went wrong because of the row with John Lyall, the West Ham manager, when I allowed my feelings to be known on radio and television. As a result I read in the *Daily Mail* on 1 April (sic) that Clive Thomas was said to be facing a Football League inquiry as the League frowns upon referees making personal television appearances. League secretary Graham Kelly was quoted as saying, 'There is still the possibility that the League will take this matter up but it is no more than a possibility at this stage.'

The date of the replay was 1 April but Graham Kelly did not mention it that night at Villa Park. Instead, he sent a letter the following day to tell me that Mr Lord would like to meet me on 13 April.

Here we go again. Once more the meeting was at the Great Western Hotel, Paddington. Once more Graham Kelly was present to meet me in the foyer and told me to cool things down as Mr Lord was on the warpath. Once more I said I was frightened of neither of them. Once more I took notes straight after the meeting and once more I reproduce the conversation as verbatim as I can.

Bob Lord: 'Why did you speak to the press after the Football League Cup Final at Wembley after the League had told all officials at the Portsmouth Referees' and Linesmen's Conference that no official should speak to press, television or radio after a match?'

Clive Thomas: 'I was not aware of it. In fact, I'm sure that this was not said at the conference meeting.'

BL: 'You are a liar and a cheat. Now what are you going to say about that, Mr Big Clive Thomas?'

At this point I stood up and said if that was the way he was going to speak, then I was going.

BL: 'You can go if you like.'

Graham Kelly: 'Please sit down and let us talk this over.'

CT: 'I don't want to speak to that man if that is his attitude.'

BL: 'Are you telling us we did not say that at conference?'

CT: 'Yes. What you did say was "watch what you say to the press after a match. It might well be better if you say nothing". Therefore that was guidance and not a directive.'

BL: 'You're a liar.'

I stood up to walk out again.

GK: 'Please sit down.'

BL: 'Who do you think you are? Everything Clive Thomas does is right. He never makes a mistake. You never say sorry or apologise, but Alan Hardaker called you a liar, didn't he?'

CT: 'Yes, and Alan Hardaker apologised.'

BL: 'No, he didn't.'

CT: 'With respect it is obvious you have forgotten the meeting you chaired. The meeting was held here and the full referees' committee was present. Graham Kelly was there with George Readle and Alan Hardaker was wrong and he apologised. Can you remember it, Graham?'

BL: 'Anyway, I've looked after you for thirteen years although I've never liked you.'

CT: 'I'm amazed.'

BL: 'The great Clive Thomas is amazed.'

CT: 'Yes, how people can be so two-faced. Only last year we three had a very good meeting and last December I met you to put some ideas forward. Now you tell me you can't trust me.'

BL: 'We have all done what Clive Thomas has said. Now it changes.'

CT: 'Are you saying I'm off the referees' list?'

BL: 'Please yourself.'

CT: 'I'm prepared to go off the list if my president and secretary of the Association of Football League Referees and Linesmen say that you gave us all a directive and not guidance about speaking to the press.'

BL: 'That is what you want, isn't it?'

CT: 'No, I want to stay on the list but I am prepared to accept it if I am wrong.'

BL: 'But Clive Thomas is never wrong.'

CT: 'Come on, let us talk some common sense.'

BL: 'Why? Because Clive Thomas says so?'

CT: 'Grow up.'

BL: 'I am warning you that no one had better know of this meeting.'

CT: 'I am not the type to tell people of all my meetings. I never told the press about the last two meetings.'

BL: 'I'm telling you that was a directive at the conference and you have taken no notice of it. I will want to know your views so that I can take them back to the referees' committee and they will make a decision.'

CT: 'It was not a directive, only guidance. I am prepared to meet any committee.'

BL: 'I will tell you if we want you. Anyway, you go out for twenty minutes to think things over.'

CT: 'I don't need twenty minutes.'

BL: 'You go out and think it over.'

CT: 'It seems you need the twenty minutes to cool off and talk to each other.'

I did in fact leave for twenty minutes and spoke with George Parrott, a friend in industrial relations, who advised me to 'stay on the list and beat him at his own game'.

Then . . .

BL 'What if it was guidance not directive? Why did you take no notice?'

CT: 'If it was a directive, I would have made a decision on that last July before the start of the season.'

BL: 'What would you have done?'

CT: 'I would have accepted not to speak to the press.'

BL: 'Why did you then?'

CT: 'I was so incensed with John Lyall's remarks, but it seems now that I should have accepted them because the word "cheat" has now been used by the acting president of the Football League and secondly there was a very controversial decision made and I wanted to explain – right or wrong.'

GK: 'Would you do the same thing again?'

CT: 'No.'

BL: 'Clive Thomas is saying "no".'

CT: 'If I have upset anyone, then I would quickly apologise.'

BL: 'Good God. Clive Thomas has apologised. Mr Kelly put that down, we have waited over an hour for that.'

CT: 'Come on Mr Chairman, the trouble with you is I'm the only referee who is not afraid of you or anyone else in the League. In fact, some might say you are a bastard.'

BL: 'Did you hear that, Mr Kelly? Clive Thomas calls the acting president a bastard. You know I could have you up for that?'

CT: 'And I could have you up for calling me a liar and a cheat.'

BL: 'It is not as bad as a bastard.'

CT: 'That is a matter of opinion. Might you know what I said was a figure of speech.'

BL: 'Because Clive Thomas said it is a figure of speech.'

CT: 'If you have taken it the wrong way, then I apologise.'

BL: 'Clive Thomas has apologised twice.'

CT: 'Where do we go from here?'

BL: 'I don't know what the committee are going to say when I tell them that Clive Thomas has called me a bastard.'

CT: 'Well, Mr Chairman, I still believe I have a lot to offer the game, and I am still prepared to help refereeing. I am telling you I shall not be talking to the press.'

BL: 'You won't keep it up.'

CT: 'In two years time you will apologise to me because I will show you I can do it.'

BL: 'I won't send you flowers or a telegram in two years time. I will shake your hand.'

CT: 'Then you will have to come to Porthcawl.'

BL: 'I will come to Porthcawl.'

CT: 'I am going out from the meeting and opening the door, not crawling under it.'

BL: 'Well, we will see what is going to happen.'

And with that I shook hands and left.

Mr Kelly's silence during the meeting may well be explained by the fact that he had appeared on television with me live from Wembley on the day of the match and that we had been taken to the stadium in a Football League car for the appearance.

I offer no further comments on that other than to quote a Football League circular of 15 December, 1978. '(The Management Committee) for their part are taking steps to curb press criticism of referees by persons inside the game and ask that all match officials exercise the greatest caution when contributing to the press.' This, in effect, was also what was said at the Portsmouth conference.

By July of 1981, just a month or two after the meeting with Bob Lord, I was writing to commiserate with his illness and to say how much he was missed at the AFLRL conference. In his reply, he said that 'deep down, we know one another'. I am sorry to say I never met Bob Lord again. But I'd have lost the bet because, let's face it, there was no way in which I could ever remain silent.

Later in 1981, the League took what I believe to be another retrograde step and it is really a part of the same syndrome as talking to the press or appearing on television. Referees are as much a part of the game as anyone and it is up to all of us to project the right image of football. Heaven knows, the game is suffering enough without bringing down a curtain of silence. So I was not amused to receive the following circular from Mr Kelly on 10 August.

'It has been brought to my attention that match officials are being caused some embarrassment by being invited into public rooms after matches. Many officials, although aware of the difficulties which may arise, are loth to refuse invitations because they feel it would be discourteous to do so. In view of this, I would remind you that it is the opinion of the Management Committee that it would be in the interests of all concerned if clubs, in future, did not invite match officials, or their guests, into public rooms after games.'

I responded:

'I have always been prepared to discuss the game with football supporters and therefore have always appreciated the opportunity to speak to these people at the conclusion of the match. Of course there have been some supporters who have not agreed with my decisions, but I would certainly not say that they have been an embarrassment to me.

'In the light of the dwindling support to the game, I honestly believe that it is more essential now than ever that all of us involved in the game act as public relations officers and with this in mind I respectfully ask you to reconsider this decision which I know has not been taken lightly.'

Graham Kelly in return replied:

'I fully understand your concern and reasons for writing – all of us in the game must accept that we have an obligation to sell it – and I know that you personally would be able to deal with any situation that might arise.

'However, I must say that the particular restriction to which you refer has to remain. We feel that the inherent dangers would outweigh the marginal public relations benefits to be obtained from match officials entering into discussion with a limited number of people.'

I still believe it is a backward step not to allow those referees who are prepared to to discuss the game while those who are embarrassed need not become involved and can remain quiet.

The whole question of hospitality and socialising reached, I feel, absurd heights – or depths, depending on how you look at it – on 3 January, 1984, when I was due to referee an evening match between Bristol Rovers and Wigan. Because of appalling weather I drove to Bristol in the morning, decided the game could not be played there and then to prevent

Wigan from having to travel and had a coffee with the Rovers chief executive, Gordon Bennett, manager David Williams and his assistant, my old friend Wayne Jones from Treorchy. It was all very friendly.

I could not guess, then, why the press were seeking me when I returned home. It turned out that an article had appeared in the *Western Daily Press* that morning, saying that the Football League had refused to allow the Bristol directors to give me a farewell drink in the boardroom after what would have been my last match at Eastville. A harmless gesture, you may think. Indeed, Graham Hole, a Rovers director, told Peter Jackson in the *Daily Mail* that 'we need to open up more lines of communication to build up a better rapport with referees. Thomas may have been controversial in his time but at least he has always been consistent, something which is lacking in many officials.'

I had known nothing about the proposed invitation. But, really, it is an idiotic attitude by the Football League which prevents referees from meeting directors, let alone supporters. Surely, the game today needs close and harmonious communication at all levels.

By March 1982 I was *persona grata* once more as I was asked to join with a couple of English FIFA referees, an assessor, the president and secretary of AFLRL, a Football League Advisory Committee, comprising Sir Matt Busby, Jimmy Hill, Bobby Charlton and Graham Kelly, who wished to discuss with referees the entertainment value of a league game, how referees could contribute to it and what problems there were. At the meeting Graham Kelly circulated to everyone suggestions of new laws or possible new interpretations. Lo and behold, they were almost the same as those I had put on paper for Bob Lord in 1979. I took exception to this new committee wheeling them out as their own suggestions and Jim Hill did not disagree but hoped that they would accept in principle what they were trying to do.

My colleagues seemed reluctant to back me on my personal points of view in respect of assessors, the regionalisation of referees, increasing the number of matches for referees and decreasing the number of referees and linesmen on the lists, possibly because of the presence of Mr Kelly. Jimmy Hill, though, was trying hard to move ahead and ensure some desperately-needed changes in football, but there were no further meetings, another backward step. On 30 March, after receiving the minutes of the meeting, I wrote to the League to ensure that it was in writing that four of the five suggestions placed by the committee had come from me.

On 2 April, Graham Kelly thanked me for my letter and said: 'I take the point. Kindest regards, Graham. PS: Glad to see you accepting late appointments still.' This was because on the morning of Friday 2 April, the League had asked whether I would officiate at the Brighton versus Southampton match the following day in place of Clive White. I pointed out to Pat Callon that this was outside my normal geographical area but she said they were in a spot, this was a local derby and she wanted me there. Strangely I was asked belatedly again to replace Clive White a short while later, on 6 May, for the Hereford–Crewe game. A different lady at the FL said she was not sure why Clive White was unavailable, whether it was for personal reasons or because he had the Cup Final on 22 May. They did not ask me to replace him for that match, nor the World Cup Finals in Spain. He took part in those glamorous occasions, but, for personal reasons, never again refereed in the Football League.

For the 1982–83 season, I was in the thick of an early clampdown on players which was implemented by the AFLRL at their conference and which I discuss elsewhere. 'I'm booking players right, left and centre again', I told John Sadler of *The Sun* in October. 'And I'm going to carry on doing so for my last two seasons in the game. After seven games my bookings are up fifty per cent on last season. And unless the Football League kick me out or players and managers get the message, that's the way I'm going to operate.' I was quoted as saying in 1976 that I was turning my back on the style that gave me the nickname, Clive the Book.

'I have shown restraint. For six years I have purposely avoided being book happy ... I don't want to be "the book" again but if that's what it takes to improve the game I shall carry on.

'And I'll tell you something else. Any referee who is not prepared to work in the same way should get out.'

For a time everyone in the game appeared to be in agreement. But then cracks began to show and the united front put forward by the Football League, referees and even players crumbled in the face of a circular sent to referees by the FA in October. It said:

'The recent change in Law Twelve, Paragraph 5(a), concerning the so-called "four step rule", together with the new interpretations in respect of the taking of a throw-in and of "serious foul play" for cynical fouls, appear to have all been working extremely well. Each has made a successful contribution to our continuing effort to improve the image of the game.

'A little unease has been expressed, however, in the narrow area of the interpretation initially adopted in respect of serious foul play in those situations involving intentional handling of the ball.

'It has, therefore, now been felt appropriate to disregard the specific phrase "including intentional handling of the ball" from the recommended interpretation. The effect is to remove what may have been thought to have been an undue emphasis on this aspect of unfair play.

'A referee, in accordance with the Law, must decide what is, *in his opinion*, "serious foul play" and should use his discretion in considering every aspect of an incident and the particular circumstances in which it occurs.

'We refer to the final paragraph of the Law Amendment Information Sheet for Season 1982–83 which read:

"The Football Association are confident that referees will use common sense and not over-react in the application of these interpretations."

– and trust that this may continue to be the case.'

I agreed with the AFLRL that all referees should continue to implement the decisions that were passed at the conference although I felt it was the start of the inconsistency shown by referees for the remainder of the season.

The debate rumbled on under the surface but in the summer of 1983, quite literally a few days before the season began, referees were told that as the result of a decision by FIFA they must not send off players who prevented a goal by deliberate handling of the ball.

The chaos and consternation caused by this retrograde step inflicted upon us by an organisation where our influence is now minimal came as no surprise to me. I had already taken serious issue with those FIFA gnomes of Zurich.

·13·
THE GNOMES OF ZURICH

Dr. J. Havelange,
President,
FIFA,
Hitzigweg 11,
8030 Zurich,
SWITZERLAND.

19 July, 1983

Dear Dr Havelange,

As a FIFA referee and a disciplinarian, I am concerned that millions of people throughout the world are leaving our game of football, and therefore, I am appalled at your decision that England's interpretation of The Laws of the Game are out of step with the rest of the world. You are of course correct because you and your Committee are not able, and probably not capable, of recognising the problems that exist in the game of football.

I am concerned about your interpretation of the professional or cynical foul and the handling of the ball in appropriate situations where it denies the attacking side a probable goal scoring opportunity. Yes, I have been an instigator for years in trying to stop players cheating by stopping a goal being scored by unfair methods. Law 10 clearly defines that a match is won or drawn by goals being scored. Therefore, would you not in your very limited experience of football feel it justifiable for a player to be sent off the field of play if he deliberately stops a goal being scored by an unfair method?

Our interpretation of this law was a success in the Football League last season. This was proved at the beginning of the season by the number of goals that were scored and although more players were sent off the field, they were beginning to accept the referees' new interpretation of Law 12, paragraph 5N.

Unfortunately the Football Association, probably with FIFA in mind, sent a circular to all referees in October asking them not to over-react in the interpretation of the new application of this law, resulting in my opinion, in some referees, like yourself and your Committee, taking the easy way out.

I ask you to look at the television and see the matches played in the

World Cup in Spain 1982 and the last two European Championships where there is clear evidence of the number of professional fouls committed by players who were not even shown a yellow card.

Dr Havelange, you and your Committee are condoning players cheating on the field of play. I now ask you how many members of your Referees Committee, including yourself, have ever refereed a football match and how many have refereed a game of football within the last 10 years?

I await your comments with interest.

Yours sincerely,
Clive Thomas

Dr Joao Havelange, known as 'Avalanche' in some secretive corners of football, did not reply to my recorded-delivery letter. You may feel that I was being unnecessarily offensive, but I stand by the letter, every single word of it. Indeed, I could have sent more pungent thoughts, so angry was I that the footballing gnomes of Zurich were not only burying their heads in the snow or fishing in the wrong pool or whatever gnomes do in Zurich, but were also interfering with the running of football in England and Wales.

Any changes in the laws of the game are worked out and agreed by the International Board, which meets every year. It consists of representatives from FIFA and the four home international countries. In 1983, FIFA were adamant that the clampdown by referees in the Football League during the 1982–83 season on the professional foul, which is more accurately a 'cynical' foul (or even an 'amateur' foul, insofar as it can be seen by everyone and you can't be more amateur than that), was a misinterpretation of the rules. Despite the success of the clampdown, and the fact that the FA and the FAW were well aware that the game had improved immensely in entertainment value as a result, with more goals being scored, FIFA instructed all the home countries that the stricter interpretation must be withdrawn with immediate effect.

In its circular the FA said it was essential that we in this country did not continue procedures that were contrary to those practised throughout the world, and we had an added responsibility in that English league matches were so widely televised abroad. (The FAW, incidentally, asked the FA to send its version of the circular to Football League referees in Wales, the first time I had ever received a circular from the FA concerning rules since my governing body is the FAW.) I have to put this challenge to the members of the home associations: you were not prepared to go against Dr Havelange and his henchman for fear of your positions within FIFA and UEFA.

My letter to the Brazilian President of FIFA summed up my frustration with soccer at international level. But we should perhaps start at square one if you are to understand fully the problems that lead to that kind of outburst.

Each country nominates, or at least can nominate, up to seven referees to UEFA (the Union of European Football Associations) and to FIFA (the Federation of International Football Associations), each of whom is expected to be refereeing at the highest level in his particular country. But Wales, for example, has never had seven referees on the Football League list, with the result that they always included Football League linesmen. When you consider, too, the inexperience of referees from, say, Malta and Cyprus, you may imagine why there are difficulties in reaching competent standards for all matches.

On appointment, referees must – quite rightly – take the FIFA fitness test (details of which are included elsewhere) but, surprisingly enough and again in Wales, the linesmen whose names have been submitted by the FAW do not take the test. I cannot understand this because, through the referee's injury, they could well be called upon to referee a UEFA cup-tie without passing more than a very basic medical. I am not particularly proud to say that I am the only Welsh referee who has for the past eighteen years had a full medical by the FAW's medical adviser. Others nip down the road, as it were, to have a word with their local GP. This can't be right: every person on the UEFA list should have an organised and thorough check every year by the same FAW-approved examiner.

UEFA also organises a course each year for new referees on the list. But, after attending my first in Switzerland in 1972, I have received from UEFA only the annual congratulations on being selected again along with any changes in the rules of their competitions. Every season, however, the secretary, Hans Bangerter, points out that successful control of matches in the competitions will depend as in the past upon the quality of refereeing in the early rounds. Referees must be stricter, paying even closer attention to instructions they have been given and ensuring there is no violence or poor sportsmanship. Negative attitudes and inadequate performances will result, it says, in referees not being appointed to another match for a while. Fair enough. Yet the same problems arise with the same referees who receive the same plum appointments.

The UEFA Referees' Committee had been controlled for a time, until his death in a car crash in August 1983, by Artemio Franchi, whom we have met before on the World Cup scene. He was also president of UEFA, which meant that he had crucial and almost total control of vital areas. On his committee were Giulio Campanati, a fellow Italian, Rudi Glockner, an East German (known by all Welshmen for his performance in the notorious battle of Ninian Park between Wales and Yugoslavia in 1977), a West German, Johannes Malka, and an Englishman, A.D. McMullen.

I have discussed earlier McMullen's qualifications for important positions, but at one time he used to speak to me about the reasons why I was appointed for certain matches. He would go out to Berne for a couple of days, after the draws for the next round matches were made, to help choose the officials. There were some matches in which a strong referee was required, to ensure that violence was prevented or cured, and inevitably these seemed to be given to me. Since about 1980, though, these conversations have ceased, possibly because McMullen is responsible for my geographical area and was embarrassed about my outspokenness on the laws of the game. As a result of my views I was excluded from the European Championships in Italy in 1980, where the standard of refereeing was nothing short of a disgrace – and some of the worst performers were still given important appointments the following season and thereafter.

But McMullen's 'qualifications' are almost equalled by the men who are used as assessors, called delegates by UEFA: people like Sir Harold Thompson, Ted Croker, Trevor Morris, Ernie Walker and Dick Wragg, who, like him, have never refereed a Football League match. They are the people who have the audacity, without real experience themselves, to mark referees. I have never asked these assessors what marks they have given me, but I have invariably met them at airports on my way home and been mildly amused by their comments as they seem to have attended an entirely different game. They also seem to have had an excellent three days away from home, all expenses paid, generally in a better hotel than the referee's, and often go home with a gift, which they then compare with yours.

Someone in UEFA's executive should have had the courage to discover why Dr Franchi was able to be chairman of the referees' committee when he was also UEFA's president. If ever there was a closed shop in football politics, here it was. No one, apparently, was prepared to query it, presumably because their own position might be at risk if they asked too many questions.

I pointed out to McMullen once while we were having lunch before a game at Luton that I had problems with Dr Franchi and with Friedrich Seipelt. He admitted that he always found it difficult to put my name forward for matches as Seipelt, because of his personal dislike of me, would vote against it regardless of my suitability. But an Englishman still seemed to do well and I believe McMullen has much to answer for in respect of my few matches in Europe and especially for no European Cup Final. In the first round UEFA matches in 1983, Englishman George Courtney had a UEFA cup-tie in Yugoslavia and a second leg two weeks later – yet I didn't have a match that month. McMullen was clearly looking after his boys. Courtney had previously refereed a UEFA Cup Final in May 1982 when I had been in Europe more than ten years longer, and, by the marks I received, with more ability. McMullen would contend that ability is not everything, but McMullen is as powerful in European football in UK terms as Havalange is within FIFA, and he has achieved his position from being an administrator at schools' level.

The biggest mistake made by the FA in my opinion was in not promoting Ken Aston in place of McMullen. Ken had all the qualities, the ability and experience to promote refereeing round the world and would have been far more successful in running the UEFA courses for referees. At the course I attended, McMullen's performance was so poor that even his own referees from England were laughing – behind his back, of course, because they would not wish to harm themselves in the eyes of such a powerful man. Perhaps it is just as well then, as we have already discovered, that UEFA has no referees' instructors' course: it might be a disaster.

I believe that the ability of the referee is not always a top priority in the choice of appointments and that other considerations must be taking precedence. Nor am I alone in this belief. Why, even Herr Seipelt in his report of the standards for the World Cup in Argentina in 1978, which were criticised severely round the world, said that although he was reasonably satisfied with the first-round referees, he was not with the second round and thereafter. Perhaps, then, I should be pleased that I only had that one first-round match. Yet the second-round referees were appointed to the finals.

Closer to home, an astonishing attack was made on them by Terry Casey, who was at that time FA coach for the north-west of England. He was sent as an official observer by the FA and his comments, he said, were not made simply to have a go at referees but because he felt very strongly about the manner in which some of the games he saw had been allowed to be played and controlled. Out of twelve matches he faulted six referees on their control and handling of the game.

His report makes fascinating reading. For example, he says of Nicolai Rainea, of Romania: 'As the game (Italy v France) progressed, the manner in which it was played deteriorated and the referee should have taken a firmer grip on the situation earlier. A poor refereeing performance by any standard. A good referee would have sent off Italy's Bonetti.' Of Argentina v Brazil (refereed by Karoly Palotai of Hungary) he says: 'Several players should have been cautioned early on and, in fact, at least three players should have been sent off. The referee was completely incompetent. He allowed play to go on after serious fouls had been committed. The display of refereeing was disgraceful and the match suffered because of it.' Of Brazil v Italy (Abraham Klein, of Israel):

'Many fouls went unpunished by the referee and once more we were to see a refereeing performance that was below par. Some of the tackling was violent but no positive action was taken.'

Two of the other three referees mentioned, Barretto, of Uruguay, and Gonella (Italy), who took the final, retired. But the other three continued not only at UEFA level in cup finals but also in the World Cup Finals in Spain. It is clear that the referees' committee did not agree with Mr Casey. Indeed, the FA appointed the 'completely incompetent' Palotai for international matches at Wembley after that report.

Why do Football Associations do this sort of thing? And how on earth are the referees chosen at international level?

In the 1982 World Cup, one of the most important matches, Italy v Argentina, during which I lost count of the number of fouls, was refereed by none other than Rainea of Romania. In a similar game vital to both teams, Italy v Brazil, who was the referee? Why, Klein of Israel. And with Austria and France? Palotai of Hungary.

The linesmen chosen for the third place play-off match between Poland and France were Rubio of Mexico and Lacarne of Algeria: the assessor was Arriaga of Mexico. Should a man be assessing his fellow countryman at this level? And are officials from Mexico and Algeria really qualified – do they have the necessary experience for such a game? Arriaga in fact assessed both that match and the final. Who was the assessor for the brawl between Argentina and Brazil, the politically-fraught Poland v Russia, Brazil v Scotland, USSR and Scotland and Brazil v Russia? A certain O. Sey from Gambia. Who? Where? While F.G. Alvarez from the well-known soccer nation, the Philippines, assessed three England matches, against West Germany, Czechoslovakia and France.

At the start of the series, and because I was more worldly-wise about football politics, I told a journalist that there were four referees who would be involved in those final games, depending on which nations were involved: Palotai, Klein, Garrido of Portugal and Coelho of Brazil. Garrido did the third place match between Poland and the unlucky France and it was a racing certainty, once Brazil were out of the tournament, that Senor Coelho would be the representative of that country in the final. Just as Dr Franchi had made sure that an Italian refereed the 1978 final, so did 'Avalanche' make certain a Brazilian had the 1982 honour. And we know what a mess they both made of the games. It all makes me wonder: what on earth did I ever do to upset Brazil?

Talking of being upset, one of the real problems of refereeing at international level is, of all things, hospitality. I deplored the action a few years ago of the Scottish FA when they banned one of my colleagues who was deemed to have accepted from an Italian club gifts which were above and beyond the norm. If the person who reported the incident is whom I think, I know full well that he also has accepted expensive gifts. Much more important, why was the club concerned not suspended rather than merely fined by UEFA, when their action was if anything more grave and their responsibility more serious? Was it perhaps because it was an Italian club? And why did Scotland take such severe steps? Was it to show how pure they were immediately after the drugs scandal and their disastrous performance in Argentina? A man's future in football – and outside it – was sacrificed at the altar of Scotland's dubious morality.

The Companion of the UEFA Referee, an information booklet of advice, states: 'Any offers of excessive hospitality and exaggerated generosity are to be refused politely but firmly. Under no circumstances must you accept gifts which are more than souvenirs – objects such as valuables, articles of everyday clothing etc.' And a UEFA memorandum says that 'referees are requested not to use the hospitality of the organisers in excess and to eat and drink in an acceptable way. Extras such as telephone calls etc shall be borne in all cases by the referee himself. Traditional mementoes such as badges, pennants and so on may be presented to the referee only after the match has finished. These points will always be especially carefully watched by the UEFA Executive Committee and the referees' committee and these authorities will take severe action wherever necessary.'

They must, of course, be joking. Ninety-nine per cent of referees and delegates on the European circuit have cabinets full of glassware and other 'trophies' in their living-rooms which they have received before matches. Many times gifts are left discreetly in the hotel for your arrival, others are presented openly at a lunch reception before the game, sometimes by the home clubs only and other times by both teams. I have always accepted the gifts, yes: afterwards you'll be fortunate to receive a lapel badge from the losing team.

Let us for a moment go to Barcelona, where a public relations agency, complete with attractive lady escorts, looks after you with an apparently unlimited expense account. Champagne and nightclubs are the normal perks, and any talk of football concerns only the cleanliness of the home side and the low depths to which the opposition will stoop, particularly, say, the tough number five and the vicious number three – have another drink. It is big business and it is wrong and I have always refused to discuss a game with any individual.

I believe that referees and linesmen should be met at the airport on arrival by members of the host country's referees' association and should be hosted by them for the three days in the country. Instead of champagne and nightclubs, they should meet the local referees to promote mutual understanding of the current problems facing the game. They should not meet club officials until, perhaps, two hours before the kick-off, and all expenses should be paid through the referees' association.

UEFA are apparently not short of cash. Although I have never attended one of their disciplinary hearings, I have attended boards of appeal – and expensive affairs they are. I was detailed to attend such an appeal on Friday, 21 November, 1980, at the Hotel Hilton Airport, Zurich, because the Yugoslav club, Sarajevo, were objecting to the penalties placed on them after a match in Hamburg. Because I was due the next day to referee the Brighton-Manchester United match, I asked whether I would be able to return to London that same Friday night. No trouble, predicted UEFA delegates I approached, you won't be in the meeting for more than an hour. They were wrong, by fully forty minutes. I left Heathrow on a Swissair flight at 9.05 am, arrived Zurich 11.10 to be met by a UEFA representative and a chauffeur-driven car. The meeting was due to start at 2.30 pm and my return flight was at 4.30. No problem, said the UEFA man. I had a sauna and a massage at the hotel, paid for by UEFA, lunched and was told the meeting had been delayed until 3 pm. By 3.14 the chairman had heard my report, by 3.20 the Sarajevo representative said he had no further questions and by 3.30 I was back at the airport. I reckon that twenty minutes cost someone close to £500. And that was just for me.

The hearing that made me really furious took place on 2 May, 1983, when I was supposed to be officiating at the major promotion-seeking derby between QPR and Fulham, on Bank Holiday Monday. Paris St Germain were appealing against the four-match suspension of two of their players in a match against Waterschei. When the FAW phoned my secretary on 12 April to tell me about the appeal, she told them about the QPR match and, the next day, Eddie Harrison of the FAW confirmed a discussion with UEFA who had said I could be on the 12.40 out of Zurich which would arrive at Heathrow at 1.15 our time. With the help of the Metropolitan Police I was prepared to guarantee to the Football League that I could arrive at Loftus Road at 1.30 – a bit tight, but possible. Later that afternoon, when I was refereeing a police international match at Ninian Park, the FAW phoned to say that the Football League were releasing me from the vital second division promotion match. They would not reconsider the decision.

I flew out on the Sunday night (at a total cost of £459), stayed again at the Hilton, attended the meeting at 10.45 next morning, left twenty-eight minutes later, caught the plane and was listening to comments on the car radio about the QPR game as I drove home down the M4. The Board of Appeal confirmed the decision taken by the first disciplinary hearing. To add insult to injury, I received a letter from UEFA saying that they had made a mistake in my expenses and they would be more than satisfied if I returned £25 due to the rate of exchange – and this after losing the best part of two days of a holiday weekend, missing the most crucial promotion match of the day and the fee of £40! Really, though, the UEFA hearing should have been changed earlier but no one had bothered to ask about my availability, and who cares about referees anyhow?

The referee is always the last person to be considered but, when you think of the people in charge, this is hardly surprising. I accept entirely that a paid administrator should be an expert in that particular discipline, but I believe that the whole structure nationally and internationally should be changed to ensure that referees are in control of referees. Because of the current politics within the game, referees have to spend their time looking over their shoulders to keep in with their representatives on the UEFA and FIFA committees, with the result that they often think twice before giving honest views. If they are not honest off the field, will they be trustworthy on it? A referee should be free from external pressures and worries of the political variety.

My proposed new structure would start on the bottom rung of the local referees' association, the secretary and chairman at national association level would be ex-international referees, as would the members of the referees' committee. The representatives on the UEFA committee would therefore be senior referees from the major footballing nations whose duties would not only include the appointments for European cup matches but would include also the monitoring and recommendations for changes in the laws and the responsibility of organising coaching throughout Europe. At least six members of the UEFA referees' committee would be members of the FIFA referees' committee, to ensure a majority on a committee of ten. Retirement age would be sixty, to ensure an inflow of new blood but giving long enough for the referee to make an impact after retirement from his active role. That way, perhaps, the referee would no longer be a second-class citizen.

*   *   *   *   *

Finally, though, let us move to a lighter subject; I return to hospitality. Only once have I received a gift I did not particularly want. Size, of course, is no guarantee of value or acceptability and it was therefore with no little suspicion that I viewed the present I was given, in full view of the delegate by the way, after a match involving Kiev in deepest Russia.

It was a huge urn, about two feet high and a foot wide, known to the experts in *objet d'art*, I understand, as a samovar. I looked for help to my interpreter as the members of the Kiev committee applauded me at the presentation after the match, either because I was accepting their gift or because they were delighted to be rid of it. I asked reasonably politely how the hell I was going to carry it across Russia, across Moscow and home to Britain. More, what was it for? He pointed out that to receive such a samovar was an honour, a reflection of the respect held for me by the people of the USSR. To reject it . . .

At Moscow airport, to my instant delight, the authorities and security guards in customs refused permission for such a masterpiece to be taken from their country. They inspected it for a considerable time until my interpreter, curse him, had a quiet word and they allowed me to take it. When I arrived home, Beryl asked what we could do with it and, before I could answer, she said I had told her the Russians thought highly of me.

In fairness, I should say that it is worth a considerable amount of money though it has been on loan ever since to our friends, Gary and Fred, in their pub, *The Llangeinor Arms*, in the Blaengarw Valley, where it does look rather more at home. But the samovar was not the only problem I encountered in Russia . . .

·14·
WHISTLE-STOP TOURISM

*'To travel hopefully is a better
thing than to arrive'*

Many people will be aware of the quotation from Robert Louis Stevenson. Less well known is the conclusion to the statement: '. . . and the true success is to labour'.

As the result of my refereeing career, I have been fortunate enough to travel in some forty countries, including just about every nation in Europe, east or west. Because of this, people understandably tend to think that I have seen every museum, every beach, every monument and every nightclub the other side of the Severn Bridge. The reality, of course, is nothing like the dream, and my true success, if that is what it is, has been, as the man said, to labour. In short, I remember my performance and the match rather more than the place.

Oh yes, I am worldly-wise, much travelled and vastly experienced: but the experience tends to be of airline terminals and timetables, the wisdom is of hotel facilities and the tourism of quite literally the whistle-stop variety, so short is the time in any given city. And, believe me, the fact that you are travelling for a major event at the invitation and behest of UEFA or FIFA does not make you immune from bureacratic bungling or from the problems facing the average unsponsored visitor or businessman.

Don't misunderstand me. I am very grateful for the opportunities I have had, but as I sit now and look at an atlas and at a list of matches at which I have officiated overseas, not all of the memories are happy. The first time you travel to Russia to referee a match, for example, is a curious experience. In March 1976, I was delighted to be given the European Cup quarter-final between Dynamo Kiev and St Etienne as it was undoubtedly the plum match of the round. Yet that pleasure was tempered somewhat by the fact that I had difficulty in explaining to my wife that I had only a one-way ticket. Apparently, I would be supplied with the return ticket on leaving Moscow after the match. There were clear, if sinister, possibilities . . .

With my linesmen, Gwyn Owen and Vic Lewis, I left Heathrow on BA 990 at 10.35 on the morning of 2 March and we were duly met at

Moscow's Sheremetyevo Airport, dour and snow-shrouded as it was, at 5.15 that afternoon by a representative of the Kiev club who was to accompany us on the further flight to his home town. Alas, he said in fluent English, there was so much snow in Kiev that no planes were flying and that, anyhow, conditions were so bad that the match venue had been changed to Simferopol. We could not fly out from Moscow until the following morning. Would we therefore sleep at the airport?

Would we what? He refused my request that he should phone UEFA, at which point I informed him that I was prepared to sleep at the airport, certainly, but that I would then be flying back to London first thing the next morning, match or no match. All of which was really an academic threat because I did not have a return ticket anyhow. He left us standing forlorn and lonely with our bags at our sides for an hour or so. Gwyn Owen was growing even more agitated than me because there is a demand by immigration when you fly into Moscow that you have no more than £25 in sterling in your possession and, as a consequence of doing some business on his way to Heathrow, he had very much more.

In fact, the police did not pick Gwyn up, and we were finally taken to quite the dingiest hotel that I have ever seen – or that I have never seen, insofar as it was in total darkness when we arrived. We were given a room – and for the first time I actually wanted to share a room with two male companions, and they with me – and told we must be awake at 5 am for a 6.15 flight. Awake indeed … we didn't sleep. No breakfast, out to the airport, a journey in one of the smallest planes imaginable and eventually arrival at Simferopol, where there was if anything more snow than in Moscow. But there was at least the very welcoming Mikhail Oshemkov, who was somewhat surprised to find us arriving on the actual day of the match, technically against the rules of UEFA. He pointed out that referees coming to his part of the world always travelled two days before the game and was baffled because the FAW had not recommended this to me even after they had been notified.

Before going to the hotel, and because of the amount of snow on the ground, I wanted to see the stadium. So at 9.30 am Mik took me there to find at least six inches of snow: as I saw it there was no way that the game could be played at 6 that night. I explained this, and Mik asked when I wished to inspect the ground for a final decision. I said 4 pm.

We were taken to the hotel (the equivalent, possibly, of a one-star in Britain) where as usual there was a lady of considerable bulk in the corridor on permanent watch. Tell me, are they there to keep you in or to keep others out? Either way, she watched over us like the proverbial hawk until we went to the stadium, where we were confronted with an amazing sight. More than five hundred people, including soldiers, with buckets and wheelbarrows, were finishing the clearance of the snow. In the middle of the pitch there were huge military fan heaters like those used to clear runways at airports. I do not believe there is any place in the world where the ground could have been cleared so quickly or the pitch made in more perfect condition. The players did those conditions full justice and it was a splendid game.

Gwyn Owen, in fact, was lucky to receive his return ticket. The Russians were so impressed with his continuous singing that they wanted him to stay. But we finally returned to Moscow – every plane has to go through the capital – with the St Etienne team, in their special aircraft, and then travelled home. A fascinating trip, indeed. But I would warn future referees about the food (I ate only Russian bread and Welsh honey) and would sincerely recommend to UEFA that future matches in Russia, but outside Moscow, should become four-day visits.

Lack of a return ticket may be one thing: lack of a passport is quite clearly another. I am, or at least my friends tell me so, a methodical person not usually prone to inefficiency or forgetfulness, and so it was with no particular thought or worry in mind that I set off one day early in 1983 to travel to Belgium for the match between Waterschei and Paris St Germain, which is described elsewhere. I had made all the arrangements as usual for the tickets for my linesmen, Frank Roberts and David Delaney, and when we put our cases through the check-in, I asked them to produce their passports. This was a formality, and they were of course ready to leave on flight SN 606 in ninety minutes at 14.45. But then I realised that I did not have my own passport. There was no immediate panic, and I asked how I could overcome the problem: the security men pointed out that I would be allowed out of Heathrow, but that they could not guarantee that I would be allowed to enter Belgium. Nevertheless, they would notify Brussels of my predicament and, sure enough, the interpreter from the Waterschei club was ready when we touched down.

We explained my problem to the police and, presumably because I was to referee the most crucial game in which Waterschei have ever played, they accepted me into the country on the basis that I was well known to them, though I was a shade concerned as to whether this was in my favour or not. On my return they duly let me out of Belgium, helped possibly by the fact that the game achieved much publicity and possibly by Waterschei's victory. And so back to London, where I again explained my problem, to a young lady at passport control who was somewhat sceptical but who would speak with a higher official. She asked first, though, what I had been doing in Brussels. When I told her, she said, yes, of course, she would have recognised me if I had been wearing my shorts. I told her that I would happily change into shorts if I would be allowed back into the country. She did not take up the challenge but I was home.

I did, on the other hand, have my passport firmly with me when I first visited East Germany. The FAW in September 1973 gave me the match between Carl Zeiss Jena and Mikkelin Pallalijat, which meant travelling through Berlin and crossing the Iron Curtain through Checkpoint Charlie. We actually had to pay to go through but when I made a comment to that effect and that I didn't particularly want to go through anyhow, the border guards fortunately could not understand me. So be it: we were met by two representatives of the host club and had to drive through a colourless and dreary part of the country for more than two hours.

A bad introduction, then. But at the end of the day I have to say that the hospitality and general efficiency and standards in the country were as high as anywhere I have been. At the hotel there were bouquets of flowers and bowls of fruit in our rooms. More surprisingly, perhaps, at a dance in the hotel that first evening there were more women present than men, they asked men to dance and it was perhaps this that made me wonder if there was anything sinister about it. Certainly I always felt we were being closely watched. But in general East Germany left a very favourable impression on me.

Talking of ladies and the Iron Curtain, I would also speak highly of the arrangements in Czechoslovakia, though to this day I am a little baffled by one incident. One of my linesmen for the match between Sparta Prague and Schalk of Holland in March 1973 was Idwal Williams of Neath. A few days before we left Wales, Idwal asked whether I minded if he took a parcel out to Czechoslovakia for a friend. I told him that unless he knew exactly the contents of the parcel, I would not take the chance: as he could not be sure, I refused permission. Twenty minutes out of Prague he announced he still had the parcel with him.

I was very annoyed, but there was little I could do at that stage. I must admit it was with some surprise that I heard Idwal ask our host as we were being taken to the hotel how the parcel could be delivered. The man was unmoved: the address was only five minutes from the hotel and, yes, they would deliver it. So while I changed, showered and prepared for dinner, Idwal delivered his parcel and came back full of smiles. Indeed, our interpreter had allowed the person to whom he delivered the parcel to come back to dinner. Because this was highly irregular, I said that Idwal would have to look after the person himself. I should, of course, have been suspicious when he happily agreed.

When we arrived for dinner, there was the interpreter with a very, very attractive young lady. I immediately pulled rank for the only time in my European travels and ordered that she accompany us as assistant interpreter for the next two days. More's the pity, therefore, that as we were leaving Prague's Ruzyne Airport to return home, the lady concerned took me aside to ask whether I would make sure that neither Idwal nor Cliff Brooks, my other linesman, kissed her goodbye as certain people would be watching. It is such a shame that in Eastern European countries either they are not allowed to behave naturally or feel that they cannot. On the other hand, I still do not know what was in that parcel.

Mind you, I appreciate that it is not only the Eastern bloc countries that have their problems. San Sebastian, for example, is a highly attractive part of northern Spain: the old city is particularly beautiful. But it is also in a very volatile part of the country, and on the day I arrived to referee a match between the home side and KSC Locheren in December 1980 a policeman was shot dead as a result of the Basque dispute. Because of this, the representative of the home club was ordered not to let us out of his sight for the whole visit. Politics and sport are inevitably and intricately connected.

You may think that as a Celt I might have sympathy with the Basques. I can understand their motives, but I can never accept their methods because I believe in discipline and in law. It was a shade surprising to find that in the south of Spain, close to Marbella – where much of this book first found its way on to the typewriter and where you will always find British soccer personalities relaxing out of their season – there were road blocks on the major highways in connection with bombing incidents at the other end of the country.

Northern Ireland, of course, is another problem area. In 1972, when Scotland refused to play in Belfast, the match was transferred instead to Glasgow. No one bothered at the time to ask whether I, the appointed referee, had any views or would travel to Belfast. It was another case of the authorities taking the referee for granted with the FAW making the decision on my behalf. Indeed, at Belfast in 1980, my linesmen and I travelled from Wales for a similar fixture to discover that Scotland were flying in on the afternoon of the match and returning immediately after the final whistle. Once more, no one bothered to ask the poor old referee.

I have officiated in only one match on the other side of the border and that was a friendly, between Eire and Switzerland. It was one of the few occasions in my career that I have refereed a soccer match on an international rugby ground. I was not helped by the fact that, just a month before, Wales had come the most humiliating cropper at the historic Lansdowne Road, Dublin. Little wonder that the groundsman, in proudly showing me his ground, introduced me to each particular patch of turf on which Ireland had scored their tries.

I had a tremendous welcome, however, and in my regular business negotiations in Dublin, where I make frequent visits for the OCS Group who have businesses there, I have always been received with humour, goodwill and hard but fair dealings. I look forward to further visits.

Beautiful as it is, though, I am not sure that I want further dealings with Cyprus, which is a real pity. Spoiled as Cyprus is, once more by politics and jealousies, it is nevertheless an idyllic island and I had every right to believe that the two games we had to encompass would make the visit memorable. Memorable it was, as it went wrong from the very beginning.

We were due out of Heathrow, my linesmen, Gerald Morgan, Walter Williams, and myself, at 4 pm on Tuesday, 2 October, 1979, but the flight was delayed and then delayed further. Clearly something was up – or, rather, not up. Finally, we were told the flight would not go out that evening and so I 'phoned Trevor Morris at the FAW to recommend that he telex UEFA. His response was that, knowing me, he was sure I would find some way to Cyprus. I suppose he was right.

Back to British Airways. They eventually found room for us on the last flight to Athens, with the assurance that we could have a flight on to Cyprus next morning, the day of the match. And so, with our baggage still on the stationary plane, we darted off for the Athens flight armed only with a promise from a young Chelsea fan on the BA staff that he would somehow ensure that our luggage caught up with us. Off we went, then, out into the blue (or black by now), with no baggage, no currency (as it was provided by the host club) and no hotel booked. But in Athens, we were taken under the capable and sympathetic wing of Olympic Airways and they fixed the hotel and an ongoing flight the following morning. Not surprisingly, there was no one to meet us next morning in Cyprus: they simply did not know we were there.

With no little difficulty, and remember we were unshaven, without money and looking thoroughly dishevelled, I persuaded an official of Cyprus Airways to contact the local club secretary, who was in the process of contacting UEFA for a replacement referee because he believed we were still in London. The FAW, of course, had failed to pass on the news of our predicament – but we were finally booked into our hotel. The luggage also turned up two hours before the match: thank you, BA and Chelsea fan, to whom I presented the match ball on our return. If he reads this perhaps he will re-establish contact.

All's well that ends well, they say. Alas, it did not. For the first time, we were due to cover two matches on consecutive days with Gerald Morgan to referee the second and myself running the line. What should have been his most memorable day was doomed to disappointment. The dressing-room at the ground was quite the worst I have ever seen, a mere shed with two zinc sheets on the roof and with a toilet not fit for a dog. The whole set-up was a disgrace to European football: it would have been a disgrace to Rhondda League football. The total lack of professionalism makes me wonder whether the smaller nations in UEFA really should qualify for the major tournaments.

However the game, played in the afternoon because naturally there were no floodlights, ran its course and at last we could relax. Relax? Hah! The secretary of the club recommended a restaurant to which he would be pleased to take us for dinner, and, at about 7.30, with him driving and a lady friend alongside him in the front of the car, we set off. After about quarter of an hour, we realised we were driving on sand, and finally it became obvious, as we drew up at the water's edge with nothing but sea between us and Egypt, that we were lost and in total darkness. I told him, sensibly really in view of the fact that there was no going forward, that we should go back. He had forgotten the way as there was no road and, the more he revved the engine, the deeper we settled into the soggy sand. We were stuck.

Leaving the lady in the car and with Walter Williams, an ex-police driver, at the wheel, we had to take off our shoes, roll up our trousers and push. And push. We had agreed that once the car was moving Walter should keep going. He did: but what we had not anticipated was that he would keep going for half a mile or more. With sodden sand up to our knees, we eventually caught up with him. He smiled widely.

Not surprisingly, on our arrival back at the hotel we were greeted with considerable ribaldry from the Romanian team involved in the match as we slunk past. Would we, the club secretary asked, care instead to go to a nice little restaurant he knew . . . ? No, we would not.

In fact, our visit to Cyprus ended with some slightly hysterical laughter which must have puzzled other passengers on the flight. Shortly after take-off next morning we looked down as the plane banked for a farewell sight of the island of Aphrodite. Below us was a beach. With a perfect set of car tracks leading down to the water's edge. And back.

A slightly more difficult problem arose one day in March 1975 when I was due to referee with linesmen Vic Lewis and Brian Cox the match between FC Amsterdam and Cologne. We arrived fairly late in the evening with the result that we booked quickly into the Amsterdam hotel and went straight out for a meal. It was only the next morning that I realised that the hotel was one of the worst in which I had stayed. I mentioned this to Vic and Brian as we went down to breakfast and we agreed that we would pack our bags and leave when the interpreter came to take us for our preliminary look at the stadium. I explained when he arrived that the hotel was unsatisfactory and I suppose I should have realised something was amiss when he appeared somewhat agitated. It was, he said, out of his control, but that he would arrange for me to speak with the secretary and president of Amsterdam when we reached the stadium. The president apologised, listened politely to my complaints about the quality of the hotel, explained that other referees had been satisfied but that alternative accommodation would be found for us at the Hilton. He then said that he was very concerned personally about my complaints. He owned the hotel.

Not that I always drop bricks with the heads of clubs I visit. I remember once taking full advantage of the hospitality provided by that excellent Belgian club, Anderlecht, when, on the morning of the second leg of the European Cup semi-final against Twente Éntschede in April 1978, I was taken with linesman Keith Cooper to a private sauna while our other colleague, Ieuan Thomas, preferred a tour of Brussels. I know who had the better time ... Certainly, I was well toned up for the game.

After the match we went to a nightclub with Anderlecht representative Raymond De Deken, who is now very much a close friend, and the president's son, Roger van Den Stock, who is also a UEFA official. During the evening, I had reason to tell him that I worked for an office cleaning company and he told me in turn that he and his father had a very close friend in Britain in that industry. I nearly fell from my chair when he said the name of the friend was Derek Goodliffe, my governor from the OCS Group, and that they stayed at the company flat, as I do, when they visited London. From that moment, I was a different person: no more drinks, no more saunas, sober-minded and altogether a solid and upright citizen. Nevertheless, within twenty-four hours of my return to Britain, my boss had a full report on my activities, sauna and all. It's a small, small world.

It always seems so, too, when I go away on holiday and find inevitably that the people in the villa across the swimming pool are in football or, as happened in the case of one quite extraordinary coincidence while preparing this book, I wrote about John Bond in the morning and then quite literally bumped into John and his son, Kevin, on the seafront of a Mediterranean resort in the evening. This reminded me of the story of the enemies meeting after a long time and shaking each other warmly by the throat.

But my family and I tend when possible to head for Portugal for our holidays where we find peace and quiet in the sun, staying in private villas not for reasons of snobbery but because it can, I'm afraid, become a little wearing in a hotel where every fellow guest in the bar or round the pool wants to talk about soccer or particular incidents or clubs. I like to be recognised, of course I do, and I'm always prepared to sign autographs because I feel that any such rapport is for the good of the game. But it's not really fair on my family if I'm talking football all the time.

So, as I say, we head for Portugal, where we also get tremendous value for money – though I have not always felt quite so benignly about this part of Europe. After refereeing a match between Benfica and Ujpest Dosza in November 1975 we were paid out as usual at the splendid Hotel Don Carlos in Lisbon in the currency of the country: 15,750 *escudos* to be exact. It seemed an enormous sum, but on our return to Britain we found that the exchange rate left us with 'a negative cash-flow situation', or something like that. The FAW raised the matter with the referees' committee of UEFA, who suggested merely that I took it up with the Portuguese. I wrote to the secretary-general of Sporting Lisbon Benfica pointing out that I was £40 in the red on the trip, Idwal Williams was £31 down and Hugh Bishop £37. After months of letter-writing, Benfica decided finally that it was impossible to consider my request.

I thought I was heading for Greece once. After refereeing a Henri Delaunay Cup match between Germany and Greece in Düsseldorf – a 1–1 draw in which I had, incidentally, one of the best linesmen I have ever known in Gordon Harrhy, along with Desmond Southall – the Greeks were so delighted that they invited us to come to Athens. I never went. Maybe I should not have made it so clear that if I were going to referee a friendly, I would anticipate that my wife would also have an invitation.

I'd like to have seen more of Italy too. Although I have refereed in many matches in the old Anglo-Italian tournament, for some reason I did only one European Cup match, and that was Torino v Bastia in December 1977. Little went right: except that because the official assessor was fogbound an old friend, Gigi Peronace, stood in and gave me a glowing report. But I wanted badly to be back in Bridgend next day for a very special appointment with Frankie Vaughan. With the airport closed, the Italians fixed for a potential Jackie Stewart to drive me through the Alps to Switzerland for a flight home. I'm told it's a beautiful journey. I saw nothing of it – my eyes were unashamedly closed most of the time.

Yes, it's better to travel hopefully, whether to Turin or Torquay, Anderlecht or Aldershot.

·15·
HALF-TIME

Benfica 5, Feyenoord 1. Sounds a convincing enough win, doesn't it? And although a journalist immediately after the match muttered something about money and Feyenoord, I paid no attention to him: whatever it was he was saying could have gained or lost a great deal in translation. I slept soundly in Lisbon on the night of 22 March, 1972: but next morning I was awakened somewhat abruptly by big Jim Orpin, my genial linesman, who was brandishing a copy of a newspaper I later discovered was called *A Bola*, which I probably dare not translate.

'HAPPEL ACUSA O ARBITRO RECEBEU DINHEIRO DO BENFICA' read a headline. Now you don't have to be fluent in Portuguese to get the gist of that. Happel was the Feyenoord manager, *acusa* speaks for itself, *arbitro* I knew to be the referee (Thomas in this case), *recebeu* must surely mean receive. After that, it was a question of deciding whether *dinheiro* meant money, sports cars, exotic ladies, diamonds or what have you. The trouble was that this *arbitro* had not *recebeu dinheiro* or anything else.

Seriously, though, I took a very grave view of this allegation. I went immediately to the Portuguese Football Association offices in Lisbon, where the president and his assistant translated the article for me. After returning home to Treorchy, I wrote to UEFA to demand some action, even though the FAW had advised me to forget the whole matter. In time, Happel was reprimanded and fined.

*　　*　　*　　*　　*

I thought we might have some moments of miscellany at this point in the narrative and come off the pitch for a breather, a sort of half-time when we can relax with a few idle thoughts and jottings. Having started with money, I'll stay with it for a moment.

I receive a fair number of letters one way and another, but few have amused or rewarded me more than the one I received from a gentleman called Jack Smith, of Bishops Way, Sutton Coldfield. Jack wrote a somewhat rude letter to me in July 1983, suggesting in effect that I didn't know what I was doing, that it was time I packed it all in, and that I should resign. He enclosed a pound for my retirement fund.

But he made a fatal mistake, did Jack. 'If I was a betting man', he said, 'I'd bet a pound to a penny that you will tear this letter up and throw it away.'

'Dear Jack', I wrote back. 'Thank you for your letter of 19 July the contents of which are noted, and also for the enclosed £1 towards my retirement fund.

'By rights you should now send me another £1 as you have lost your bet in that I have not torn your letter up. In fact I am very interested in your comments ...' And I went on to answer the points he had raised.

Fair play, almost by return of post came another £1 note, with the comment, 'I withdraw my suggestion that you should retire. After all, if a man in your position can take the time to reply to my letters, he can't be all bad!'

Jack, if you have bought this book, let me know, and I will return the two oncers. They're still pinned to your letters.

*   *   *   *   *

Anonymous letters are not so good. Try this one for size:

'I pray God will forgive you for what you have done to Ipswich Town football. The people in East Anglia never will, how could you cheat an honest team the people in East Anglia are really disgusted at you, you are no better than those crooks in London but however much your bank book has swelled ... God don't repay his debts in money you will live to regret what you have done.

'There's too many crooks in sport today and we don't want any down here ... You are indeed a horrible horrible man. What did the crooks threaten to do to you? Many people here wish you the worst. So do I.'

Any more anonymous letters will go straight into the waste paper basket, which is all they deserve if the writer does not have the courage to give his name.

*   *   *   *   *

When is a referee not a referee? The Welsh FA Disciplinary Committee had to answer this soccer conundrum. Following the Welsh Cup semi-final when Rhyl were beaten by Cardiff City 2-1, I booked the Rhyl wing-half, Howard Smart, in the car park some thirty minutes after the game. He made some comments about my refereeing in front of witnesses and refused to apologise. He was fined £25.

The case is not unique: Port Talbot referee Gerard Lewis once reported the Stoke City manager, Tony Waddington, at London's Liverpool Street Station for allegedly criticising Gerry's refereeing as they left the train following a Stoke match at Ipswich. The disciplinary committee of the FA took no action ...

*   *   *   *   *

Don't smile please. I once took the name of Bristol Rovers full-back Phil Bater in a match against Shrewsbury for smiling. In a dissentful manner, of course.

* * * * *

The goal that got away: Cardiff City v Wolves, pre-season friendly 1979. Did the ball hit the stanchion in the goal and bounce out when City's Ronnie Moore scored? As a referee, I said that I did not give a goal because I had not had a clear view of the ball, and neither had my linesman. Wolves players had already complained. Cardiff City secretary Lance Hayward denied later to the press that the floodlights were not working. Now, I confirm that I asked for the lights to be switched on but was told by Lance that the man in charge of the lights had not turned up. It didn't look good for me when I read Karl Woodward's report in the *Western Mail* next morning but I felt it right at the time that the club was not severely criticised. So now you know why we played in near darkness.

* * * * *

Friendly nonsense 1: Some referees actually tout for business for those pre-season friendlies, to such an extent that once when Cardiff City wanted me on another occasion Lance Hayward wrote to ask me to apply for the match as they had already received one application from another referee. No way: if a club secretary wants me for a friendly, he can ask me. I'm not going cap-in-hand to him, and I didn't.

Friendly nonsense 2: Even if you are asked, that doesn't mean that everyone is happy. I once found myself in the middle of a storm between the Merthyr Tydfil club and the Merthyr Referees' Society, because the club had asked me to referee a friendly match with Middlesbrough. The local society wanted their own men to referee and to run the lines. Seems I couldn't keep away from trouble even close to home.

* * * * *

Ambition achieved was when I refereed at arguably the most revered ground in the world: Cardiff Arms Park, otherwise known as the National Ground. The match was between soccer and rugby stars in the Welsh Rugby Union Centenary Year, the rugby team included J.P.R. and J.J. Williams, Gareth Edwards, Phil Bennett, Gerald Davies, Tommy David, Bobby Windsor, and John Bevan amongst others. Although I did for once try desperately hard to let a particular team win, the rugby lads lost

7-4. My regard for the hallowed ground was such that I actually knelt on the turf.

* * * * *

Second-class citizen 1: My grateful thanks to good friend Salah Ouri, a manager at the Royal Lancaster Hotel in London. On the eve of my League Cup Final between West Ham and Liverpool in 1982, referee and wife, linesmen and wives had been booked into a hotel just off Bayswater Road. It felt as if it were in the middle of Bayswater Road, such was the traffic din. I wondered whether the players were having to put up with such conditions and decided to move rooms. The helpful manager could offer no alternative, so we moved hotels, to the Royal Lancaster, where Salah greeted me as 'the greatest referee in the world', almost certainly because he was a QPR fanatic and I was shortly to referee one of their games.

George Readle at the Football League took great exception to the move but, since then, my colleagues in more recent League Cup finals have been booked into the Royal Lancaster. I believe that even the management committee have had their meetings there: so I've done some good.

* * * * *

Second-class citizen 2: Because the FAW are reluctant to pay overnight expenses, I often used to stay with some very close friends of many years, Barry and June Williams, in Wrexham when I had a match in North Wales. This caused Jimmy Scoular to have some grave doubts about me when he was manager of Cardiff City, who were playing at Chester in the Welsh Cup: he watched me with great suspicion when I left the train at Wrexham, and greeted me with even more suspicion and lots of smirks at the thought of my supposed infidelity to Beryl when I caught the same train as the Cardiff team next morning, looking somewhat dishevelled and bleary-eyed. Jim, if you read this, I promise you it was all innocent: I had been up in the attic in my pyjamas all night helping the Williamses to repair a burst pipe. Honestly. I can let you have their 'phone number if you want verification.

* * * * *

Breaking and entering: Barry was guilty once of aiding and abetting when I broke into the Wrexham ground quite unlawfully one night. I was due to referee an FA Cup replay against Tottenham and, when I arrived at Wrexham the night before the game, Barry told me the ground would be hard through frost. Tottenham had requested a decision by 10 the next morning, and so we tried, to no avail, to find someone in the

Wrexham management to open the ground that evening for a preliminary look. So we went off down to the ground, found a hole in the fence near the supporters' club and, after going all round the terraces, found access to the pitch where the moon was so bright that we could have been under floodlights. A ground staff member had left a fork in the ground and I was just able to pull it out but quite unable to put it back. Barry shouted from the deserted terraces 'What a referee', and for once I responded to the barracking – 'If you're not satisfied with the refereeing, go home.' We did – but I often wonder what would have happened had we been caught. I certainly must have looked sheepish next morning when I asked John Neal, the Wrexham manager, about the state of the ground.

* * * * *

After he had left Wales, John Neal wrote in the Chelsea programme of 6 November 1982, in respect of a recent Chelsea match I had refereed: 'Clive Thomas gave an immaculate performance, using the advantage rule to perfection and handling the players in just the right way. His man management is excellent and he is prepared to talk to the players instead of, or sometimes before, throwing the book at them. And this is the difference between the really top referees and the ordinary ones. Many good referees of Clive's stature have recently retired and are now given the job of assessing. I think they would be much better employed going on to help and teach new referees just coming into the League and passing on their experience.'

I couldn't agree more, John. But the League don't seem to see it that way and neither does the training committee of the Association of Football League Referees and Linesmen.

* * * * *

The training committee and the association have come under tremendous fire from former World Cup referee Kevin Howley, who quit as an assessor because of a 'general revulsion' against all the things that have spoiled football. He knocked the association, knocked the players, and complained that referees were becoming robots. 'The game is losing ground fast', he told the *Daily Mail*. 'Sadly, today's game is governed from offices whereas the best products come from workers. Football's workers are referees. So I say to football, "Get off their backs and let them get on with it."' Nice going, Kevin.

* * * * *

Trial by television: In an article headed 'The unacceptable role of television', in the Autumn 1981 issue of *Football Today*, the official quarterly of the Football Association, Allen Wade wrote that towards the end of the season 1980–81, 'television revealed another side of its power – a power for which it has no mandate from the public or sport – its power to act as judge, jury, public and press. The ruthless way in which Clive Thomas was pilloried, not only over his alleged error in awarding a penalty against Spurs in the semi-final of the FA Cup but also by dragging up other controversial decisions, surely has to be unacceptable.'

Allen went on to say he believed I was right in most of my judgements, as I saw them at the time. That should be an end to it. 'If that isn't the case, then *all* decisions on the field must be subject to action replay at *every* match and who is to interpret what the camera shows?

'Unfortunately for Clive Thomas he has to decide and he has never shirked decisions. I know that Clive Thomas is one of the best half-dozen referees in the world and I would sooner have his judgement than television's.'

He concluded: 'It will be a sad day for football when we concede the judgement of football to television (or the judgement of anything else for that matter). We may be in danger of doing so almost by default if we are not careful.'

I wrote to Allen: 'With respect to the BBC, there are two people I hate at the moment and Jimmy Hill is both of them ...'

In fact, I can't really complain, because television has generally proved me right. And, Jim, I didn't really mean it – I am sure you still have much to offer the game.

*   *   *   *   *

Finally, as we prepare to take the field for the second half of the book, an article by Malcolm Macdonald in the *Daily Mirror* on 11 March, 1983, which was headed 'Courts to act if the refs won't'. Malcolm based his piece on a tackle by Tottenham's Graham Roberts on Clive Whitehead of West Brom and warned that 'if referees don't give protection, the courts will'. He went on to ask what player is going to have a leg shattered, lose wages and his job through the stupidity of another player. 'There is only one way to stop the farce before it begins: clamp down on referees – insist they listen to the pros – get their bosses to revoke the stupid rule of "not being sociable at clubs" – and appoint Clive Thomas as a supremo. Thomas isn't everyone's favourite. But you always knew what he was going to do. He stuck by the rules. He would be perfect to act as a flying doctor, ready to patch up any quarrels between club and referee. Clive could break down barriers, knock down doors and talk with sense. Football is on collision course.'

Malcolm could also break down barriers. I have tremendous respect for him as one of the game's forward thinkers. We badly need people like

Malcolm, Terry Venables, Howard Wilkinson, Graham Turner, Frank Clark and Alan Durban, all managers with real talent, to lead us into the future. Mind you, even they can on occasions be affected by the stresses of their position. In October 1983, Terry Venables approached me at half-time in the vitally important QPR–Liverpool match to question whether I 'was being fair to both sides'. Nevertheless, if I had not written this book for a year or two, they would, I'm sure, have found a way into the next chapter.

·16·
THE GOOD...

Lawrie McMenemy should immediately be appointed General Manager and Public Relations Director of the Football Association, a post just made for his type of personality, charm, knowledge and ability and a post badly needed for the benefit of the game. This would stop administrators and council members commenting on subjects clearly outside their knowledge.

I start this chapter with the large ex-Guardsman because his is a style which any would-be manager might emulate and because, having spent much of the book so far in criticism, I would like now to mention some of the personalities who maintain and enhance the standards of the game and to whom youngsters can look with admiration.

Lawrie is one of the most diplomatic managers in the game and one of the most liked; he has a tremendous following on television, particularly among women, and is a most understanding and human being. Yet he has a tough streak. On one particular night after Southampton had lost at home, I went as usual to his office for a chat and had been joined by some journalists when we heard Lawrie approaching after he had spoken with his directors. He's such a big man that you can hear him coming half a block away and I rushed to sit behind his desk on his huge seat, acting as if I were chairman of his board. 'The game was a shocker, McMenemy has to go', I joked as he came in. 'Get out of that chair, Thomas', he said. 'You'll never be big enough to sit behind my desk.' He then laughed it off and we were able to discuss the game, as ever, with no holds barred.

I have mentioned earlier a match when Arsenal won 1-0 at the Dell on New Year's Day on a pitch made suspect by frost. Early that morning, my friend Brian Truscott, the Southampton secretary, 'lent' me seven of their apprentices to have a five-minute four-a-side trial match to test the surface. My team won 1-0, incidentally, perhaps because I refereed and played. I decided the other and bigger match was on. Lawrie was not there for the inspection and trial, possibly because he would always accept my decision, but as I was driving home that afternoon with my wife – the match was in the morning – I heard Lawrie being interviewed on the radio. Should the game have been played? If Clive Thomas said the ground was fit, then it was fit, he replied. He made no mention of a suspected hand-ball that brought the winning goal for Arsenal: a true sportsman.

There is, in fact, much to admire among managers in the game. I would also single out Brian Clough, who to my mind should have been made team manager of the England side but who was overlooked by the Football Association: one of their bigger mistakes.

Cloughie, unlike McMenemy, is not the greatest of diplomats and has many enemies, which may explain why you do not need a private detective to discover the reasons for the FA's failure to appoint him. It is obvious that he would never be tied down by people within the establishment. Brian's track record, however, spectacularly illustrates his class: I have no doubt that with total financial support he would have been the greatest manager of all time. Yet when I first met him, I thought he was an ignorant so-and-so.

It was just before a Derby County–West Brom match over a Christmas period when referees were still going into both dressing-rooms before a match to tell the players what was expected of them and to define how they would referee. As I was leaving the Derby room Brian, who had been lying on a table during my talk, said, 'I hope you do better than the fellow with us last week.' As he hadn't moved from the table, I asked him, 'And who are you?' He jumped up quickly and said he was the manager of the club. 'Next time you speak to me', I said, 'you'd better be standing up'.

I went back to my dressing-room. Minutes later, there was a knock on my door. It was Clough. 'I like the way you talk', he said. 'Keep on like that and you'll be the best in the world.' We've had our good times and our bad times since then.

I remember the day Forest were due to play Leeds in the second leg of a League Cup semi-final after the first game had not been played in the best of spirits. Brian was buoyant as we had a cup of tea in his office during the afternoon: he was so sure of winning the second leg that he invited Beryl and me to the final. When I declined because I had a company conference on the same day, he volunteered to come to speak at the Friday evening session because 'it's the team that's playing, not me, and I can see them later on'. However, back to that game with Leeds, and his view that Forest would 'hammer them because we have a full-strength side and they have some injuries'. I knew he had never forgotten his forty-five brief days as manager of Leeds United and I expected tension.

There was such a fog and a freeze-up that evening that I had to cancel the match. Instead of arguing, as I thought he might in view of what he had told me that afternoon, he said simply, 'Clive, you'd better ring up your wife and explain. You can't drive home in this.'

During my career I have spoken to Brian about my performances on many occasions. It was he who recommended a few years ago when I was having a particularly bad spell with the authorities that I should not pack up the game but stay in there and fight it out. His advice has been crucial, always constructive and optimistic, which is no doubt why he extracts the best from his teams.

Referees know that Clough is one of the few managers who will invariably back their decisions. After matches he used to come in to ask what players had given me trouble in the game. I knew he would deal with them. But referees were, alas, quick to forget after they had agreed with a speech at an Association of Football League Referees and Linesmen's Conference in which he told them to back me all the way. I also knew that Brian would never let me down whenever I was trying to raise money during my involvement with the boys' clubs. Every time I asked him to attend an event, he said yes.

You can't talk about the good things of football without coming round to Liverpool. The late Bill Shankly, Bob Paisley, the chairman John Smith, the secretary Peter Robinson and the supporters ... every aspect of their game, even if one or two of the players are not of quite such admirable cast.

Bill Shankly was a wily old bird. On one occasion I had the temerity to send off his beloved Tommy Smith in a match at Maine Road, Manchester. Smith had behaved quite incredibly foolishly, arguing long after the incident – a free kick I had awarded to Manchester City. He continued abusing me while a corner was taken, while the ball went out of play and while Clemence went to retrieve the ball. 'Another word from you', I warned Smith, 'and you'll be off'. I suspected he wouldn't stop and I was right. Because I had cautioned him earlier in the game, I had no option but to dismiss him. It was difficult for the Liverpool players to understand because they had not heard Smith's complaints. 'Please Mr Thomas', asked Emlyn Hughes in his usual polite way, 'would you tell me why you are sending him off?' 'For continual dissent', I said, and Emlyn, knowing me well, stopped any other player from pursuing it.

After the match, there was a knock on the door. My linesman opened it and I heard the Scottish accent, 'Errr, I would like to speak to Mr Thomas.' I yelled, 'That's Bill Shankly and it's the first time you've ever called me Mr Thomas. It's always Clive and if you're not prepared to call me that now, I'm not speaking to you.' He wanted to know why his boy had been sent off, and when I told him he said, 'Right, Clive, I'll fine him.' He probably did. But he also fought like hell at the FA disciplinary hearing when the decision was a two-match suspension. His appeal lasted more than three months, at which point the suspension was confirmed. But Shanks had achieved his aim: Smith played in a European Cup final while the appeal meandered on.

During that appeal, incidentally, Bill was cross-examining one of his directors who had been called to give evidence. Maybe they had not done their homework correctly but Bill was becoming a little warm under the collar as he tried to make sense from the director with the usual help of a Subbuteo board showing the stand in which he had been sitting. Exasperated, Bill finally pointed and said, 'And that's the stand ... and this is the bluidy car park, where you come in with your Rolls-Royce.'

Who better to succeed Shanks than Bob Paisley, a much less flamboyant character and nothing like so outspoken, but who nevertheless was always prepared to have a few private words and offer a bit of advice and help. Not just for referees either: on one visit to Anfield I was showing round a colleague and his sixteen-year-old son. The Liverpool dressing-room door was locked but Bob left his lunchtime sandwiches and flask of tea not only to open the door but to chat with my friends for quarter of an hour.

Both Bob and his henchman, Joe Fagan, who took over, were quick to let you know on the pitch what sort of game you were having. Generally their comments were worth noting. During one game at Southampton, they relayed through Emlyn Hughes the belief that one of my linesmen did not know what he was doing. They were absolutely right, too, and at half-time I told the linesman that I'd find a replacement if he didn't improve. He did – and I received a slight bow of the head in acknowledgement from Bob Paisley.

A totally different type of manager again, but one who stands out as one of the nicest, was Joe Mercer. Perhaps his gentle approach was the reason for the lack of trophies although I gather that Joe as a player was rarely passed. Joe and I had our differences but there was one time when be backed me up to the hilt. He was a director of Coventry at the time and his big centre-half, Larry Lloyd, was quite literally and regularly marking Manchester United's Pancho Pearson. I spoke to Lloyd and later cautioned him while I also had a quiet word to let Pancho know that I was aware of what was going on. Despite warning Larry Lloyd as we left the pitch at half-time that he would be off if he didn't cool it, the second half was only four minutes old when Pancho Pearson went sprawling yet again. I stopped play and, after Lloyd had gone through a Norman Hunter-like display of politeness by picking up Pancho and dusting him down, I sent him off.

After the match I was discussing football generally with the directors and their wives in the guest room when the subject of refereeing cropped up with Jimmy Hill, the man we love to hate.

He had a strange theory. Apparently, I should have been aware that

Larry Lloyd was having his first match after a long-lasting injury. He was also renowned as a slow player marking one of the quickest in the game, and I should have taken that into account. His remarks were greeted with rapturous approval by the assembled Coventry entourage: except, that is, for Joe Mercer, who sat in the corner without comment, while Jim expressed surprise that I had also 'threatened' Lloyd at half-time. I sought permission from Jim to answer his criticism. It was not my job to know who had been injured and who had not (although I did, in fact); next thing, I said, you'll be asking me who is having a row with his wife. I admitted that I had done my homework on players and knew that Lloyd was much slower than Pearson, which was why I had given him a helpful warning – not threatened him – at half-time. If the club wished to report me to the FA for threatening behaviour, they should go ahead but, for the life of me, I could not understand why someone in management did not give Lloyd the same advice, whether threatening or helpful. Larry Lloyd is very much a friend today.

As I was leaving, Joe Mercer said: 'Thomas, you took a chance coming into the lions' den but all credit to you for sticking to your principles.'

Joe always used to say in after-dinner speeches that I was the most brilliant technical referee, but he wished to God that they had never invented the notebook and pencil. I met him a season or two ago at a fourth division match at Sealand Road, Chester, where the 1,400 spectators and management seemed delighted to see me. So was Joe, and I thought, 'If it's good enough for Joe Mercer, it's good enough for me.' He said later, 'I watched you very closely today and it's good for the fourth division and their crowds to see a referee of your calibre. I was so pleased to see you not fetching out your book and pencil without losing any of the respect.' My respect for you is even greater, Joe.

Three other managers who should be sought out by any young referee, player or would-be manager wishing to learn about the game are Ron Saunders, John Neal and Frank O'Farrell. Ron's worried appearance does nothing to hide a worried man: over the years I have known him since that match when I took both Manchester teams from the field, I have learned that he has had reason to worry. Even when I was delighted to referee his testimonial match between Aston Villa and Birmingham, he looked worried: not at the amount of money he might be given but about the entertainment value of the game. But his knowledge of the game and his willingness to help others are of value to everyone.

As for John Neal, he is one of the coolest managers in the game. During one match with Bolton at Stamford Bridge, the big, rather cumbersome, if wholehearted Chelsea centre-forward, Colin Lee, was over-robust, and I had to caution him. Because I was concerned at the way in which Lee had responded, I tried to speak to John, his manager, after the match, but was unable to do so. I therefore telephoned John on the Monday to talk about the incident, as this was not the Lee I had previously known. 'Unfortunately you were not aware that Colin had one or two problems and it was certainly through these that he spoke to you as he did', said John. It is not your job to be aware of these things, he said, but he should have known better. That is typical of the cool way he manages his players. Maybe managing Chelsea, Middlesbrough and Wrexham, you have to be cool . . .

Frank O'Farrell, the former West Ham player now general manager at Torquay, is one of the finest motivators and thinkers in the game. Just because he is at the tip of the country does not mean he is a forgotten man. On the contrary, he is a good reason to have an appointment at Torquay. The advice he gave me many years ago in his broad Irish accent – and he knows better than most the problems I have had – I have always followed: be your own man. You may not receive the appointments you deserve but, far more important, you will be able to walk down the road with your head held high and sleep peacefully at night.

And what about players themselves? First of all, a man who has not once queried a decision, a man who has never moaned either about me or his colleagues, a man who is a credit to soccer but a man who may be just too nice ultimately to make his way in football management: Pat Jennings, whose behaviour on and off the field should be noted by every schoolboy, goalkeeper or not.

I was delighted when in 1982 I was invited by the BBC to contribute to a film they were making on his life. I travelled on the same aircraft as Pat to Belfast once, me on business, he to visit relatives. It was only a short journey, yes, but the opinion formed on the pitch was confirmed off it. I would rate him on a par with John Charles: a gentle giant.

I have never heard Pat blame his defenders when he has conceded a goal, rather more than I can say for Ray Clemence who, to me, often seems to take the view that it was someone else's fault. Peter Shilton, incidentally, lies somewhere in between. Those watching on television may be under the impression that he is playing hell with all and sundry, but he is not; he is not apportioning blame, but marshalling his ranks to make sure it does not happen again.

Then there is Trevor Francis, one of the most exciting and competent players in the game today. What a tragedy that he has been lost to English league football, because his skills are an enormous spectator attraction and his behaviour on the pitch impeccable, always respectful. He never queries a decision but equally is not too shy to ask questions: a model to youngsters in every way. He passed me once on the way down the M4 to Llanelli, where his wife comes from. A mile down the road, there he was beckoning me to stop, just to have a chat about the game. Trevor always wants to talk football. That's why he is a true professional.

Now try John Wile for size. He may not have been the most skilful footballer of the last decade, but he was certainly one of the most courageous captains. What he lacked in skill was certainly made up by sheer competitiveness and determination. He was having an outstanding semi-final for West Brom against Ipswich once at Highbury when he cut his head so badly that I gave him my handkerchief to prevent the blood streaming into his eyes. He then had to leave the field, I thought probably for good. No, within minutes he was back. By the way, John, I still have not had that handkerchief back – or are you still telling people it's the only thing that Clive Thomas ever gave you?

Another captain and respected professional who could be a blueprint for youngsters is David O'Leary of Arsenal. Maybe we got on well because I had difficulty in understanding his Irish while he had problems with my Welsh. A fatherly figure on the field and an inspiration to his teammates, he is tough and yet respectful.

Then there's John McGovern, a player of tremendous skill and tenacity who led by example, always immaculately dressed and a marvellous ambassador for his club when he was at Nottingham Forest, and for his manager. Phil Thompson of Liverpool was the idol of the Kop, and there can be no higher praise than that. I was privileged to referee his testimonial match at Anfield, at which I was disgusted by the lack of effort shown by Souness, who is frequently unnecessarily hard, and Dalglish, who should perhaps remember that they are star players and have a duty to reward the people who pay to see them as well as a colleague they are allegedly honouring.

Phil Dwyer, too. Who's he? I can hear them asking in the more rarefied areas of the first division. Phil, otherwise known as Joe, Dwyer is what professional football is all about. He has been with Cardiff City since he was an apprentice, I trained with him for many seasons, and I know full well his crunching tackles. Joe Dwyer does not know how to give less than one hundred per cent. His name may have found its way into the notebooks of several referees, while his villainy has been acclaimed and his parentage doubted around the countryside. During a Boxing Day derby with Newport County in 1982 in front of a crowd of more than 17,000, I had reason to shout at Cardiff's very promising goalkeeper, Andrew Dibble, for wasting time at a goal-kick. 'Don't be like that, Clive', said the redoubtable Dwyer. 'He's only a youngster.'

'That's what worries me', I replied. 'He may grow up to be like you.'

Quite seriously, though, he could do far, far worse than grow up like Joe Dwyer. If loyalty, determination, spirit and humour are to be admired, then look up to this one-club man.

A similar player was Stoke City's Denis Smith, who moved to York as player-manager. Denis would never accept that either he was beaten or that his club were. When he tackled, he tackled with every bit of effort; when he kicked, he kicked with every . . . Not that I condone kickers, but I'd rather have a hundred Dwyers or Smiths than the surreptitious types. He'd a sense of humour too, had Denis. In one match in which he was playing I pulled a muscle with only half a minute gone. Amidst jeers and cheers from the crowd, I collapsed on the ground. 'What's the matter, Thomas?' asked Smith. 'Tired already?'

Finally, possibly, a surprise inclusion but one has to speak as one finds. Bob Hazell was never the easiest of players to handle. Playing for Wolves against Arsenal at Highbury one afternoon, he was the first player I had seen blocking (not knocking) out Malcolm Macdonald for eighty-nine minutes. I awarded a corner to Arsenal and saw, just over the goal-line, Hazell attempt to strike a home player. Something must simply have snapped. I sent him off and, with Wolves in disarray, Macdonald headed in the corner. Rough justice? I believe that Bob learned a lot from the mistake and has never looked back since. I have refereed him many times since and on each occasion I would give him nine out of ten for ability and discipline.

On the other hand, some people never learn . . .

·17·

...AND THE BAD

It speaks volumes about Bobby Robson and his England side that I walked out a full quarter of an hour before the end of their important match with Denmark at Wembley in September 1983, hoping for a quick getaway after watching one of the worst and most gutless displays I had ever seen from a home international side. It gave me no satisfaction that the man in charge was one of the very few managers in the league I could not stand. Nor could I understand him: any man who airs his complaints to the press rather than talking man to man lacks courage in my view.

Robson first made a bad impression on me at a semi-final replay at Chelsea in April 1975. I took the names of four Ipswich players – Burley, Hamilton, Beattie and Wark – as they were losing to West Ham. After the match, during which I had disallowed a goal, Robson stated to the press: 'The referee was in absolutely no position to give an offside decision. The linesman was in a perfect position and he signalled it was a goal ... There were several FA administrators at the game and I challenge them to take action against the referee. If they don't, they are failing in their duty to professional soccer.'

Such an outburst by a manager does no good to the game. I would agree with Robson that the administrators failed to do their duty – but only by not taking a grip of him and giving him a warning. A member of the appeals committee that heard the players' case was Mr Bert Millichip, chairman of the FA, who appointed Robson to his England post. I wonder whether they said even a single word to Robson.

Some seasons later, when one of his Ipswich team had been sent off, Robson made another strange outburst, this time against Kevin Keegan, who was then playing with Southampton. I had the match the following season and I was ready for Robson to behave in the same manner. Luckily he didn't, but it is sad that you have to prepare, albeit with reluctance, for such outbursts. It is wrong, to my mind, to blame the referee, the opposition, anyone rather than your own shortcomings. I fear this attitude spread through the Ipswich team, too.

Robson's captain, Mick Mills, never seemed to forgive me for that semi-final replay, either. It's not that he says anything: the way he looks at me when a decision goes against him is sufficient to ensure that our relationship has never been good. Mills seems not to understand that it would have been easy for me to accept both the goals I disallowed in the semi-final but West Ham and, more importantly, I would have known that it was dishonest.

Whenever I refereed Ipswich thereafter, Mills would not speak to me, even at the toss-up. Right, I felt, if that was the childish way he wished to behave, so be it – but I would not tolerate a dissentful attitude to linesmen. The very next time I was at Portman Road, for an Ipswich Town/Nottingham Forest FA Cup replay, the home supporters acted as foolishly as Robson and his players. They didn't even send me to Coventry, but let me know full well what they thought as soon as I ran out on to the ground. It was not long before Mills showed his dissent at a linesman's decision and I rightly cautioned him, to the chagrin of the crowd. (A small incident in the second half: I had to caution another Ipswich player, took out my pencil but . . . no notebook, as I had left it in the dressing-room. I had to pretend to go through the motions and, later, found an excuse to go to the linesman and borrowed his. Happily, the incident was not picked up by Anglia television.)

But back to Mills. In my last season or two, he was gradually starting to acknowledge me. I wonder whether this was because he had moved to Southampton and had a manager with a more mature personality, or whether he had realised, belatedly, that Thomas would stand no nonsense.

Other players from the Ipswich side who should never in my opinion be near the England squad – they would not have been ten years ago – are Russell Osman and Terry Butcher. Butcher appears to have no particular skills other than to ensure that no one passes him. I would certainly have sent him off for one tackle during the World Cup in Spain. He committed a very typical professional foul to prevent a likely goal.

Now I'm not saying that these four, nor the other people in this chapter, have nothing to offer. They may be perfectly good husbands and fathers and remember their mothers' birthdays. But they are also people who by their attitude do very little to help the game and who should not be copied, I believe, by young people.

The criticism of Bobby Robson I would level also at the man who may be in line to be his successor. I refer to Watford's Graham Taylor, who in my experience is not senior management material though in view of the track record of the FA in their appointments he may be right for them.

I have had two major altercations with Taylor after he has criticised me to newspapermen. The first came when I was due to referee Leicester and Watford in the 1981–82 season in what could have been an important promotion match. Leicester's secretary, Alan Bennett, telephoned me on the Friday morning to say there was six inches of snow on the pitch and the match must be in doubt. Here was a chance, I thought, to try out again my belief that managers should participate in deciding whether the pitch was playable. I told Alan that I would be travelling to Leicester that afternoon to have a preliminary look at the ground but that I hoped a final decision could be made at 8.30 am on the Saturday in ample time to prevent the Watford supporters or team from travelling. Would he make arrangements for the Leicester manager, Jock Wallace, and a police official to be present at that time?

I then telephoned Watford and spoke to the secretary, Eddie Plumley, as Taylor was not available. Eddie passed on my message and Taylor phoned back to say he wouldn't come up to Leicester for the 8.30 inspection and would leave it to me. I pointed out that this was an opportunity to have the Football League ruling changed but he still declined as he was travelling with his team on the Saturday morning.

While I was having dinner at the Holiday Inn that evening with one of my closest friends from my army days, Tom Shield, Hugh Johns of ITV inquired whether the cameras should move to an alternative match, in view of the conditions.

Nearly everyone of importance was at the ground at 8.30 the next morning, except Graham Taylor. The police were concerned about the snow on the terraces; the groundsman, whom I had known for years, was for once non-committal because he didn't know what was under the snow. Jock Wallace was prepared for anything. To cut a long story short, apprentices, volunteers, Tom, Jock and myself started on the clearing. By 10.30 I was fairly confident we could play, so the news was conveyed to Watford and the League that a final decision would be taken at midday. We played. It wasn't perfect, naturally, but I have seen many worse pitches.

Imagine my surprise, then, when Graham Taylor was quoted as accepting my decision but wondering why such frantic efforts were made to get these matches played: not a word about his chance to help make the decision or even clear the snow. Was this a case of another manager just looking for excuses?

The Watford manager did exactly that in 1983 when his team were playing West Ham at Vicarage Road. Before the match, when the managers brought in their team sheets, I took the chance to speak to both Taylor and John Lyall. No dissent, I said, and, I made abundantly clear, no encroachment at free kicks, otherwise there could be cautions and sendings-off. If the four defenders in the wall encroached, yes, I'd send off all four if necessary. Both managers said 'Thanks, Clive, you'll have no problems with our players.' I didn't with John Lyall but I did with Taylor.

The game was only a minute old when a free kick was given to West Ham on the halfway line. Luther Blissett stood only five yards from the ball. I was thirty yards away, awaiting the kick, when Billy Bonds protested to me about Blissett, who would not move away. I ran back, the kick still not taken, and cautioned him, with the home crowd baying their disapproval. One of two things had happened. Either the manager had not conveyed my instructions to the players, in which case he had only himself to blame, or the player had paid no attention to the manager's warning.

Taylor had a press conference after the game and complained: 'You are playing to one man's rules. He just does things on the spur of the moment.' Not a word, of course, about my pre-match warning – I felt sick that a manager of repute, England material in that he was the person in charge of the youth side, should make such remarks without having the courtesy to speak direct to me. It is no good Taylor saying he is not allowed to either: he's done it before, even to the extent of bringing champagne into my dressing-room with his chairman, Elton John, when they won promotion.

I did, on the other hand, think at one time that John Bond might have a great deal to offer the game. Flamboyant, outspoken, forthright, yes, all of those things but, it appears, not a winner, perhaps because he allowed himself to become bigger than the game. We have had several upsets but the example I give of his difficult temperament concerns a Football League Cup second leg at the Dell, Southampton, in 1982, where torrential rain threatened a wash-out. Indeed, after twenty minutes, we had the worst downpour I have ever played in. I asked Joe Corrigan if he could see all right. 'At the moment I can only see you, Clive', he said, 'but don't stop the game because everyone's enjoying it'. Down the other end, I asked Peter Shilton, who said laconically: 'It's a bit wet, isn't it?' Any thought of abandoning the game thus disappeared because no player objected, and everyone floated on. Southampton won 4-1, the players received a standing ovation and I made sure that my linesmen went in at the same time to share it: everyone deserved to be part of it.

But waiting outside the visitors' dressing-room which we had to pass was the huge frame of John Bond. 'That was a disgrace', he said. I honestly looked round to see to whom he was talking. 'The refereeing was a disgrace', he said.

I could have ignored him. I could have reported him – and told him so. Instead I asked him to elaborate.

'How can I do that here?' he asked.

'I'll come into your dressing-room' I said, to his surprise. It was indeed a dangerous suggestion because his team had just been outclassed and most players look for excuses under those circumstances.

I told the linesmen to carry on to our dressing-room while I, still sodden, followed Bond into the City dressing-room and closed the door. The players were despondent but looked up in astonishment when they saw me. There was silence.

'Right', I said to Bond, 'you've just said I was a disgrace to refereeing. Substantiate it.'

He said a goal I had disallowed for an offence on Shilton was valid. I said Shilton was obstructed – and how could Bond have seen the incident clearly when he was forty yards away in the dug-out, in the pouring rain? He then asked why I hadn't booked Southampton's Chris Nichol after I had spoken to him in the first minute and told him he would be off if he committed the offence again. I told him I had said no such thing and, again, how the so-and-so could he hear from twenty-five yards or more?

The only criticism from a player came from Bond's son, Kevin, who looked up and said he did not think he should have been cautioned. I agreed with him: I had made a mistake: he should have been sent off.

There was no protest from players I respect like Joe Corrigan and Asa Hartford, though I have never in my career found them shy when they feel they have a fair complaint. Bond was now in a spot: in front of his players he had found a referee prepared to take him on. As I was leaving I told him, 'Get your players one by one into your office tomorrow and ask them what they thought. I am prepared to gamble eight out of eleven will say I had a good game.'

Within minutes Lionel Smart, chairman of the FA Referees' Committee, came into my dressing-room to say that was one of the finest performances of refereeing he had seen for a long time: which makes it even odder that I did not referee a Football Association cup-tie that season, as I told you earlier.

Bond later went on television and was asked by Gerald Sinstadt what he thought of the refereeing. 'Clive Thomas says he's the best', replied Bond. Gerry then asked him what he thought I did wrong. 'You saw the game, what do you think?' responded Bond. Gerry said he thought I had a good game and so did many others. 'That's up to them to judge', said Bond. I was interviewed separately by Gerry and told him that Bond would not enjoy any of my decisions in the eighty-nine minutes after Manchester City had scored in the first but that he must have been about the only person at the ground who did not enjoy the game. His remarks were typical of the man: to me it was another example of a manager clutching at straws to find consolation in defeat. The straw could not hold his weight and, within three months, he had left Maine Road in some disarray.

Of all the managers, though, I would not want anyone to take his lead from Don Revie. Many say that his Leeds United side of the seventies was the most professional we have ever seen in Britain. It depends on what you mean by professional. Each time I refereed Leeds United I experienced hostility, disobedience and dissent from players and from staff. Is that professionalism? During matches the players would shout comments on your performance and then claim they were talking about their colleagues. I had more trouble with that side than with any other twenty teams added together.

Billy Bremner was a player who would never admit that he had committed an offence. It took him a few seasons to accept that he could not control me. He might have been a small man but he had an awful lot to say and was no doubt the right sergeant-major to take charge of the infantry from the commanding officer, Revie, whose sole concern seeemed to be to win matches – or, rather, not to lose them.

In one particular match at Highbury on 2 December, 1972, I booked five Leeds United players in another attempt to clean up the game and they appealed of course to the FA. I was very pleased with the way the subsequent FA disciplinary hearing went under the chairmanship of the late Vernon Stokes, a solicitor who was trying to bring sanity to such hearings. Revie attempted to defend all and sundry and to impress the media at Lancaster Gate but the commission accepted my version of every incident.

Bremner's statement in defence of his caution makes fascinating reading for those who know or think they know the man. 'I asked the referee in a nice manner', it says in part, 'to please consult the linesman. All I wished was for him to appease everybody by doing so, and thus avoid bitter feelings. Had he been co-operative and then awarded a penalty he would have satisfied everybody . . .' Nice try, William.

In the last case, Alan Clarke thought he should not have been cautioned and also claimed that during the match I had kicked him. Pat Rice, the Arsenal full-back, would be a witness. Unfortunately Pat was unable to be present at the commission but the allegation by Clarke was clearly made to blacken my character. It was also making football history as no referee had ever been charged with kicking a player though, in junior leagues, there have been many examples the other way round.

I was absolutely flabbergasted when the accusation was made. Even though Clarke made his claim in his written defence I never seriously thought he would use it. I was further shocked when the chairman pointed out that it was not the FA's responsibility to judge this issue but only the caution. I contended that it was and wanted to be given the opportunity to disprove the accusation. Vernon Stokes refused and said that the Football League would be notified.

A few days later I received a letter from Dick Hall, secretary of the Association of Football League Referees and Linesmen, of which I was a member, pointing out that Leeds United had requested the association to take disciplinary action over the allegation but I told Dick that the matter was too hot for the association to handle. Stay out of it, I said, as I am going to take on Leeds United and Alan Clarke myself. I then contacted the League and asked Alan Hardaker what he intended to do. If the answer was 'nothing' I would take on Clarke privately, as I had taken legal advice from my cousin, solicitor Wayne Thomas. Hardaker later confirmed that a full inquiry would be held in Sheffield on 6 August, 1973, and although I was on holiday in Cornwall on that day, I was prepared to go to Sheffield. I had also been asked to attend a meeting in Stoke the same afternoon. I couldn't understand how the League believed I could attend both meetings but I was determined to be in Sheffield. Then, forty-eight hours before the hearing, Hardaker 'phoned again to say the Sheffield meeting was off. Leeds United had admitted that the allegations were unfounded. After telephone calls to Wayne, we told Hardaker we would accept the cancellation but only if we received a letter from Leeds United within twenty-four hours dismissing the allegation.

The letter duly came, dated 6 August, from Mr Keith Archer, secretary/general manager, of Leeds United FC. It read:

'I have to refer to letters which were sent to the Association of Football League Referees and Linesmen and to the Football League Limited in April of this year making certain allegations against you during the course of the League match, Arsenal v Leeds United, on 2 December 1972.

'I am instructed by my club and the player concerned to inform you that we wish to withdraw unreservedly the accusations made against you in the letter and to extend to you our apologies for any inconvenience or embarrassment which these letters may have caused.

'Copies of this letter have been forwarded to the secretary of the Association of Football League Referees and Linesmen and to the secretary of the Football League Limited, and I hope that you will accept the sentiments expressed herein and regard the matter as closed.'

I never thought anyone would go to such lengths to damage a person's reputation and career: if I had not been strong enough to fight, I wonder what would have happened.

Sadly, but because it is only human nature, I am now suspicious of Alan Clarke as a manager and, therefore, of his players. Indeed during a match between Plymouth Argyle and his Scunthorpe United in the autumn of 1983 (and he avoided bringing the team sheet into the dressing-room) I had to caution three of his United players in as many minutes, not for kicking but for offences involving lack of discipline. Even before his playing career was over, though, I was refereeing at Elland Road a match with Liverpool, who were a goal up with just thirty seconds left, when Tommy Smith fouled Clarke far out on the touchline, level with the Liverpool penalty area. Knowing Clarke as I did, I was not watching the ball as Terry Cooper took the kick and, as I had guessed, with the ball about ten yards away Clarke tapped Smith on the ankles in retaliation for the foul. Jack Charlton nodded the ball into the Liverpool goal but I was awarding the free kick for Clarke's sly infringement. There was predictable uproar. Television that night, however, showed the incident very clearly from behind the goal.

Revie, of course, was appointed manager of England, which must have set the game back twenty years or more. The Football Association with this decision deserved all they got; and no one can tell me they did not know Revie's background, because he had attended as many commissions as me.

Just one final point about that Leeds side. I cannot understand how a player like Paul Madeley could have been a clean fish in that murky water, an honest and quiet man who was vicious in neither word nor deed. And, in fairness, perhaps time has been a healer: Terry Cooper is certainly putting back into the game as much as he was able to take out. Without his enthusiasm in preaching the football gospel, Bristol City might well be in the Alliance League today.

Gordon Milne is another manager I can do without. He told Bill Anderson of the *Leicester Mercury* newspaper about my refereeing of the Leicester–Leeds United match on 9 September, 1982, that 'a perfectly good, entertaining game was ruined by the dismissal of Lynex and, with referees being given new interpretations vastly outweighing the situation, we must ask ourselves in which direction the game is heading . . . perhaps, at another ground, the decision could have caused a riot'. What he did not state was that I had warned both managers before the match that I would not tolerate encroachment at free kicks. I would do the normal things, cautioning the player the first time but sending him off if the offence was repeated.

I was surprised when Milne asked: 'Are you serious?'

'You know what I'm like', I said. 'If I say it, I mean it.'

He gave an example of four players in a wall moving forward. 'Would you honestly send all four off?' he asked.

'Yes.'

Incredibly, he then said we could be having seven-a-side football tonight and that the pitch was too big for that.

'How do you know?' I asked. 'Maybe we'll find out tonight.'

Sure enough, Steve Lynex encroached early in the game and, in the second half, committed another cautionable offence, so he had to go. He may have thought he had been harshly treated – but only if his manager had not passed on my clear warnings. It would be interesting to know whether any action was taken against Lynex by Milne for not adhering to his instructions, if there were any. If there were not, should action have been taken against the manager by his directors? Graham Kelly at the Football League, by the way, asked me to take no further action over Milne's comments. I didn't, but only with reluctance. Then again, Gordon Milne is hardly a winner, is he?

John Toshack, on the other hand, was a winner for a long time, both as player and manager. He is one subject on which I disagree with Brian Clough, who thought at one time that Tosh was one of the top managers in the game. Some would say that I am not competent to judge successful management but I have been at the top of my profession for many years longer than any manager in the Football League and I have seen them all come and go. I remember Tosh way back with Cardiff City, I trained with him and came to know him well. He was a referee's nightmare, not on the physical side because I am sure John would never kick anybody but because of his moaning. The result was that I never formed as good a relationship with him as with other Welsh players. He would complain bitterly about tight marking, and I would tell him not to be such a big baby.

His petulance may be his undoing. It's very easy to be magnanimous when you are riding high: to behave the same way on the downward path is not so easy. I have never seen Tosh as a general in charge of troops and his attitude towards referees and linesmen before he had been suspended from the trainer's bench by the FAW made me question his reaction to discipline. I could give you a list of linesmen who should have reported him for his comments from the bench: I hope only that he will have learned his lesson from his many experiences, good and bad, as manager of Swansea City.

At a regional referees' meeting at which he was guest speaker, I was very surprised that Tosh reaffirmed what he had told me on the telephone the day after the FAW suspension for his action in a match refereed by David Letts. Tosh said the referee had admitted at the hearing he had made a mistake in his report and that what he said was contrary to the linesman's evidence. He thought in view of this conflicting evidence some action should be taken against David Letts and wanted to write both to him and to AFLRL. After pointing out that David was a colleague of mine, I advised him to leave the matter alone as it was quite feasible that the referee would have a different view from a linesman – it proved there was no collusion. He might, I suggested, lodge an appeal with the FAW but that establishment had told him there was no right of appeal.

And what of the players? I suppose the most publicised of my battles was with Alan Ball and I am certainly not proud to say that I cannot remember the number of times I have cautioned or sent off this diminutive player. I am genuinely delighted now to claim him as a friend for he has been, despite his disciplinary record, a credit to the game to such an extent that I might have wished to include him in the previous chapter on the goodies, so much has he given and so much can a youngster learn from him.

Even Bill Shankly from Liverpool defended Ball from Everton at one disciplinary hearing (though he had by then moved to Arsenal) to no avail. Nor did the transfer make any difference. I cautioned him again at Highbury when he indicated that he thought a linesman was crazy. That was enough for me because I protect my linesmen whenever possible. I walked over to Ball and he said: 'You've been waiting for this, haven't you?' 'You never learn, do you?' I replied.

On the following Monday, I was leaving for a European match when I read the headline, 'Ball accuses Thomas of vendetta'. I reported him not just for the caution but for unjustified statements to the press. The Football Association duly took action and Alan apologised to the FA which was not, alas, publicised.

I never sent off Alan for anything other than dissent by word or action. Things changed dramatically when he went to Southampton. He was still the terrier snapping at everyone's heels, legally though, and always wanting the ball, to such an extent that I believe he was Lawrie's best buy, even better for the club than Keegan. Down at the Dell one afternoon, a linesman flagged for offside and Alan half turned with arm in the air as if to say, 'never'. I blew my whistle and said to him, 'Hey, that was offside, you know.' 'Sorry, Clive', he said and ran across to the linesman to apologise. The press put this down to good refereeing. To put the record straight, it was no such thing. Ball apologised on his own initiative. He was a changed Alan Ball, perhaps a more mature one. Many problems could perhaps have been avoided if a manager early in Ball's career – perhaps Alf Ramsey after that match all those years ago at Aberdeen – had shown understanding and firmness.

Somebody should have a similar word with two Manchester United players, Remi Moses and Norman Whiteside. I remember Moses at West Brom as an average player, with the usual firmness you expect in midfield, but at Manchester I was shocked at how he had changed. He was now tackling from some ridiculous positions with no chance of winning the ball and I told him so in no uncertain terms. 'Carry on like that and you'll not only be sent off but you'll break somebody's leg into the bargain.' What, I wondered, was Ron Atkinson feeding him on?

In one game I refereed at St Andrews, Birmingham against Manchester United, he was sent off, suspended and missed the FA Cup Final in 1983. As I say, someone, somewhere should take him to one side – along with Whiteside – and have a little chat.

That match at Birmingham was the first time I had encountered Norman in the middle. After watching him in the World Cup series where he was undoubtedly one of Northern Ireland's dramatic successes, I saw in him a player of immense ability, with colossal skills, but with an attitude that I dislike in a footballer so young. His tackling was far too robust and he was short on discipline. Someone must tell him that the game is bigger than he is for I would hate to see another George Best arise from Northern Ireland. Management has a lot to answer for in the tragic Best saga.

I'm also a little concerned about Brian Robson. Although I accept he is the best midfield man in the country, he goes into tackles where even saints would fear to tread, with no chance of winning the ball. The change has come within a year or so. But Whiteside, like Best, needs a father-figure as well as a manager. I wonder whether Ron Atkinson is the man for this role just as I wonder whether he will curb Moses or Robson.

One referee is reported to have described Ossie Ardiles as the most professional player he had ever met. That certainly is not my view: I have thought of him as an excellent player, yes. But Ossie, a little man, can still manage somehow to look down at you. His expression when not being rewarded for taking a dive after a perfectly clean tackle in itself justifies a booking – either from the Royal Shakespeare Company or from the referee. In his book *Ossie – my life in football* he has apologised to me for an outburst once when I gave a penalty. 'I called him every bad name I had learned in England and should have been sent off', he said. It is typical of him to make such a statement after the incident: every pro knows that if he deliberately swore at me for whatever reason, he'd be down the tunnel without even being asked his name. This particular player would never have the courage to swear at me – and didn't.

Ardiles was fortunate I did not send him off – and not for swearing – in that controversial semi-final between Tottenham and Wolves at Hillsborough and, if he had been, I doubt whether Spurs would have gone on to win the Cup. He was involved in a tangle with George Berry. The two sized each other up, then Ardiles was said to have queried Berry's race and legitimacy: Berry was alleged to have answered with a mouthful, but not of words. Certainly an offence was committed on each side. I told them what I thought without mention of race or liquid response and in my wisdom let them stay on the park.

Someone who stayed on the pitch when I would have sent him off if I had seen the incident was Sammy Nelson, the former Arsenal full-back. He not only took the view that nobody would pass him but ignored any advice that you gave him. On this particular day, though, Sammy Nelson had actually scored a goal against Coventry, an event rare enough for me to assume that he would be fully and lengthily congratulated by his colleagues. I turned away to the halfway line. After the match, I was invited to speak to the press but I could not think of anything controversial that had happened. 'Will you be reporting Nelson to the Football League?' I was asked. 'Why?' I countered. After scoring, Nelson had apparently run behind the goal and bared his backside to the crowd, as shown next day in photographs which quite genuinely shocked me. I never saw the incident so Nelson escaped censure for a most degrading offence, that was at the least ungentlemanly conduct and certainly brought the game into disrepute.

Another Arsenal full-back who will find himself in trouble if he's not careful is Kenny Sansom, a pity because I rate him as one of the best since Jimmy Armfield. The sooner that Kenny realises that he will never beat referees with a quick and sarcastic comment against a decision, the better will be his game.

Cantankerous rather than sarcastic is the word I use to describe two other players who have given the game so much in their respective ways. Step forward, firstly, Kenny Dalglish, who has all the talents, skills and entertainment value to have been in the 'good' chapter. He may be one of the greatest of players but he is also one of the most difficult to referee. I have had to caution him on a number of occasions, mostly for dissent, despite the fact that I have always tried to look after the ball players. The type of thing I have in mind occurred at an international in Belfast when Kenny received the ball when he was offside but ran on fully forty yards before stopping and leaving the ball where it was, after throwing up his arms in disgust. No lessons for the young here.

A further point about Dalglish which is not his fault: he is said to be the best screener of a ball in the game. Rubbish, I say. The FA manual, in referring to screening, does not say the player is allowed to stick out his arms and his backside. That is plain obstruction but too many referees cannot see it is breaking the law.

The other cantankerous man is Brian Horton, possibly the best captain in the Football League in many ways. It is a pity that he allows his over-enthusiasm to rule him with referees. He is so difficult that when the Luton manager, David Pleat, comes into the dressing-room with his team sheet, he will explain that Brian does not mean the things he says and asks that you do not caution him or send him off but merely tell him to get on with the game. David sometimes acts like a solicitor on behalf of his client and, knowing and respecting him as I do, he is not trying to con you but simply trying to help Horton. Brian is a master at controlling referees and the only way to deal with him is to make it clear that there is but one man in control of this game: me.

Finally, two other men who might have appeared in either of these two chapters. The first is Kevin Keegan, who has taken more dives than many an Olympic high-board gold medallist, but who is such a gentleman in so many ways that, with the exception of those penalty-seeking moments, he is a model for everyone.

The other is one of the really exciting players in today's game who may well be a driving force one day behind a revitalised England team. I have watched Steve Williams since his apprenticeship, I know that Lawrie McMenemy has worked on his fiery temperament and, as I write, there are certainly increasing signs of maturity. His position as captain should ensure steady growth.

I have worked on Steve's attitude to discipline for years. You name it, I've done it. I have chatted with him in a restaurant, explaining where he is going wrong on the field; I have spoken to him on the day of a match to give him guidance for the next ninety minutes; at the kick-off I have threatened and cajoled him. I wonder sometimes if I am fighting a losing battle though, because I am still not satisfied that he gives one hundred per cent co-operation on the field. There have been times when I have been cautioning him while Lawrie has been trying to defuse the scene from the touchline. Will he ever achieve his potential – and captain the full England side? I know no other manager, other than Lawrie – apart perhaps from Brian Clough, in view of what he was able to achieve with Kenny Burns – who could harness the talents and break in Steve Williams. He is a great player in prospect ... and it will be a great shame if he's not more careful.

·18·

WHISTLE WHILE
YOU WORK

Shortly after a close colleague, Colin Seal, had refereed a 1980 FA Cup
semi-final between West Ham and Everton – during which he awarded
Everton a disputed penalty and later sent off the scorer, Brian Kidd, to
earn himself a wave of criticism for his handling of the game – the thought
of taking the replay (it had been a 1–1 draw) clearly worried him. 'I feel
like a pilot who has been in an air crash and has had to climb back into
the cockpit', he confessed.

Depending on which newspaper you read, he was apparently a little
punchdrunk. 'I'm shattered and hurt by the criticism after the most
important match in my life. I feel like boxer John Conteh, regarded as a
complete failure', he told the *Daily Mirror*. And in *The Sun*: 'I feel as if I
have been ten rounds with Muhammad Ali. I'm on my knees, almost
out, but I must come back again. One mistake by me in the replay and
I'll be lambasted. I plead through your newspaper to the players and
public. Please give me a break. I'm a very honest person. If I make a
mistake, I do it honestly.'

Similarly, take the case of Alan Robinson, now a FIFA referee, who
has stated that he was nearly killed by the black crowd after awarding a
penalty while refereeing for the FA in South Africa. Later he temporarily
failed his FL referees' fitness test and broadly puts that down to the events
in South Africa.

A number of Football League referees take tablets before a match:
others have a tot of whisky to settle their nerves. I have a spoonful of
honey in a cup of tea. To me, if you can't stand the heat, you should get
out of the penalty area.

These stories illustrate the lack of what I believe to be the necessary
components of a good referee: fitness, the right attitude, skill, ability to
manage, will power and honesty. Give me a youngster who loves the
game and who has these qualities, or is prepared to acquire them, and I
will make him a Football League referee.

Naturally, the laws have to be known forwards, backwards and side-
ways – but this knowledge will be of little use unless the referee is fit. It is
essential that he has a regular medical to ensure he can last an hour and
a half, running approximately nine miles. I recall wearing a pedometer
once during a match between Chelsea and Bolton at Stamford Bridge in

order to help research at Cardiff Training College. I clocked 11.25 miles that afternoon, though in fairness I should point out that this included a ten-minute warm-up.

On my appointment to the World Cup in 1974, I was not totally satisfied with my overall fitness. So I scoured the country for someone who could really prepare me properly. I was fortunate to choose Tom Hudson, ex-Olympic athlete and director of sport and physical education at the University of Bath. I not only went to Bath weekly for three months before the competition but also received from Tom a special programme for the duration of the finals themselves.

To quote a German, Helmut Schoen, from his paper at a UEFA conference for leading referees in 1976: 'We take it for granted that top-class referees undergo an adequate physical training to be able to keep up with today's football. One of the assets which make a top-class player is the physical fitness gained through hard training. As a consequence the same is necessarily required of a modern referee. Especially today's fast game with its ever-changing actions of play requires that the referee … is able to keep up with the pace of the game. Research shows that referees, particularly in Britain, have little knowledge of how to prepare themselves for today's modern game.'

Helmut Schoen was absolutely correct. It is only during the past four or five years that the Football League has brought in a fitness test that every League referee has to pass. Yet as a FIFA referee I have been tested every year for some eighteen years, one of the few examples of positive thinking by FIFA. UEFA have no such test, and it shows: many referees I have seen in European football would certainly not pass a FIFA test.

The FIFA 'exam', known as the Cooper Test, operates like this:

Minimum Requirements

COOPER TEST: The number of metres run over level ground for the duration of 12 minutes (style of running optional)

25–39 years . . . . 2300 metres
40–50 years . . . . 2000 metres

Basic values of Cooper:

Age	18-29	30-39	40-49	50-59
Very poor	-1750	-1500	-1250	-1000
Poor	1760-2240	1510-1990	1260-1740	1010-1490
In condition	2250-2750	2000-2500	1750-2250	1500-2000
Excellent	2760	2510	2260	2010

400 m. run (track) .... 75 seconds
50 m. run (track) .... 8 seconds
shuttle run 4 × 10 m .... 11.5 seconds

Normal weight:

$$\text{Weight} \quad \frac{\text{height (cm)} \times \text{av chest measurement (cm)}}{240}$$

The chest measurement is calculated by measuring over the mamillas and is the arithmetical average between maximum inhalation and exhalation.

The Football League test is taken in the middle of July, which could mean that a referee is fit in the middle of summer but could then, in theory at least, enjoy himself overmuch on holiday and not be toned up for the beginning of the season. It is difficult, I appreciate, to choose an optimum time for the test, but in my opinion there should be a 'refresher' in January when matches are more crucial, grounds are heavier and total and mental physical alertness is required.

I also believe that backward-running should be introduced into the test. I must query the research done in 1982 which gave the following figures for a Football League referee's work rate:

Walking	1309 yards
Jogging	2939 yards
Sprinting	382 yards
Running backwards	1024 yards
Aggregate	5656 yards

The aggregate is just over three miles. H'mm!

The tests themselves have their moments of farce. I remember taking the eyesight section one year when the examiner pointed at a car, for me to read the number plate at twenty yards. 'That's my car', I said. 'That's all right', he replied, 'it does not state in the regulations *whose* car number you have to read'.

Fitness is crucial. Without it, none of the other necessary attributes will be of great use. I was caught out once. I don't know what Tommy Docherty and Tommy Kavanagh fed the Manchester United team before a match with Aston Villa in 1977 but they came out like racehorses. By half-time I was shattered, and foolishly said so to Lou Macari as we came off for the interval. 'How long are you going to keep it up?' I asked. 'Right to the end', he replied, 'and if you can't keep up with us, hand over to your linesman'. I was not surprised that United went on to win the cup that season.

I train the day after a match, which is not the norm. This habit was first suggested to me by Tom Hudson, but I also learned its value from the German national side during the European Championships one year. They finished a match with Holland at about 11 pm local time and were back training at 8.30 the next morning. I don't think there are many British players who would welcome such stringent discipline.

For my part, I have an annual physical with Graham Jones, medical adviser for the FAW, and I am also a patient of Gordon Latto, a former Harley Street doctor now at Caversham, who checks me about three times a year and who changed my pre-match diet by suggesting honey and salads. My job with OCS means a very early start to the day, as I have described, with the result that I am often to be seen jogging around the cliffs near Porthcawl at six in the morning. The milkman laughs but it is worth it.

Ever since my early days as a referee on the mountain of Blaengwynfi, I have maintained that it is essential to have the right attitude, starting with the necessity of being at the ground in plenty of time to discuss your instructions with the linesmen. Some referees seem more concerned when they arrive that their wives or girlfriends have decent seats, apparently placing more importance on the social scene than the game itself. In a fairly recent Division One match, I had started to speak with my linesmen about an hour before the match when the reserve linesman came in with his ten-year-old son. I suggested as diplomatically as I could that his son should leave and he reluctantly agreed, but only if he could make sure the lad was in his proper seat. He therefore left while I continued my instructions. A month later, the editor of a Referees' Association magazine sent me a copy of his monthly issue and apologised for a story that had been slipped in while he was away. Yes, it was an article by the reserve linesman, criticising Clive Thomas and saying that he felt he was left out in the cold by being excluded from the pre-match discussions. He never said a word about his son and his own unprofessional approach.

The correct attitude to a game, then, starts long before the first whistle.

I have never actually gone to a game determined to get to grips with an individual, but I certainly do my homework and work out how I might deal with particular players in particular circumstances – which is as much man management as it is correct attitude. The management of players is just as important as the management of employees in my job as an industrial relations controller. Leadership qualities, then, are important, along with good communication, firmness, fairness and consistency. Common sense – the magic eighteenth law about which they all preach – comes into it too, but I believe that too many referees hide behind the rules in order not to give decisions at all. Such is the 'establishment' referee, the robot referee, the one who before taking a decision worries about the likely establishment view. He is the one not to be trusted. The eighteenth law should be used sparingly or the ultra-professional player will take advantage of you.

These ultra-professionals have to be watched all the time. They will use every piece of gamesmanship – encroaching, gaining ground at throw-ins, appealing to the crowd, feigning injury, taking dives. They do nothing but harm to the game and, yes, I have watched them and remembered them to make sure they did not get away with it the next time. I'd rather have the physically-powerful player any day: his job may be to intimidate the opposition, the referee and the linesmen alike, but at least you know exactly where you are with him. In fact, he may not even be on the field. He could be on the bench.

One or two quick stories to illustrate what I mean. Firstly, let me introduce you to that white-haired piece of Irish blarney, the former Manchester United trainer, Tommy Kavanagh. Before a match between Manchester United and Leeds, who were then managed by the admirable Jimmy Armfield, a man who was possibly too honest for the game in that he left it to become a BBC commentator, there was a dispute over the pressure of the ball. In the dressing-room Jimmy Armfield refused to accept it, and Kavanagh asked me to check the pressure. Unlike many other referees, I have never checked the ball with a pressure gauge or measured it with a little tape and I had to tell Kavanagh that I didn't have one.

'Never mind', he said, 'we could beat this lot with a tennis ball'. That was not the sort of comment to make in front of another manager.

Kavanagh was a nightmare for linesmen, as he usually offered his opinions throughout a game. I had a match at Birmingham once when a linesman came in at half-time and said, 'He's at it again'. I told him to let me know if it happened during the second half. It did. I ran up to Kavanagh, took his name, and told him, 'If you continue, I'll put you and that bucket of water of yours out in the car park.' This may be strong talk but it is the only language that some people appear to understand.

Oddly enough, a bucket of water also featured in a match between Aldershot and Doncaster Rovers in March 1973, when I had approached the game with quite the wrong attitude. It was during the experimental but successful period when I had the same two linesmen for a season, and possibly I thought we were above this particular fourth-division fixture. Jim Sims and Gerry Faulkner told me quite bluntly at half-time where I was going wrong and I accepted their comments because I respected them.

About two minutes from the end of the match, big Maurice Setters, who was then the Doncaster manager, ostentatiously threw a bucket of water on to the pitch while I was cautioning one of his players. Jim Sims rightly drew my attention to the incident and I went smartly across to Setters on the trainer's bench.

'Are you trying to be clever in throwing that bucket of water on to the field?' I asked.

'No, Clive', he said. 'With only two minutes to go, what was the reason to take a bucket of water back into the dressing-room?'

'All right, clever boy, but for the next two minutes, I will be watching you.'

'Thank God you're watching somebody', he retorted, 'because you haven't watched anything for the last eighty-eight minutes'.

Wrong attitude on my part ... and I got what I deserved.

As I have said, it is a pity the experiment of the 'permanent' linesmen was shelved. There were so many examples of three good teams on the field being much better than two good sides with a referee and linesmen playing against each other.

It is quite obviously of prime importance for a budding referee to know the laws. It is also of importance for him to know the game – and that is a difficult subject. I would recommend that every referee should have played the game in some capacity, even those hopeful sixteen-year-olds who may follow my path. It is good that they should have had the experience of winning and, more important, losing, with good grace; it is good that they should have had the feeling of running down the line, ball at feet, and of being tackled fairly but perhaps being hurt and not expecting a free kick because of it; it is good that they should have heard the magic sound of ball hitting net only to hear the referee's whistle blow for offside against a colleague.

I was fortunate that I had reached a level of competence in the professional game before my injury and I am therefore one of the very few referees who have played for a League club. I firmly believe that this is a nonsense: we should see more footballers taking up the whistle at the end of their playing time. It is totally outdated and unprofessional of the football authority to insist that a referee must have ten or twelve years in minor leagues before he can become a League referee – which, of course, bars just about all ex-players.

I do know the problems, though. Most players during their careers have been with at least two clubs, and it would be wrong for them to be involved in matches concerning those teams, which would lead to considerable administrative difficulties. I should not, for example, have refereed a match concerning Norwich City, although I did so on just one occasion. The *Stockport Express*, in its wisdom, headlined an article 'League Cup boob: Ref is ex-Norwich' when I was appointed to referee the match between the two teams. 'In the League's view this was a piece of highly irresponsible reporting, a deliberate attempt to whip up anti-referee feeling and a story that did not justify the headline used', reported the Football League. Actually, I don't think I should have been given that game. But that was not the reason I booked two Norwich players.

But I was talking about knowledge of the game. It certainly helps a referee when positioning himself for possible breakaways, though even the best of us can be caught out at times. For example, it takes me a good ten minutes of a fourth division match to understand the particular skills. Where you might in the top leagues expect player A to pass to player B, this does not necessarily happen lower down.

Similarly, the consistent strikers of long balls, like Hoddle, Brooking, Dalglish and Robson, can give the referee hell in switching play quickly and to a great distance. The greatest of these was undoubtedly Bobby Charlton. Just about everything has been written about Bobby but on the field he was a right moaner – for the right reasons. He simply wanted the game to flow without stoppage. I'm sure if he had had his way, he would have taken all the goal kicks, throw-ins and free kicks, and to hell with the referee: not in a nasty way, but rather as we didn't need referees back in Treorchy when we played three or four hours a night.

It never occurred to me that I might be a favourite of Bobby's, and it was therefore a double privilege when I was invited to referee his testimonial match at Old Trafford against Celtic. Bobby, naturally, was a great advocate of the advantage law, and I sincerely believe that my knowledge, skill and experience have made me one of the best at allowing the advantage when others might choose the easy way and blow up. Yet I am still jealous of my rugby colleagues down in Wales, for the way their rules allow the game to proceed for some time before they need bring play back to the original spot of the offence. Soccer authorities should look again at this.

Given expertise and knowledge, given a correct attitude, fitness and total honesty and will power, that leaves only man management, a particular skill which has to be worked at, and the necessity of which is not always appreciated.

I quote from the assessor's report on an incident which took place during the match I refereed between Birmingham City and Manchester United on 15 January, 1983: 'I would ask you to consider whether it was really wise to get so deeply involved in the incident with the Birmingham manager. The problems which can result from an official making personal contact with a player – e.g. by putting an arm round his shoulder whilst talking to him – are generally recognised. Would you not agree that this principle should also be applied to managers and trainers? The gentleman concerned was momentarily very emotional and a nasty incident could have developed.'

Ron Saunders was the Birmingham manager who was said by the assessor to be 'very emotional'. The Birmingham goalkeeper had been injured but, when I queried whether he was all right, he nodded and I allowed play to go on. As it happened he was clearly in pain and the trainer came round the touchline to check with him. Ron Saunders was also worried and was at the edge of the field when I stopped play. I went across to him, put my arm round his shoulder as an old friend, and quietly told him to return to the bench.

In reply to my query of his comment, the assessor wrote further that he was pointing out the 'danger of the referee putting his arm round the manager's shoulder, culminating with a gesture which could have been interpreted as a push towards the "dug-out".' I was not amused, and wrote to the Football League asking whether I was to 'assume the comments made by the assessor were based on his experience as a Football League referee? The reason for asking this is extremely important for me to give my point of view.' More than a month later I had to remind the League that I had received no reply from them about this, nor indeed about two previous matches way back in January.

Graham Kelly replied: 'It is the relevance of the assessor's comments that should be of prime concern, not his previous status with the Football League.' I can understand the reply, because the assessor had never refereed in the Football League. But in that one small incident with Ron Saunders, I believe that I showed I had done my homework in knowing the man, I had shown man management in calming the situation and I had shown skill and experience. It was the assessor who lacked all these attributes.

But as we shall see in the following two chapters about other aspects of refereeing, such qualities are in no way vital to your progress in the game.

·19·
THE AFLRL – NO LONGER THE BEST

The objects of the Association of Football League Referees and Linesmen (AFLRL) are to regulate relations between the association's members and the Football League, including negotiating terms of service and ensuring close co-operation between the officers concerned on all matters affecting the control of Football League matches. Membership of the association is open only to referees (£30 subscription in 1983–84) and linesmen (£15) on the Football League list. Ex-referees and linesmen may become associate members. AFLRL, consisting of eight sections throughout England and Wales, is administered by a president, the immediate past-president, a secretary and a treasurer along with a member representing each section.

Tidy, isn't it? I had been a member for only two seasons of this élite organisation – élite because the members class themselves well above the Referees' Association lads whom you see on the parks and up the mountains in the lesser leagues – when I realised that its smooth surface could hide dangerous undertows. I was really quite honoured to be asked to organise the association's thirty-third annual conference: the feeling quickly faded when I found out that the section organising the jamboree, which this particular year was Wales, was expected to break even financially. We also had plenary powers to programme the weekend in conjunction with the secretary of the association. Nevertheless I looked forward to the meetings at University College, Swansea, on 5–7 July, 1968.

The first problem to be overcome was the relationship between the president, Stan Lover, the secretary, George Readle, and the president-elect, Leo Callaghan. To say they did not get on together would be to put it politely. However, as I was concerned that the name Thomas should not be connected with failure, the first thing I concentrated on was finding some money.

For the first time in the history of the organisation, I sought a sponsor. I was able to arrange a meeting with Godfrey Seager, then head of public relations at John Player, at the Europa Hotel in London. Out of courtesy I told George Readle and he immediately jumped on the bandwagon, also warning me not to inform Stan Lover. When I arrived at the hotel, I found Readle waiting in the foyer – and then in walked Stan Lover.

There was a heated exchange between the two of them and I have to say that Lover was right when he argued that he should have been told. That, however, was the secretary's duty, and I felt not in the least bit guilty as I left them to fight it out. There was no way they were both coming to the meeting. Within a few minutes Readle joined Godfrey Seager and me; he left the talking to me and John Player agreed to sponsor the conference.

It was difficult to persuade my executive to agree, as a few members were reluctant to become involved with a cigarette company, perhaps forgetting that about seventy-five per cent of referees smoked at the time! But the proposal was passed, and I was able to bring some new ideas to the conference – including keep fit displays, with the help of fitness fanatic Tom Hudson who was then director of physical education at Swansea University. We talked football refereeing, we demonstrated football refereeing, and Alan Hardaker and just about every member of the Football League management committee attended, along with their wives. Because the conference was a huge success (and it's not just me saying so: you should see the letters of congratulation) it was hoped that even greater things would follow. Sadly, though, there has never been another conference like it. I was asked to be chairman of the conference committee when it was due to return to Wales in 1984, but I had to decline: Big Brother, in the shape of the Football League, had arrived long before his literary equivalent.

Two good things did emerge from the conference. From a purely personal point of view, it could only be beneficial that my business contacts, as well as those in sport, now knew that I could organise such a conference. Secondly, not long afterwards, secretary George Readle left AFLRL to cross to 'the other side', joining Alan Hardaker at Lytham St Annes.

Each year in the association, a different president is elected, nominated by the sections, and during his year of office he and the secretary hold secret meetings with the Football League to ensure that the usual statement can be issued reassuring members that the two organisations continue their harmonious relationship. Of course it's harmonious, because our executive usually accepts what the Football League tells it. What else can they do? The secretary is an assessor, and the president invariably a referee or an assessor. If they were to argue, perhaps the assessor would have no games, while the referee might spend his time at Spotland, Rochdale, or Gresty Road, Crewe, or The Shay, Halifax, or other exotic palm-fringed resorts ... Of the ten years up to 1983, eight of our presidents have refereed in the FA Cup or League Cup finals. On the executive, assessors and linesmen outnumber, and can therefore outvote, referees.

The annual conference is now organised by the training committee, under the present chairmanship of Bob Hodgson, an associate member and ex-linesman who has never refereed a Football League match. He has the chance to invite his own committee members, these most recently being assessors – Ron Challis, Arthur Jones, Ken Ridden (whose post as national training officer for the FA should in my view have gone to the talented Jack Taylor, though Jack may conceivably not have had enough A-levels or something), and the new member, referee Keith Hackett. I understand that Keith accepted only because he thought I had also been invited.

Each section round the country has a training officer, whose duties are primarily to arrange an educational programme for his section for the year; yet these individuals have no say in the actual annual conference programme, although they of all people are aware of the problems at grassroots level. I had not realised this when I was asked to become training officer for Wales and I was delighted to accept the position: for only two months, however. I resigned in September 1982, pointing out that unless the association changed its system and made the training committee non-secret, then I was no longer interested. Curiously, there are executives on the association council who agree with me and yet nothing changes.

On the subject of training, I have made it perfectly clear to the Football League that this should be controlled from Lytham St Annes with ex-senior international referees going round the country to visit the section meetings to train referees and linesmen in all aspects of their trade.

I have to question the current training methods. In Wales, for example, training is virtually non-existent: discussion at meetings seems to be only about executive council meetings and administration when the biggest problem is that the Football League linesmen do not have the courage to convey their opinions. This was well illustrated by the appointment, for example, of Gordon Harrhy as chairman and Jack Flye as secretary in 1980. Both were assessors for the Football League and Welsh League and neither had been a League referee, although Jack Flye had officiated for ten matches in one season before he was swatted off the list for not being up to standard. No linesman would question those two officials at section meetings nor, indeed, any other assessor, for fear of reprisal. Interestingly, at the annual meeting in 1983 of the Welsh section, a nomination appeared against Jack Flye for the first time. I wonder whether this could have been because Mr Flye had just been removed from the list of assessors at Lytham?

My own problems with the association started late in 1978 when Terry McNeill of the *News of the World* sought my comments on British refereeing. He had received complaints from all over the country, and although two referees to whom he had spoken were highly critical they did not wish to have their names associated with an article. I was prepared to give my views and in the newspaper of 22 October, under the headline 'Thomas blows whistle on refs', I said our standards were slipping and 'it is time we got off our backsides and did something to improve ourselves, instead of waffling. All my association seems to do is talk about administration and appointments. Once, British referees were widely regarded as being the most efficient in the world. I would question very much whether that is the case now.'

The article raised many eyebrows and, on 5 November, there were some fireworks. I had just arrived home from a three-and-a-half-hour South Wales section meeting when Peter Jackson of the *Daily Mail* telephoned to say the AFLRL president, Ray Tinkler, had told him the association were asking the Football Association of Wales to charge me with bringing the game into disrepute because of the article. This puzzled me to say the least because at the meeting I had just attended my representative member on the executive council had not even mentioned the matter. I can only assume that it had been discussed by the executive council during the past week.

I then received a letter from the FAW, dated 6 November, to say that their attention had been drawn to the article written by Terry McNeill, and asking whether I had been quoted correctly in it.

On 9 November, I replied to the FAW secretary, Trevor Morris, that the piece was indeed a true reflection of the interview. Further, I would appreciate him telling me who had brought the article to his attention. That night, incidentally, I attended my section's annual dinner and dance, during which I was presented by John Gow with a silver salver for my World Cup appearances in Argentina. 'I hope', he said, 'that you will referee in the 1982 World Cup finals'. John Gow was my representative on the executive council.

Then came the following sequence of events:

23 November – Letter from Trevor Morris, confirming that his attention had been drawn to the article by the secretary of my association, John Goggins.

28 November – I wrote to tell Trevor Morris that I was surprised, as an established referee, that the FAW could not have told me the name of the informant from the beginning. I suggested that he should have asked Goggins to write direct to me, as I felt the transaction between the two associations was not good for the relationship between establishment and referee. I certainly did not expect the following letter, dated 15 December, that I received from Trevor:

'I consider the contents of your letter of 28 November to be somewhat brash, even after allowing for the fact that modesty is not one of your particular traits.

'Let me make it perfectly clear that I don't need you to tell me what my administrative rights are as Secretary of the FA of Wales. I suggest you stick to refereeing – at which you have few peers!!

'In the circumstances, Mr Goggins was perfectly at liberty to write to me. Whether or not we were prepared to act on his advice was, of course, an entirely different matter. Our first thoughts were that this is primarily a matter between you and them and I have written accordingly.

'As a champion of free speech over many years, I feel that I am in a position to give you a little friendly advice. You would be well advised to contemplate beforehand what reaction some of your more liberal comments are likely to arouse, particularly with the "establishment" as you put it.

'Seasonal greetings.'

I had to make some reply and did so on 20 December.

'Thank you for your letter, the contents of which I have noted. It would be only fair for me to tell you that I find the paragraphs of your letter to be unnecessarily offensive. Seasonal greetings.'

What a Christmas present from my own Football Association when they were agreeing that I was, in effect, right and that the article should have been a matter between the AFLRL and me. The AFLRL then became involved again with a letter written on 1 February, 1979. They clearly thought they had failed with the FAW and at their own council meeting, because the letter, from Goggins, said he had been asked to write to suggest that while the comments in the press were appreciated and the points taken, it would have been wiser and more prudent for these matters to be aired at a meeting of my section or at the annual conference. Goggins concluded the letter: 'With every good wish for continuing successful whistling.' Yet again, decisions had been reached without the person most concerned being consulted.

In December 1979, I then received an invitation to address the association's annual conference in Portsmouth the following summer. I agreed that I would take a look at refereeing in the eighties but refused to enlarge on what I was going to say, which did not amuse the president and his executive. I worked very hard on the lecture, even interviewing five top club managers – recognisable, though their names were not mentioned – for inclusion on tape to illustrate where the referees were going wrong. The chairman of the training committee, no less, wrote afterwards to say that 'my professional presentation impressed everyone. I only hope', he continued, 'the referees have the courage to carry out what was decided'.

And Goggins himself said: 'As well as the positive character, the professional manner of presentation was quite superb and everyone is grateful.'

Basically, I had pointed out in the lecture that we must change our style of refereeing with regard to the cheats of the game. I suggested that a more positive attitude should be taken towards serious foul play, gamesmanship, treatment for injured players and encroachment at free kicks. The laws of the game should be applied with consistent thoroughness and accuracy. All the points I raised were agreed on and they were circulated to all referees.

A year later, after I had told newspapers that there were cheats in the game, I was disappointed to read a headline 'Thomas is out on his own'. John Goggins said: 'It must be emphasised that such statements are the expression of a member's personal point of view and do not reflect the association's view.' And this after our agreement at the 1980 conference about gamesmanship! A spokesman was disagreeing, I believe, with the proposals that had been passed.

Cheating, though, was only one of the points that was worrying me during that summer of 1981. I wrote to Goggins asking (a) whether a letter had been written to the executive council by the secretary of the West of England section, regarding an alleged remark I had made about Derek Nippard's appointment as FA Cup Final referee; (b) whether he had received a letter from a linesman, Montacute, concerning myself and what action council had taken without my evidence; (c) were the Goggins quotes on cheating his personal opinion or had the council's feelings changed; and (d) what had happened if anything in respect of the 1980 conference recommendations for changes in the laws.

His reply, on 21 July, said my information on (a) was incorrect, that there had been a request from the London and Southern Counties section to make investigations on the alleged remarks but substantiation was required before council could act and there had been no subsequent action. On (b) he agreed that correspondence had been received from Mr Montacute and Graham Kelly of the Football League but no action had been taken. The statement on (c) had been made after consultation with the president and (d) officers of the Association and the Referees' Association were to include the item on the agenda for a forthcoming meeting. The correspondence rumbled on but it turned out that items (a) and (b) were three years old in the one case and a year old in the other.

Was justice seen to be done? No it wasn't – and I believe the executive have a lot to answer for.

There was a chance that the 1982 annual conference in Birmingham would be rather more lively than usual and, after a lecture from Arthur Jones in which he rightly warned of too much tackling from behind, the emergence of the hard man and the professional foul, I chaired a referees' seminar and asked whether we should change the interpretation of the professional foul – the wilful prevention by a player of a goal-scoring opportunity by illegal methods, either by a physical foul or through a hand-ball. The result was seventeen for, seventeen against. Graham Kelly, who was sitting in as an adviser, explained that he was a Class C referee and asked whether he could vote. I could not accept this and I gave the casting vote in favour of change, so that we could get a grip on this problem once and for all.

The referees then asked me to speak on the subject and explain why I felt so strongly. I referred back to the 1980 conference and my reasons. I was then asked to take another vote. Now there were thirty-two in favour of change and only two dissenters. Graham Kelly, who would have supported me with his vote, thanked me later for what I had said – but my reaction was that there had to be something wrong with referees who could change their minds so dramatically within three minutes.

Another seminar took place under the chairmanship of referee Gilbert Napthine, who required answers to notes he had been given by the training committee. We started on the ten-yard encroachment but, after a few minutes, he tried to use his power as chairman to move on to other issues. To hell with that, I argued, with the backing of my colleagues: encroachment, which occurs possibly six times a match, is more important than, for example, the professional foul which occurs perhaps once every ten games. We all agreed we needed more time on the matter: I stated that whether I had the backing of other referees or not, I would implement the laws as they stood, meaning that in any encroachment I would warn, caution and then send off.

I was pleasantly surprised when it was unanimously agreed that we would adhere to the law. Alas, some referees did not have the courage to stand by this decision throughout the season. Although we saw in the first six weeks of the new season more players being sent off than ever before, referees were being inconsistent. I called for a special referees' conference in October to discuss four specific points: the new law on goalkeeper's steps, the professional foul, throw-ins and encroachment.

To some degree, the Football Association, in a circular of October 1982, forestalled the conference by watering down the treatment of the professional foul, asking for common sense to be used and warning of over-reaction in the application of the interpretation.

The referees' conference – held in Coventry in November – I'm afraid turned out to be another day of frustration and inaction. Many referees simply did not have the courage to operate on the cancers in the game.

I have to say the same about the 1983 annual conference in London. It was hopefully entitled Consistency, Co-operation, Control. It might just as easily have been entitled Inconsistency, Unco-operative and Uncontrolled. In fact, if you want to go and make a cup of tea now, or even go to sleep, don't worry because you won't miss anything if I give you a full report of the conference before I decided to leave it at the halfway point.

*   *   *   *   *

Feeling better? In that case, I'll tell you one final story about the Association of Football League Referees and Linesmen and a banning for life.

Ricky Nicholson was a Football League referee, and a former secretary of the association, who became an assessor. He was not my favourite person but that is beside the point. In the *Daily Express* he gave his analysis of a match I had refereed between Millwall and Aston Villa on 29 September, 1974. He wrote that I was a law unto myself on the field, spurning both the edicts of the Football League and the spirit of the game. Although he pointed out that my control of the game was blameless, he went into deeper issues of refereeing. I did not come out of it very well but I did quite honestly accept his comments as I would accept any criticism which was constructive.

Then, in a letter dated 5 October, 1974, from Dick Hall, secretary of our association, to Nicholson with a copy to me, deep concern was expressed at the article in the *Express*. The association would be pleased to hear Nicholson's comments. I heard nothing further until I read an article by James Lawton in the *Daily Express* that confirmed that Ricky had been banned for life by a sub-committee that met in a Cheshire hotel. The sub-committee was composed of Pat Partridge, who is now a FIFA instructor, Gordon Kew and Vince James. Told of the ban, Nicholson said simply: 'This is a sad business . . . referees should be just as liable to criticism as anyone else.'

Ricky, I agree entirely. At no time, and I repeat at no time, was I given the opportunity to convey my feelings and my views. Once again, I was not invited to any meeting, just as with the other examples I have given.

Finally, a look at the bitchiness and the total disregard for one's colleagues to be found among the fraternity.

A referee at a crucial relegation match in 1983, when the home team had to win to maintain its status in a certain division, inquired before the match whether there was any possibility of purchasing FA Cup Final tickets. He was obviously very pleased when, threequarters of an hour before the kick-off, a director of the home team came into the dressing-room to give the referee two complimentaries. He also offered one each to the linesmen. One took his with gratitude, but the other, to his credit, refused. The team, coincidentally, did avoid relegation.

Not very long afterwards, another referee who had heard about the episode was busy retailing the story around his colleagues and expressing surprise that the referee concerned should have placed himself in such an embarrassing position. I do not condone the referee's bare-faced request, though he was clearly opening himself up to future questioning, but I really do criticise the actions of the director, who holds a senior position in the game.

What would the AFLRL have done with the recipient had they heard about the story officially? A warning? A ban? Or would they regard as a worse offence the public statements of an assessor, whom we will discover in the next chapter to be strange people.

·20·
ASSES OR ASSESSORS

'It was by no means an easy game, they never are at Bristol, but there were very few grumbles about the officials after the game and that is most unusual.' Extract from an official assessment on Clive Thomas for his handling of the match between Bristol City and Hull City on 28 April, 1973. In opening the chapter on referees' assessors with this brief excerpt, I have two objects in mind. Firstly, to draw attention to the purely gratuitous comment about Bristol and, secondly, to illustrate the point that some assessors are so ignorant and rude that they have to rely on the 'grumbles' of others to make their reports.

When I raised this point with the Football League, they agreed completely. 'This comment was unnecessary. The matter will be taken up with the assessor.' After receiving further details from the assessor, Alan Hardaker wrote to me that 'by letting the League know about these comments made by assessors, we are all a little wiser'. And I had always thought that somebody up there in Lytham read the reports. What was the point of them if nobody at the League bothered to see them?

It would be an exaggeration to say that this was an isolated case. Some assessors will inform you that it was a lovely, sunny afternoon; others will lyricise about the amount of excitement for a fourth division game; yet others again try to read a player's thoughts. Some think they should be writing leading articles for *The Times*. But then, I have never liked the present assessment system.

For those who may not be aware of it, the system came into force back in 1970. Referees were generally in favour because, previously, there had been in operation a method whereby the clubs involved in a match would mark the referee out of ten, and this could clearly produce biased marking depending on the result of the match. I have always believed, in fact, that a good referee will come out on top whichever system operates.

But the problem facing the Football League was quite apparent: where to find the right calibre of assessor? The answer was simple: jobs for the boys. But they did not appoint only experienced ex-referees. We found that they were giving the jobs to men who had never refereed in the Football League at all and who therefore could have no idea of the pressures of a big game. Nobody other than the referees' committee knew who they were: allegedly they attended matches *incognito*. I say 'allegedly' because you can frequently see them in directors' boxes around the country, pencil and clipboard or notebook in hand, or with portable tape recorder perhaps in the grandstand. They make out their reports on Sundays for the Football League and the referee receives from the League a copy but without the number of marks awarded and without the name of the assessor.

In those early days, the assessor's form included thirty points for his study. If the assessor wanted to draw your attention to a particular failing, he would put a tick alongside such juicy items as 'Your whistle should be blown harder, or, alternatively, you should get a louder whistle', or 'Smarten up your appearance' – as if a referee would take the field with holes in his socks. And even 'Do not talk to the players except in carrying out your responsibilities.' What do they think we do out there? Discuss last night's episode of *Coronation Street?* Then there was the dangerous item number thirty-one: Additional comments.

It was a ludicrous form and the Football League recognised it as such, bringing it down in 1972 to six headings: Application of laws and control, Positioning and fitness, Advantage, Stoppages and signals, Co-operation with linesmen and General remarks and summing-up. Now, instead of merely marking ticks, the assessor has the chance to feast himself eloquently on each item before succumbing finally to literary diarrhoea under General remarks and summing-up. Assessors tend not to waste the chance, either, writing at great length about trivialities.

Referees do have the right to question an assessor's comments but most are reluctant to do so. The Football League does not encourage additional administrative burdens, the assessor may be an influential person and the referee fears being assessed by the same person again. I frequently receive calls from referees asking for guidance as to whether they should accept without comment an assessment with which they disagree totally. They do not wish to speak to the League because they lack the confidence that they will get help and encouragement from the staff. One referee admitted to me, indeed, that three assessors had told him to disregard where players were taking throw-ins and that he felt that this was the way he had to officiate – taking notice of the assessors and disregarding the laws of the game. What an indictment! I could not agree with him and told him so. He hasn't phoned me since.

But let us take a random selection to show you examples of the genre and my reason for treating assessments with suspicion and cynicism.

30 MARCH, 1974, TOTTENHAM V EVERTON: 'I thought you were unwise to blow your whistle to stop play at half-time when the ball was dropping in the penalty area from a corner-kick. Perhaps my learned tutor was wrong but one of his golden rules was "Never blow when the ball is in the penalty area". On one occasion when I was linesman at Tottenham

the referee blew for time exactly as you did and the ball was headed in the net. Pandemonium reigned.' Full marks for his clairvoyancy – but it was a typical indictment of the honesty and integrity of referees and what they should be doing, even if Jack Taylor did make a similar remark about me in Argentina.

13 SEPTEMBER, 1972, LUTON TOWN V BIRMINGHAM CITY: 'Cautioned another Birmingham player ... spectators near me seemed puzzled by this as indeed from my position in the stand I was too.' I wrote to Alan Hardaker to ask whether 'the referee should also take into consideration the spectators' comments'. A reply, via the FL, came from the assessor: 'I had the feeling in common with other people that there was an element of inconsistency. I'm sure Mr Thomas would agree with the old cliché that justice must not only be done but must also be seen to be done. Incidentally, the spectators I referred to happen to be some very eminent managers seated behind me whose comments I could not help but overhear ...' I wrote a further letter emphasising that an assessor should not be concerned with the opinions of others, eminent managers or not. But I received no reply.

14 OCTOBER, 1972, SOUTHAMPTON V LIVERPOOL: The assessor stated that the weakness of one linesman was subject to a separate report but was not for my consideration. I rang the Football League to inquire further and was rather bewildered to discover he had written a detrimental report, certainly – but not about the linesman I had had to tell at half-time that he had better get dressed if he could not do better in the second half, I would find a replacement. In short, the assessor had mistaken the two linesmen and, if I had not raised the question, the wrong man would have had his career threatened.

23 AUGUST, 1975, COVENTRY CITY V MANCHESTER CITY: Assessor stated that my five cautions were justified. Because this was supposed to be the new Clive Thomas, full of leniency and understanding, I wrote to the League to say that this was my third match and that I had intended to change my style of refereeing and would not be wielding the notebook about. But the assessor was absolutely right here and I had to point out to the League that some players in the matches did not care about myself or their colleagues. 'In fact', I wrote, 'they acted like animals'.

1 NOVEMBER 1975, OXFORD UNITED V HULL: 'At the termination you stood by the exit and clapped several players off.' And 'you indicated emotional involvement when you often put both hands on your head. Do you consider such idiosyncrasies reflect impartiality?' I replied that 'this was a ridiculous point for the assessor to have brought up. I also react like a human being and saw nothing whatsoever wrong in congratulating two teams for an excellent display of football.' And why should I not react to a near miss, for example?

18 DECEMBER, 1979, WIMBLEDON V PORTSMOUTH: 'To sum up, keep up this standard and you will not only do a service to the games to which you are appointed, but also to refereeing, by example.' No comment other than that this assessment was given by the training officer of the Football Association, Ken Ridden. And by 1982–83, I was not having a single FA Cup match.

30 JANUARY, 1980, TOTTENHAM HOTSPUR V SWINDON: The assessor for this FA Cup match took a page and a half to explain where I went wrong. Secretly, I had asked Lawrie McMenemy to write an assessment of my performance also. What an enlightened report from Lawrie: more factual, more professional, more constructive and looking into the deeper aspects of man management and emphasising control of individuals.

5 SEPTEMBER, 1981, NOTTS COUNTY V COVENTRY CITY: 'Do please look at the question of fitness. My experience is that once you are worried about your limbs responding less quickly, then lack of concentration follows.' I wrote to the League on 11 September: 'As this assessor had had refereeing experience and feels that I am worried about my limbs, perhaps he could suggest a fitness programme for the season to ensure that I "do not lack concentration".' His reply to Graham Kelly said 'The comment I made upon fitness, in Section 6, was intended to be generally impersonal: it would have been better had I replaced the word "you" with the impersonal and formal "one" and "your" with "one's", a much more stilted and hardly conversational form. Or I could have written "... my experience is that once a referee is worried about his limbs responding less quickly, then lack of concentration follows. This I believe to be true. No fitness programme can prepare for this situation ..."'

Geddit? This assessor finally beat one, me or you, or should I use the less personal us? Either way I suggested to the League that this correspondence should now close. It did.

But perhaps the assessment from which the most important lesson should be learned was one given on a match between Manchester United and Manchester City at Old Trafford in March 1978, when there were so many comments on the form that I suggested to Alan Hardaker that a meeting with the assessor might be of benefit both to me and to him. The League sent his reply on to me and revealed for the first time that it was Bob Matthewson who said that he 'had no objection to a meeting if this could be arranged, preferably in Argentina'.

'Seriously though', he continued, 'I know from information received on the grapevine that he is fully aware that I was the assessor at the game and if he cares to pick up a telephone at any time I would be happy to endeavour to enlighten him on any points relative to the assessment.'

In fact I had not known Matthewson was the assessor when I first wrote but I asked the League whether they would agree to my 'phoning him. George Readle telephoned to advise me to drop the matter as he thought nothing would come of it. The embarrassing thing for the Football League and to my 'union', the Association of Football League Referees and Linesmen, was that Bob Matthewson was president of the association at the time.

I cannot believe it is right that any executive member of the association should be an assessor because, if I am not satisfied with an explanation given by that assessor/Football League, I should be able to take it up with my association. I can't now because I would be judged at an 'appeal court' by the same person who passed the original sentence. The executive must surely be under the thumb of the Football League, who are their employers as assessors. Because of this fear, too, you can imagine I was not particularly pleased when my AFLRL secretary, John Goggins, recently moved home to Lytham St Annes from Manchester. I hope it is only for the fresh air, John.

Referees, though, do play into their assessor's hands. There are those who will phone a club secretary to see who is the assessor at their game; there are those who will inquire as soon as they reach the ground and then check with the files they have brought with them to see what points that particular assessor looks for; there are others who will actually take their assessors in their cars to matches and then home afterwards. And there are yet others who fear that they will be seen to be giving lifts and will actually drive a hundred yards or so from a ground to pick up the assessor after the match. Linesmen can fall into the same traps.

I caused controversy again at the 1982 AFLRL conference in Birmingham when Graham Kelly asked the four hundred delegates, consisting of referees, linesmen and assessors, how the assessment system could be improved. I said frankly that it was a waste of time and should be killed off. To replace it, I would bring back club markings with assessors being called in to examine a referee only after he had received, say, three consecutive unsatisfactory reports. The assessors themselves would all be former Football League referees and should resign automatically when they had been out of the game for ten years.

I can understand why I received so little backing. Two referees in particular were greeted with tremendous applause. Gilbert Napthine said he was all in favour of assessors and, with the new interpretation of the professional foul coming in the following season, referees needed all the help they could get from assessors. George Tyson, in expressing delight at the system, went so far as to say it was the greatest thing since sliced bread. But could such support for assessors have anything to do with the fact that there have not been more than six referees taken from the list in any one year for the past ten years? No one can convince me that there are only six below-standard referees out of ninety-odd each season.

Are the marks being given by assessors too high? Are they looking for the right characteristics in a referee?

Ridiculous, too, is the fact that a retiring referee who may have been at the top of the League's list for many years has to apply to the Football League to become an assessor. No application, no invitation – and yet we still have linesmen as assessors, chosen by people who have never blown a whistle in the Football League.

But nothing beats the system operating in some of the contributory leagues. The top referees in the Welsh League, for example, are watched by Football League assessors for a number of matches. At the end of that season, the leading referee on the basis of those assessments is invited to the League for an interview if there is a vacancy in that area. If that referee is successful and promoted to the League, he is then sent the batch of assessments made on him during the previous season. But the unsuccessful referees are left to wonder where they have been going wrong: they are not presented with their assessments and are left to continue their bad habits.

I cannot understand this any more than I can understand why the AFLRL training committee has not demanded from the Football League that the assessments should be made available to all referees as a necessary part of training and improvement. While the current incestuous system operates, referees throughout England and Wales will continue to be ignorant of their deficiencies.

·21·
TV THOMAS

Perhaps it is because I am Welsh. Perhaps it is my simple belief that I am an entertainer, a performer who refuses to accept that there are on the field only twenty-two players. You have only to look at the number of my fellow countrymen in politics and pulpit, in show business and in the classroom to realise that we love the centre of the stage. On the soccer pitch there are twenty-two players, yes, but there is also me – with two colleagues to assist me, of course. The result is that if I arrive at a ground to find all the paraphernalia associated with television coverage festooned around the stadium, then I am unashamedly delighted.

Some referees and linesmen shudder when they see the cameras: they hate so much to be in the limelight that they make elementary mistakes because they are apprehensive and tense. Others wear their Sunday-best kit. But my adrenalin flows the more quickly when I see a television camera – or even a radio microphone – and so I have to accept the criticism frequently levelled at me within the hierarchy of the game that I am a showman, an extrovert. The fact is that I believe some of my best performances – and I use the word here in a professional rather than a dramatic sense, though there is a hint of that too – have been in front of the cameras.

The characteristic way in which I start each match, where I lift up a leg and give a little kick as I blow the whistle, picked up almost unerringly by the television cameras, was not specifically introduced for their benefit. I have been asked countless times why I do it: I even receive fan mail, almost entirely from women, presumably on the basis that they appreciate my hairy legs. The answer, though, goes back many years, and once more to my old friend, Frankie Vaughan. During his singing tours and whenever he came to Wales, we would as fitness fanatics inevitably go to a sauna, where he would go through his exercises – including that idiosyncratic high kick of the leg which older readers will associate with *Green Door* and his many other hits. I thought, well, if he can do that sort of thing at his age (sorry, Frank), then surely at mine I can think of something similar. So I gave it a whirl in the Rhondda one day, some of the players thought it a good gimmick, and it became a trademark which, although referees have copied some aspects of my game, has remained mine alone.

You may think there is little harm in such a tiny indulgence. Certainly, although it was something I was determined to continue as a part of making myself a personality, I was considerably surprised at a UEFA conference in Macholin, Switzerland, in 1973, to hear my old friend Friedrich Seipelt, the chairman of the referees' committee, single me out during a lecture about the gimmicks of referees. He had criticised Italian referees generally for positioning themselves behind the goal for the taking of penalties on the basis that they were certain that way to be in the camera shot, when I heard him say that there was one referee among the most influential in the world who picked up his foot at the start of every match and every half. No name was mentioned but those British referees present all looked at me. I wonder where Seipelt received his information: could it have been a criticism passed on to him from Britain?

The point is that television has helped to give me whatever name I have – good or bad. I believe that I have always attempted to help the media, newspapermen or television people, and they have undoubtedly helped me in return. I have never, ever criticised television, for example, for showing slow-motion action replays where a referee could be proved wrong. The result of this relationship with the media is that I have always been happy to see television commentators in my dressing-room before a match: with just one exception.

That man was Barry Davies of the BBC. Barry still believes I was wrong: I believe, of course, that I was right. The incident happened during the 1982–83 season in a crucial match between Brighton and Everton at the Goldstone Ground when he arrived as usual for a pre-match chat. I explained that I had no wish to talk with him unless he apologised for the way in which he had interviewed the Tottenham manager, Keith Burkinshaw, after that controversial semi-final at Hillsborough the previous season when I had given a penalty a minute before the final whistle for a foul by Glenn Hoddle on Kenny Hibbitt. Wolves duly scored the equaliser. It was then that Barry, on television, asked Keith what he thought of the decision. Keith, true to form, said simply that Clive Thomas gave the decision and we accept it – a reply I respect, for Keith was also ensuring that his players would not comment on the decision. Barry's reaction was to finish the interview by saying that this must be the understatement of the year. Now, I believe that Barry's job was to seek the views of the manager and not to add his own comment for the millions who were watching but, down at Brighton, he said he felt he had done no wrong. It was stalemate.

As it happened, during that game at Brighton which was vital with regard to relegation in the first division, I gave a penalty to the home team – the first on the Goldstone Ground, incidentally, for two years – and the Everton goalkeeper made a brilliant save. As he was clearly helped by the fact that he had moved before the kick was taken, I ordered Brighton to retake it – the type of decision that players rarely agree with as just about all goalkeepers move but few referees penalise – and they scored from this second attempt. Curiously, and with only a minute or so left, Everton stole a winner and Howard Kendall, their manager, and a friend of many years, congratulated me on a good game. I know this was not simply because his side had won: he had on many previous occasions told me if he felt I was wrong with the result that he is a manager to whom I will always listen.

But within ten minutes of the final whistle a BBC representative was asking whether I would be interviewed. I asked by whom, was told it was Barry Davies, and said I would be interviewed only by someone else. The go-between left but returned later to say that they still wished to speak to me but could not agree to my suggestion. I appreciate fully the BBC's point of view. What right does a referee have to nominate his own questioner? My right was to say yes or no and to stick to my principles, with the result that for the first time I refused to go on television. In Barry's favour, I should add that at no stage during his commentary on that game or in his after-match comments would you have known that there was any kind of difference between us. On the contrary, he acted like a true professional. And in my final season our friendship has been restored.

Penalties inevitably play a major role in the slow-motion replay syndrome. Rightly so: they are frequently the talking point of a particular match.

My mind goes back to Anfield in March 1975 and a game between Liverpool and Birmingham City. I was certain that the incident was inside the penalty area when Steve Bryant fouled Peter Cormack but when I whistled for the offence I was told politely but firmly by the Birmingham players that one of my linesmen was indicating that the incident happened outside the box. I overruled Burnley linesman Graham Boothman, and Kenny Burns of Birmingham inevitably could not accept it. That was nothing unusual for Kenny: it took him seven years to accept me but now we are such friends that when he was unfit to play in a match in the 1982–83 season he actually regretted the fact on the basis that I was in the middle!

On this occasion, however, he disagreed, but the decision stood, Kevin Keegan scored from the spot and Liverpool won 1–0. Freddie Goodwin was City's manager at the time and he was waiting for me at the tunnel at the end of the game. He had apparently seen the incident, as with any manager sitting in the grandstand or in the dug-out fifty yards away, rather better than I had done. Because this book is, as it were, for family viewing, I will not repeat his exact words; he made it eminently clear, however, that he disagreed with a decision that had cost his side the match. I was furious when I entered my dressing-room, not with Freddie, but with the linesman who had let me down by not adhering to my pre-match instructions. Once I had acknowledged his signal then my decision would stand.

Within a few minutes, Freddie Goodwin was at the door, still disgruntled and seeking the linesman's view. I told him I was not prepared to discuss the matter. 'But I'll bet you £1 I was right', I said, 'and as I am at Villa Park next Saturday, don't bother to post it. Just drop it in at the ground.' Freddie left, still feeling robbed. Then came another knock at the door. This time it was John Motson of the BBC who said he had looked twice at the incident and the tape showed I was wrong and that the penalty should have been a free kick outside the area. I questioned his angles and those of the camera and, although I had not intended to watch *Match of the Day* (I like to give my wife priority on a Saturday evening when I return home and take her out for a meal), I knew I could arrange to see television at the social club at Polikoff's at Pentre where the steward and his wife, Gwyn and Pam Lewis, would make the arrangements in between dances as it were.

The press were also waiting outside my dressing-room at Anfield and I knew I had to meet them or to make 'no comment' - two words which are not in my vocabulary. So I showered and prepared for the questioning. Another knock at the door: John Motson again, to report that he had now watched the incident six or eight times and that I was, in fact, right. Because I am no different from anyone else, I was elated when I held the press conference ten minutes later.

On the Monday, Colin Wood wrote in the *Daily Mail* that 'the film of the match showed that Cormack was right on the line when he was flattened and so Birmingham's claims as summed up by Freddie Goodwin were groundless'. Mike Ellis believed in *The Sun* that 'if the championship trophy returns to Anfield ... Liverpool should invite referee Clive Thomas to the celebration'. And Chris James of the *Daily Mirror* wrote that: 'Clive Thomas's mailbag could be bulging this week with letters of apology from Freddie Goodwin, Birmingham players and Burnley linesman Graham Boothman.' I had, in fact, two notes that week. One was from John Motson saying, well done, you're right again. And the other? It was a compliment slip from Freddie Goodwin, with a £1 note attached. I still have that £1 note and the letter from John.

I said a moment or two ago that there was only one occasion on which I recall turning down a television appearance. But there was another major occasion when the establishment attempted to gag me and that was on my appointment to the World Cup final series in Argentina. The invitation from FIFA was accompanied by a lengthy contract and by a form requesting measurements as Adidas would be supplying the clothes. In fact I received so many that I gave them away to Argentinian friends. But the other part of the contract was similar to insurance forms, as there was plenty of small print. Because of the experiences I have had with football administrators and because of my position as an industrial relations executive, I am well aware of the need to scrutinise thoroughly those small-print clauses before signing. I could not accept some of the points, especially that section which referred to talking with the press. I understood fully the political problems associated with the host country and the potential dangers inherent in speaking off-the-cuff – but this was football and not politics. Besides, I considered myself experienced in dealing with the media. I had built up substantial rapport with the press and in return had been dealt with sympathetically and fairly round the world.

The result was that I replied to the FIFA secretary, Dr Helmut Kaser, to accept the invitation but deleted the relevant reference to press interviews and asked for the decision to be reconsidered. He in turn responded by saying the matter would be discussed at the next meeting of the referees' committee. I heard nothing further for four months until all the World Cup referees were gathered at a seminar in a Buenos Aires hotel, just before the competition. My *bête noir*, the acting chairman, Seipelt, acted true to form. He said at the seminar that no one must speak to the press: not even Clive Thomas, he said. Not unnaturally, I took great exception to this and questioned his right to say it as I was still awaiting a reply from the referees' committee. He replied that I was the only referee in thirty-two who had not signed the contract *in toto*, news which scarcely surprised me. Referees are not the most courageous people, even though they were later to make full use of their country's media services to 'phone wives, girlfriends and what-have-you in return for supplying information, albeit without the source being named.

I was attempting to have everything on the record. Then one evening we had a reception – one of far too many, incidentally – this time given by Adidas. Two days later Seipelt called a special meeting of referees to state that three of them had spoken with a German journalist who had in turn written an article about internal problems encountered by referees, which deeply angered FIFA executive council members. Seipelt then announced the names of the three referees who had spoken to the journalist at the Adidas reception: Karoly Palotai of Hungary, a German, Ferdinand Biwers, and ... me. I leaped from my seat, stating that this was totally untrue. I cannot, first of all, speak German. I know no German journalists. And I had not spoken with a German journalist. The other two referees kept quiet and so I asked for a full inquiry and requested that the FIFA executive should be involved. No further action was taken. Strangely, Palotai and Biwers always seemed to be in the company of Seipelt during our free time. In my opinion, something unprofessional had taken place.

In this country, the British press got it wrong for once when they said on 11 June that I might take an early plane home because of what had happened. And yet maybe they were right in one way because although FIFA denied that they had discussed the episode and Dr Kaser said he had also been badly misquoted by the press, it was quite obvious that my head rolled. Palotai, on the other hand, continued his career and even went to the 1982 finals in Spain.

* * * * *

Television, however, does not only involve itself with the game's serious side, with the disputes, the penalties, the sordid professionalism. It does not show only the skills, the spectacular saves and goals: it also shows the humour.

Upton Park, tucked away as it is down in London's East 13, is not the most elegant of grounds. It does not have the overt lushness and plushness of Highbury or White Hart Lane and it is one of the most difficult grounds to reach from South Wales. Yet the warm home of West Ham United has always been one of my favourites, not only on the field but also in the tea-room where those lovely ladies are so happy to provide a splendid cup of tea and sandwiches before a match – usually accompanied by some shrewd and jocular comment in a genuine Cockney accent.

Before a particular match I was having one such cup of tea and was aware that another person in the room had a face I recognised. He came across and said, 'I hope you have a good game, Mr Thomas.' I thanked him and apologised for not putting a name to the face I had recognised. 'Yes, you probably did', he said. 'My name is Warren Mitchell.' He had been filming an episode of *Till Death Do Us Part* at the ground before the match. I apologised again, little realising that I was almost to die a death later that afternoon.

You can sense when you are not having a good game, not only from the attitude of the players but from that of the crowd, of course. Any referee who claims he does not hear the reaction does so for one of three reasons: he's deluding himself, he's deaf, or the stadium is empty. In this match, certainly, I could hear them telling me to get back to the valleys and so on. Then, naturally, came the old song, *What a referee*. Typically English, too: not in tune.

The words rang round my head and I thought, possibly for the first time in the middle, 'if you can't beat 'em, join 'em'. And so I sang along, in tune, with Welsh *hwyl*. I knew the cameras were there, and I knew exactly what I was doing. The crowd reacted and, sure enough, on *The*

Big Match that Sunday afternoon, LWT's Brian Moore, whom I respect enormously, opened the programme by recommending the match itself and, later, 'we'll show the humorous side of Clive Thomas'. That's exactly what they did, with the camera catching me full face singing and conducting.

More recently, in the 1982–83 season, I was again at Upton Park when two of the most explosive players in the game came up against each other when the Hammers met Aston Villa. I shudder sometimes when I think of some of the tackles which Billy Bonds has attempted. Yet, every time, it is with the one hundred per cent intention of getting the ball: if there is a player *en route*, then that's just too bad. Indeed, I have always maintained that Bonds would have been an outstanding England player because he has a feeling for the game and, in a white shirt, would surely offer far more than I have seen from many an England player recently. The highest compliment I can pay him is to wish that he were Welsh. Then there was the rumbustious Peter Withe, a player whom I would never have thought could play more than two games for Brian Clough on the basis that Peter also thinks he is right all of the time – but he also plays with his heart and he will run all day.

In this game, as the teams ran on the field, the home crowd showed their disapproval of Curbishley, who had recently transferred to Villa and was therefore regarded as a traitor. He, when the crowd turned on me, ran alongside to say, 'Thank God you're here; they may leave me alone now.' The crunch had to come between the two big men at some stage and, sure enough, Bonds and Withe went down after a collision. Bonds was up like a shot to get the ball away, leaving Withe grounded but still trying to retrieve the ball and becoming entangled again. Bondy took great exception to this and, with me only a yard away and arguably the nearest I had been to the ball in this match, grabbed hold of him. The confrontation everyone expected was on us. The clash of personalities was about to be joined.

Suddenly, they both looked at me, paused and waltzed away, hand in hand in ballroom fashion. I blew the whistle, stopped play and called them to me. I could have sent them off but I wanted to defuse the situation. They approached me arm in arm like the men I knew they weren't – and I merely told them off and said that I would not have minded at all had they been dancing properly. I was pleased that BBC commentator Alan Parry picked up the incident for *Match of the Day* and agreed with my interpretation.

I was once more aware that the cameras were present and I wanted to show the millions watching, including referees, that common sense sometimes prevails over the strict laws of the game. Full marks, too, to Bonds and Withe.

Only black marks, though, to the anonymous assessor who made no reference to the incident but who, in his otherwise glowing report to the FL, and presumably because he had to carp about something, criticised me for walking to the centre of the players' tunnel at the end of the match because it could look as if I was wanting players to shake my hand. He advised that I step aside to let the players leave first. For goodness' sake. Is that his only real critical contribution to the refereeing of a major First Division match?

There is another aspect of television which has shaped a small part of my behaviour. When I was a young referee I watched how others were giving coins to captains for tossing up and then stooping to pick up the coins. I was determined I would never do this, not because of any arrogant way of thinking but because I believe that the least a man can do having tossed a coin to the ground is to pick it up and return it to the referee. Only once did I have a minor confrontation and that was with that fine footballer, the ex-England and West Ham captain, Bobby Moore, when he was playing at Fulham. When I asked him to return the coin to me after the toss-up at Craven Cottage, he replied: 'No Clive, it's your coin, you pick it up.'

'You dropped it', I said.

'But I don't want it now', he replied.

We stood looking at each other with the linesmen standing bemused.

Then Bobby said, 'Would you caution me if I didn't?'

'Yes.'

'You really mean that, don't you?'

'Yes.'

He picked up the coin and said, 'I don't want to be the first player you've booked before a ball has been kicked.'

It is interesting to speculate about my possible grounds for cautioning him. Perhaps 'ungentlemanly conduct' – which would have been grossly unjust for he was one of the few true gentlemen in the game.

Finally, as I think of television, I remember a tape recording sent to me by the secretary of Waterschei in Belgium of a European Cup match I had between his team and Paris St Germain. It shows clearly the leg action at the start of the match. But you also hear constantly throughout the French-language commentary, the very English words, 'Thomas the Book, Thomas the Book . . .' Could be a title there somewhere.

But even television appearances of a casual nature can be fraught with difficulties. A year or two ago I invited two Football League referees to accompany me in singing a special football carol on a Christmas edition of ITV's *On the Ball*. Eric Reid and Bert Newsome were the two referees who finally accompanied me and we seemed to go down well as we showed that the men in the middle can be human. But the other referee

I had approached said he would have to ask for Football League permission before appearing. Rather than involve the League, I felt it better to carry on without him – but I wonder what Lytham's response would have been. What I do know is that the referee concerned is now an assessor . . .

·22·
WHERE DO WE GO FROM HERE?

It may seem odd to start a dissertation on the future of soccer with a mild Monday evening in September 1969 at Bournemouth, where Rochdale were the visitors in a Third Division game. In the eighty-fourth minute of the match, when I had stopped the game for an injured player to be treated, the Rochdale goalkeeper complained bitterly that spectators were throwing bottles and coins at him. Before I restarted the game, I went over to the Bournemouth trainer's bench, sought out the manager, Freddie Cox, and asked him to have the police parade behind the goal. His reply staggered me: 'You tell them, they are standing there, you speak to them.' Even when I repeated the request, he would have nothing to do with it.

I subsequently reported the details of the spectators' misconduct and the Football Association disciplinary committee on 18 November decided that the club should be ordered to post warning notices, about behaviour, in prominent positions in the ground. But in the letter I received from the FA, dated 19 November, the last paragraph said: 'No action was taken by the committee regarding the part of the referee's report which referred to the manager Cox.'

Let's make something absolutely clear. The manager and officials of a Football League club are responsible for the safety of the referee, linesmen and players. They are responsible for the behaviour of the crowd. Before the Football Association or the Football League or the clubs criticise the police and the press, governments, magistrates, judges and the rest, they should look first at themselves. Unless they do that, unless they ensure that attending a football ground can once more be a safe pleasure for a whole family, the game will surely die. Even if some enlightened coach can wave his magic wand to recreate the missing skills and the lost excitement, the departing thousands will return only if they are secure.

If there were five hooligans among a crowd of forty or fifty watching a small Welsh League club, I have no doubt that the committee of that home team would ensure that the five would never again be seen at the ground. Nor would they be welcome as travelling supporters. For the life of me, I cannot see any difference, except in scale, between that little club and the major professional organisations.

Take the example of the match between Derby County and Fulham near the end of the 1982-83 season. The referee admitted that ten minutes from the end he was worried about crowd encroachment on the pitch: indeed a Fulham player was actually tripped by a spectator on the touchline. The final whistle was blown before the end of official time and Fulham argued that their chances of promotion were jeopardised by that decision. That is debatable but it is not the point. The decision by the Football League that the result should stand was wrong. The match should have been stopped ten minutes from time when the crowd encroachment endangered the players, the players should have been taken from the field to return only when the police could guarantee no further misconduct. If they could not give such a guarantee – and this is perfectly feasible because of the enormous difficulties in controlling thousands of people – I would then have asked the home club, in conjunction with the police, to clear the ground. Only then would I have restarted the match to play the remaining minutes with no crowd. If the police were reluctant to permit this because of potential problems outside the ground, I would have abandoned the game.

Yes, I know the problems: this could lead to an open invitation for supporters to ensure the abandonment of a match in which their team was losing. So what? Something drastic has to be done. Either the club could be 'fined' those points, or the replayed match could take place behind closed doors with the amount taken at the gate in the original match being paid, again as a fine, to the League.

The Football Association has found no answer to hooliganism. The question has to be levelled against them as to the qualifications of the disciplinary committee to take action against a club when they cannot even control their own hooligans abroad. If UEFA or FIFA were to ban the national side, then I am sure that there would be a meeting at Lancaster Gate within twenty-four hours: and action taken.

As I see it, the answer has to be found through membership of a supporters' club. Every member should have an identity card, including a photograph, before he can pass through a turnstile. He could sign in – and pay for – a guest but, as in any club, would be responsible for that person's behaviour. In applying for membership of the supporters' club each person would require a referee just as one does when applying for a passport. Furthermore the membership cards, again like a passport, could be withdrawn. Visiting supporters – or indeed fans wanting to watch a match on a 'neutral' ground – would be allowed entry on production of their club's membership card. Stewards as well as police would be able to withdraw the card while possible suspension would be determined by the supporters' club.

I accept that some additional administration would be involved to run such a scheme through the supporters' clubs, but a fee would be required for membership to defray costs and, besides, soccer is big business and should be run accordingly. The FA, in their role as judge and jury, should treat England supporters in the same way: club membership cards would be withdrawn for drunken brawls in Luxembourg, say, and the individual dealt with thereby at both national and local level.

To help members have pride in their club, I believe that a town's soccer club should also be the total sports club within the city, designed to involve basketball, hockey, table tennis and all other sports. Barcelona, although I have criticised elsewhere one aspect of the club, is a splendid example of the multi-purpose sports club: the football team has an average gate of some eighty thousand or more as a result. Match day at Nou Camp is a day out for the family.

Such an idea is essential, not only to control the problems of hooligan-ism but also to aid the future use of leisure time, which can only increase. There are plenty of examples of such clubs in Europe and both continents of America. We must accept in this country that although we may have been the pioneers of football, we have been outstripped now both on and off the pitch.

With this in mind, I cannot understand how it is accepted by people who are allegedly businessmen that a stadium should be used for profit-able purposes only once a fortnight. Artificial pitches, like that in use at the Queen's Park Rangers ground, must become the norm in order that the grounds can be used on a daily basis for other sports. And as is the case with so many amateur sporting clubs – many of the Welsh rugby clubs are good examples of this: the smaller ones usually – a general manager would be in overall business control with a board of directors (committee) running each individual sport, electing one person to the main board. Such a club clearly would seek sponsorship and there would be an income from the social side, with restaurant facilities, bars (yes, bars: as in any club alcohol would be generally respected, for misbehav-iour would lead to loss of privileges), sports shops, dance hall, concert room and so on under the stands.

The local authority must naturally be very closely involved in such a major leisure centre, both financially and to make use of the facilities for schools during education hours for training purposes – developing young people in the mould of the club, watched over by members of the club and its stars. Professional footballers, for example, would then be coach-ing during the afternoons.

The first natural targets for such far-seeing projects could well be those cities where there are two football clubs, like Bristol, Sheffield, Man-chester, Liverpool and even, in the north, Rochdale and Halifax, where there are soccer and rugby league clubs. The combined value of such clubs could be pooled to provide the centres without necessarily leading to total amalgamation since they would obviously reject the end of their own traditions.

Would not this logical progression create an enormous community spirit within a town? And would not the fact that youngsters would feel involved result in higher standards of behaviour?

The stadium itself should be an all-seater. No matter the arguments about atmosphere, about the traditional way of watching soccer and the loss of accommodation – which would affect only a few clubs like Manchester United and Liverpool. At least eighty per cent of clubs would not lose money because of the small size of the gates they have anyway and it is quite definitely a fact that there is less crowd trouble at grounds with a preponderance of seats. That seating need not be, expensive: a nine-inch by four plank set in concrete as seen on European grounds would do well.

Just a dream? I believe not: certainly, the provision of all-seat grounds and membership cards could be phased in within three years. The multi-purpose stadium with its artificial surface would clearly take longer but the greater the delays the higher the expense and, therefore, the smaller likelihood of its achievement.

To the best of my knowledge, there has been little research into the correlation of behaviour on the field with hooliganism on the terraces. I'm not even certain I would trust the results if the research was conducted because I fear there may be too many psychologists and psychiatrists trying to justify the unjustifiable. But my simple gut reaction is that the players also have much to answer for in their strange antics when a goal is scored, not content merely to kiss a colleague (which gives me and the game a bad name among the less understanding and heterosexual rugby enthusiasts in the Rhondda) but seemingly wishing to jump on his back and collapse him to the ground causing him physical as well as mental problems for the future. What are supporters of the non-scoring team intended to feel at this exhibitionism, which is frequently accompanied by the pseudo-sexual raising of the fist?

I remember Sir Harold Thompson of the FA commenting some years ago that he disagreed with the practice of players putting their arms round each other after a goal had been scored. The Players' Union took a dim view of it, and told Sir Harold, who had a totally legitimate point, that he did not know what he was talking about and that such actions were human and harmless.

I was once involved with Kevin Keegan, Mick Channon and the Southampton police over just such an incident. Chelsea's fans are never the most good-mannered in the game – in fact, some people are firmly convinced that crowd behaviour as we know it was born in the Shed at Stamford Bridge – and they had particular reason, they felt, to be incensed when six thousand of them went to Southampton for a third-round cup-tie in January 1981.

They had hoped that Geoff Hurst, then manager of Chelsea and a lieutenant of England team chief Ron Greenwood, would persuade Keegan to come to the club on his departure from Hamburg. Perhaps Mrs Hurst was not so persuasive about the beauties of West London as Mrs McMenemy was about the delights of Hampshire because Kevin signed for Magic Powers himself at the Dell. But I digress.

Before the start, the police chief responsible came to tell me that the Chelsea fans were out in force, as were the police dogs. They had been shepherded behind the goal at the bottom end – right behind the OCS advertising hoarding as it happened – and were in full voice. Within a couple of minutes of the kick-off, they refused to return the ball when a Steve Williams shot went over the fencing and into their midst. There was no way I was going to restart with a different ball; eventually I waited for two-and-a-half minutes for its return, until those who had come to see some football persuaded the bright boys to release it. I could not allow the crowd to control the situation. The same thing happened twice more, adding seven minutes to normal time, but I walked off the pitch with the same ball with which we had started.

In the twenty-sixth minute, however, came the incident that, in retrospect at least, I fluffed. Mick Channon took a corner, which was headed in for Southampton's second goal by Kevin Keegan right in front of the Chelsea crowd. Kevin ran to Mick and they stood by the goal-line, arms raised triumphantly aloft and facing the terraces. The Chelsea fans reacted like animals: I was never more glad that they were caged in. But there was no doubt in my mind that the action of Keegan and Channon had inflamed them more than the goal itself.

I remained in the Chelsea half, just outside the penalty box, while the players finished their celebrations and lined up. Only then did I call Keegan and Channon to me to reprimand them in no uncertain manner. In fairness they apologised to me and to the crowd but the damage had been done.

At half-time an angry police chief came into my dressing-room, which I don't usually allow, and asked if I would be reporting the players to the FA for incitement. I told him that as I had already spoken to the players concerned and that I was going to see their manager before the re-start, the matter was closed. I told Lawrie that I wanted no repetition of the incident, but in fact he had already warned his players. I believe now that I should indeed have taken further action against his two stars. I could have claimed quite justifiably that they had brought the game into disrepute. Because they were household names, such a charge would have been a deterrent to others and a lesson to those youngsters who copy their heroes in every way. I apologised later to the Southampton police chief. I wonder what action the FA would have taken against the captain of England, Kevin Keegan, if I had followed the matter through.

The 'live' televised Canon League match between West Ham United and Manchester United on Sunday, 27 November 1983, nearly three years after that Southampton incident, brought the kissing and cuddling into the limelight. The cameras recorded my speaking to both Ray Wilkins and Dave Swindlehurst after they had scored and telling them not to go to the crowd in their jubilation. For the next two weeks the publicity was enormous, at home and overseas. Jimmy Greaves approached me after the match when I was talking to my governor, Derek Goodliffe, to say he agreed, and that the incidents had been noted by London Weekend Television commentator Brian Moore. Indeed, ninety-nine per cent of people seemed to agree but some journalists claimed I did it because I was live on television. Simply not true! What they could not have known, for example, was that an assessment on me for a Milk Cup tie earlier in the season between Oxford United and Newcastle United included these words: 'I note your albeit general invitation to break up the kissing and cuddling between players after the home team scores ... I personally find this an objectionable habit and feel it should be discouraged at all levels.'

But I was surprised to read an article by Ian Willars in the *Birmingham Evening Mail* which stated that the chairman of the Football Association, Bert Millichip, had revealed at a lunch in London on 30 November that referees had been sent letters from the Football Association asking them to stop players indulging in such distasteful and girlish antics. 'I imagine Thomas would have received the letter two days before he took charge of the West Ham match and I am delighted he followed our instructions so promptly', said Millichip. As I understand it, all clubs received such a letter but the referees did not. Certainly, I had no such letter from the Football Association, nor the Football League, nor the Players' Union.

If I had been approached by the Football Association, I would have insisted again that I was in no way wishing to prevent celebrations, but to avoid incitement. I was therefore not astonished to read, a few days later, that a player had been charged with threatening behaviour. Magistrates at Hove had heard that Chris Hutchings of Chelsea made a double-handed salute to club supporters after a match with Brighton at the Goldstone Ground. The prosecuting solicitors said that cheers turned to jeers directed against the police and 'large numbers of supporters then climbed onto the pitch and joined in with the happening'. The defence stated that there was 'no suggestion that this man was trying to incite the crowd. He was thanking them for their support. He wants to apologise to the court.' He was, in fact, fined £250. I am certain Hutchings did not ings did not appreciate what his action caused, a clear example of the dangers of involvement between players and crowd. Unless it is stopped, not only by a circular to management but also by a directive to referees throughout the world, we will witness many more such incidents. I trust such a directive will shortly be issued.

Before every match, I have always made it clear to managers that I will not tolerate dissent. It is entirely up to them if they pass that word on to the players – though it has appeared that they frequently have not. If I were a manager, and a player had taken no notice and been booked for his forgetfulness, I would not wait until Monday morning to have him on the carpet. He'd be at the ground on Sunday. And if I were a director, I'd be finding out what action the manager took against the player. Managers are responsible to directors but how many directors have ever taken this line? I cannot go along with Len Shackleton – who included a blank page in his book, *The Clown Prince of Soccer*, to illustrate the average director's knowledge of football – but it does astonish me that some tend not to take the necessary action against undisciplined players and managers.

Some directors clearly forget their usual business acumen. It baffles me that those football managers who are fired for lack of success are given a golden handshake and then acquire an even better club a short time later. Or, alternatively, a successful manager is encouraged to break contracts. The morals of football business do not bear too much investigation, which makes me wonder whether the people who sit in judgement at the very top of the game are those best qualified to do so.

Money, either through transfer fees or wages, is at the centre of many of the game's problems. I have always believed that the individual or the employee should be paid the amount he deserves. He is then expected to work for that money. In the past twenty years we have seen a dramatic change in the lifestyle of the footballer at the same time as playing skills have deteriorated. A player may have his £100,000 detached house with lush garden and heated swimming pool while the club has a £2 million debt. How can this be? My own company would be unable to pay my salary – or that of anyone else, which is something footballers appear to forget – if they were in the same position as ninety per cent of the league clubs. Only nationalised industries appear to be able to do that.

I realise that it is generally only in the top two divisions in which these fabulous sums are paid but I was told this story during the summer break of 1983, by a manager of a fourth-division club who wanted a player to join him as he was reaching the end of his career. The player was struggling to find a club but was demanding £600 a match plus signing-on fee. I am glad to say that the manager, a wizened, gnarled, experienced, old north countryman gave him two words of wise, gnarled, experienced, north country advice.

Because of my position with the OCS Group and my relationship with trade unions, I have some sympathy with the Professional Footballers' Association. But I cannot for example accept that a relegated team has to pay its players the same money – or more, because of 'loyalty bonuses' and so on (i.e. being paid for turning up for work in effect) – when revenue through the turnstiles drops. The club board should be able to gear its salary structure to the anticipated revenue through the gates, with any sponsorship money going towards ground renovation and improvement.

In addition, players' contracts should not simply concern their playing activities. These should include promotion of the game – and not just when the player's testimonial comes round – in schools and at other functions within their community.

Players should not, to my mind, receive cash for wearing particular gear. Money from such deals should be paid to the club as should fees from television appearances, writing in newspapers and similar fee-earning activities. The club could then decide whether to pay the money out in bonuses. I admit to being paid only three times by newspapers or magazines because I believe that it is my duty as a referee to act as a PRO for the game and to give every possible assistance to the media, who, most of the time, are completely responsible in their reporting. Contrary to what some people may think, I could count on one hand the number of times I have personally telephoned a journalist to give him a specific story. But I have never been afraid to comment if one of them contacts me.

I do not seek a return to the humiliating days of the maximum wage in football – that would lead to more under-the-counter deals – but I do believe that footballers and managers must come to their senses or kill much of the professional game. They have, unlike the rugby stars, grown away from their supporters into the stockbroker belt. They now walk with kings, maybe, but have forgotten Kipling's other words about losing the common touch.

Many have also lost the common skills. I have never wanted to claim that things are not like the good old days because those good old days weren't. But as a referee who has officiated for nearly thirty years now in one league or another, I feel qualified to say that the standard of today's football is worse than at any period during that time, with the possible exception of goal-keeping where I doubt any decade has had as many performers as capable as Shilton, Clemence, Parkes, Jennings, Corrigan, Bailey and others. There has been an absolute and definite decline in basic skills – the ability to trap the ball, pass it, dribble and head it. I am very fortunate now if I see twice in a match one player actually taking on another, particularly at international level where it is positively discouraged to beat a man with sheer ball-skill and trickery.

Oh, where are the Bests, the Charltons, the Laws, Hudsons, Osgoods, Cookes, Greaveses, Hayneses, Charleses of yesteryear, let alone the geniuses of previous post-war generations like Carter, Mannion, Shackleton, Hagan, and Peter Doherty? Left on the blackboard, are they?

What I see today is the player with the ball, stationary, while he waits for support and for the opposition to reorganise their defences. Today's managers still tend to put the blame on the success of Alf Ramsey with the World Cup-winning side and his demands for more work-rate. What they conveniently forget is that there were some great players in that side. Anyhow, it is the easy way out to blame someone else. The fact is that players are becoming like some referees: robots. In all the matches I referee, I am aware that players are awaiting instructions from the bench to counteract opposition tactics. The next logical step is a 'time out' *à la* basketball. I am fed up with seeing three players round the ball deciding how to take a free kick near the penalty area and waiting up to a minute while they reach their (usually wrong) decision. Too few players are prepared to use their own initiative, or are allowed to do so.

I have always believed in football coaching but I want good coaches, people with flair who are prepared to allow the potential genius free rein. Referees have their responsibilities in protecting the ball player as anyone who saw Maradona, the little Argentinian, tackled in a Spanish league game in the autumn of 1983 would agree. And yet what did we see in the 1982 World Cup? We saw Maradona sent off against Brazil for retaliation after he had been fouled five times or more without the offender even being cautioned.

This attitude begins at school, too, where the delicate and skilful player is so often allowed by the master in charge to be swamped by a bigger bully, on the basis that it will do him good to be toughened up a bit. All this does is to make him want to get rid of the ball fast. If you ask a boy of twelve today in what position he plays, he will tell you proudly 'right flank', 'left flank', 'back four' or whatever – a sure sign of regimentation. I have yet to hear one say he is simply an attacker, with all that that word implies.

I am sure, too, that youngsters today are spoiled with success. At a presentation in the Rhondda one night, I handed out the trophies to a successful school side. Of a squad of fifteen, not one of them had fewer than eleven trophies for the season, including three certificates for attending coaching classes with the FA or FAW. There is no one who wants to be a winner more than I do, but I could not refrain from saying that

I wished the boys had not received so much because their first purpose should have been to play for enjoyment, and not for winning. There was much criticism of my remarks and it was pointed out that these lads constituted the future of the game. I doubt it. I retorted quickly that they would be lucky if even one made the grade. I do wonder what will happen to those boys when they are no longer winning every week.

I would discontinue with immediate effect the presentation to any boy under fourteen any trophy for winning: the award should be for the school or club. There would be no 'player of the year' awards, either, or 'top scorer'. Football is a team game – and did you ever hear of a schoolboy full-back being named 'top player'?

We must allow these young players, and the full-time professionals, the chance to express themselves, to think for themselves without looking to see if player a, b or c is behind them – for when b is missing, a plus c does not make the correct equation. That may be fine for algebra but not for football.

And so to the laws. If ever I had my ideal situation, with an all-seated crowd watching a team of highly-skilled footballers in a luxury stadium after a social drink in the bar with their fellow members, little of the game would be remembered unless there were goals. They are, after all, what football is all about.

I look forward, then, in the near future, to seeing:

(a) The penalty area line extended to the touchline and offsides given only when the offending player is inside the penalty area.

(b) A free penalty awarded when a professional foul is committed outside the penalty area and the offender sent off.

(c) Encroachment being penalised, as in rugby, by the free kick being moved ten metres closer to the encroaching side's goal. If this encroachment takes the attacking side into the penalty area, a penalty awarded.

(d) Goalkeepers being unable to move more than four paces once they have the ball in their control.

(e) More protection afforded to attackers in the penalty area and less to goalkeepers; possibly more penalties.

(f) Additional points for goals scored in League matches.

(g) No indirect free kicks. All must be direct free kicks or penalties.

To accompany these new ideas, I would also like to see a restructuring of the Football League. First I would seek a first and second division of eighteen teams each to reduce the fixture list. Eight teams would therefore have to go to a third division, which would also have eighteen teams. The top ten of the current third division, added to these, would form the new third division. I would then recommend a fourth division south and north of part-time professionals, clubs which would have no votes within the Football League.

Promotion and relegation in the top three leagues would be on a two-up and two-down basis; re-election would decide the fate of the bottom two clubs in the third division but, if either of the clubs had to be re-elected twice in three seasons, they would automatically be dismissed to the fourth division. The playing record over three seasons would determine which fourth division club or clubs would be promoted to the third. Promotion to the fourth division would come from the current Alliance or senior league or its equivalent.

An additional point would be awarded to teams scoring more than two goals: as an example, a team losing 4–3 would win one point, equal to a team drawing 1–1 or 0–0. Clearly this would encourage the scoring of goals and thus help to attract the paying customer, with the points being shown under a heading of 'bonus points' in the league tables, similar to the bonus points for quick run-scoring and wicket-taking in cricket's county championship.

The FA Cup would operate on the current basis, except that the clubs from the top three divisions would not enter until the third round proper. The fourth division clubs would enter from the first round proper.

In the Milk Cup, I would like to see an experiment whereby all the clubs would take part from the first round, as at present on a two-leg basis for the first two rounds, but with the club from the lower division in the draw always having first-leg ground advantage. This would ensure that there would be fewer occasions when the tie was, in effect, decided purely on the home advantage with the consequent lack of interest in the second leg because one side had established too great a lead.

Referees in the first, second and third divisions will referee only in those leagues (and cup-ties), with the fourth division referees on the supplementary list. I would be looking for, say, twenty top first and second division refereees but there would in this system be a clear career structure for the referee, with a promotion and relegation system not all that dissimilar to that of the clubs themselves.

To mastermind such changes – and, of course, to bring in other ideas, because I certainly do not think that mine are the only legitimate thoughts on the future of the game – I would form a footballing think tank of people with vast experience, and not just from soccer. Former managers and players like Bob Paisley, Frank O'Farrell, Alec Stock, Ted Drake, Joe Mercer and Ron Greenwood should be involved, a coach of great foresight like Allen Wade, along with a leading businessman like Sir Michael Edwardes or the chairman of Marks and Spencer, a top sports editor, the chairman of a supporters' club, the secretary of the

Professional Footballers' Association, and representatives from the managers and referees' associations.

Pie in the sky? Not really: certainly no more than it was pie in the sky for a boy from the Rhondda, having seen his ambition to become a star footballer killed off, to set out on a road which he wanted to take him to Wembley and beyond, to the world.

I believe it should need only a fundamental love of the game, talent and determination. Unfortunately, the harsh reality is that you need also, as we have seen, a million and one other ingredients.